CONFRONTING RAPE AND SEXUAL ASSAULT

Worlds of Women

Susan M. Socolow, Samuel Candler Dobbs Professor of
Latin American History, Emory University
Series Editor

The insights offered by women's studies scholarship are invaluable for exploring society, and issues of gender have therefore become a central concern in the social sciences and humanities. The Worlds of Women series addresses in detail the unique experiences of women from the vantage points of such diverse fields as history, political science, literature, law, religion, and gender theory, among others. Historical and contemporary perspectives are given, often with a cross-cultural emphasis. A selected bibliography and, when appropriate, a list of video material relating to the subject matter are included in each volume. Taken together, the series serves as a varied library of resources for the scholar as well as for the lay reader.

Volumes Published

Judy Barett Litoff and David C. Smith, eds., *American Women in a World at War: Contemporary Accounts from World War II* (1997). Cloth ISBN 0-8420-2570-7   Paper ISBN 0-8420-2571-5

Andrea Tone, ed., *Controlling Reproduction: An American History* (1997). Cloth ISBN 0-8420-2574-X   Paper ISBN 0-8420-2575-8

Mary E. Odem and Jody Clay-Warner, eds., *Confronting Rape and Sexual Assault* (1998). Cloth ISBN 0-8420-2598-7
Paper ISBN 0-8420-2599-5

Elizabeth Reis, ed., *Spellbound: Women and Witchcraft in America* (1998). Cloth ISBN 0-8420-2576-6   Paper ISBN 0-8420-2577-4

CONFRONTING
RAPE
AND
SEXUAL
ASSAULT

Edited by
Mary E. Odem and Jody Clay-Warner

Worlds of Women

Number 3

A Scholarly Resources Inc. Imprint
Wilmington, Delaware

© 1998 by Scholarly Resources Inc.
All rights reserved
First published 1998
Printed and bound in the United States of America

Scholarly Resources Inc.
104 Greenhill Avenue
Wilmington, DE 19805-1897

Library of Congress Cataloging-in-Publication Data

Confronting rape and sexual assault / edited by Mary E. Odem and
    Jody Clay-Warner.
        p.   cm. — (Worlds of women ; no. 3)
    Includes bibliographical references.
    Filmography: p.
    ISBN 0-8420-2598-7 (alk. paper). — ISBN 0-8420-2599-5
(pbk. : alk. paper)
        1. Rape—United States. 2. Sex crimes—United States.
3. Rape victims—United States. 4. Male rape victims—United
States. 5. Feminist theory—United States. I. Odem, Mary E.
II. Clay-Warner, Jody, 1968–   III. Series.
HV6561.C66   1997
362.883—dc21   97-16990
                                                                                CIP

⊗The paper used in this publication meets the minimum requirements
of the American National Standard for permanence of paper for printed
library materials, Z39.48, 1984.

Acknowledgments

We extend our deep thanks to the authors who have contributed to this volume. We are very grateful to Susan Socolow, the Worlds of Women series editor, and to Richard Hopper and Linda Pote Musumeci at Scholarly Resources for their encouragement and support throughout this project. Our thanks also go to Kimberly Springer and Tina Trent for their excellent research assistance.

About the Editors

Mary E. Odem is associate professor of women's studies and history at Emory University. She is the author of *Delinquent Daughters: Protecting and Policing Adolescent Female Sexuality in the United States* (1995) and is currently researching the history of sexual violence in the United States.

Jody Clay-Warner is visiting assistant professor in the Department of Sociology at Emory University. Her research interests include violence against women, women and the law, and group processes. Her recent work is published in *Social Psychology Quarterly*, and she is preparing her dissertation for publication. For the last ten years, Professor Clay-Warner has volunteered as a rape crisis counselor and educator, first in Chapel Hill, North Carolina, and currently in Dekalb County, Georgia.

Contents

Introduction

The scholarly literature on rape has grown tremendously in the past three decades, largely in response to the feminist movement of the 1960s and 1970s, which focused public attention on the problem of sexual violence and fundamentally altered our society's way of thinking about and dealing with rape. In the past, rape was considered to be a personal shame suffered by unfortunate women; it was viewed as a rare crime perpetrated by mentally disturbed men. Feminists forcefully challenged conventional understandings of rape by redefining it as a serious and pervasive social problem threatening all women, a problem that demanded immediate attention. They argued that rape is not the result of a few pathological individuals but rather stems from a system of male dominance and from cultural beliefs and practices that objectify and degrade women. Both as a physical act and a psychological threat, rape is a means of inducing fear in women, limiting their movements, and reinforcing their dependence on men.

Within the social sciences this redefinition of rape has led to an outpouring of new scholarship on sexual violence. Scholars have addressed a range of questions: How prevalent is rape? Why does rape happen? What aspects of our society encourage sexual violence? What social and psychological impact does rape have on its victims? And how do we prevent rape and sexual assault? Brought together in this volume are some of the best examples of this scholarship, focusing specifically on adult sexual assault. We have included important early articles, as well as the most recent work in the field. With contributors from a wide variety of areas—sociology, psychology, anthropology, criminology, law, public health, history, and women's studies— *Confronting Rape and Sexual Assault* provides an interdisciplinary overview of the social science literature on rape. It is designed for college students at both undergraduate and graduate levels and will also serve as a useful collection for professionals and scholars who work in the area of rape and sexual assault.

The articles are organized around four themes that have been of central concern to social scientists in this field of study: 1) prevalence and definitions of rape and sexual assault; 2) explanations of the problem; 3) institutional and cultural context of sexual assault; 4) strategies of prevention and change. The study of rape is approached from a range of different methodologies and perspectives. We have sought to address the diversity of assault experiences by including articles about groups often neglected in the scholarly literature on rape: women of color and men. This volume also features literary and personal accounts by women who have been raped or threatened by rape in order to give voice to those who have been directly affected by this problem. Rape should be understood not just as a matter of social scientific analysis but also as a problem that causes serious damage and trauma to individual lives. In addition, we have compiled a bibliography of suggested readings on rape and sexual assault and an annotated videography of relevant films and videos for use in the classroom.

Before turning to the main content of the book, it is useful to review the course of social scientific scholarship to date. This summary of the key issues and findings in the literature on rape provides a context for evaluating the articles and essays included in this volume. Glancing back also reminds us of where we have been and how far we have come in our understanding of rape.

Rape Prevalence

One important issue scholars have addressed is the prevalence of rape and sexual assault. If one were to rely on official reports of rape, it would be easy to believe that rape was a rare event. According to the Uniform Crime Reports, approximately 102,000 rapes were reported to police in 1994 (Maguire and Pastore, 1996). If this number is correct, then the only index offense less prevalent than rape is murder.* Researchers have realized, however, that these measures vastly underrepresent the rate of sexual assault (Brickman and Briere, 1983; Johnson, 1980). Many women who are sexually assaulted do not report the crime to the police because they suspect they will not be believed or because they want to avoid the social stigma attached to rape. Thus, the number of rapes reported to police is not a valid indicator of the actual occurrence of this crime. Also, police departments do not include all reported crimes in their official statistics. Instead, they count only those crimes that are "founded," meaning those crimes that the police have reason to believe actually occurred. This criterion was designed to prevent false reports from creeping into police statistics. Frequently, however, law enforcement personnel do not believe women who report being assaulted. Such a reaction is particularly common in

---

*The Federal Bureau of Investigation compiles nationwide statistics on "Index Offenses," which are the crimes of murder, forcible rape, robbery, aggravated assault, burglary, larceny-theft, motor vehicle theft, and arson.

cases of acquaintance rape, in which the police often perceive that the victim has an ulterior motive in reporting an assault, such as taking revenge against an unfaithful boyfriend. As a result of these problems with official reports of rape, social scientists have turned to victimization studies to assess the prevalence of rape.

The government realizes that many crimes occur that are not reported. In order to uncover this "dark figure" of crime, the Bureau of Justice Statistics conducts the National Crime Victimization Survey (NCVS) every six months.* For this survey, a random household sample is taken and surveyors ask each person at least twelve years of age living in the house a variety of questions regarding crime victimization. Participants are asked whether or not they have been victimized by a variety of crimes from petty theft to assault. Until 1994, however, individuals were asked about sexual assault only if they responded "yes" to the question, "Did anyone try to attack you in some other way?" Feminist scholars have argued that many women may fail to report rapes unless they are asked specifically about this type of assault. The NCVS has been redesigned to take into account the concerns of feminist scholars. For instance, all persons are now asked specifically about unwanted sexual activity. Results indicate that persons report more unwanted sexual activity using the revamped NCVS than they did in the old survey format (Bachman and Saltzman, 1995). Using the revised NCVS, the government estimates that over 167,000 rapes occurred in 1994, a figure considerably larger than the one reported by police (Maguire and Pastore, 1996).

Prior to the changes in the NCVS, however, a number of social scientists began conducting their own victimization studies in which they not only asked specifically about various forms of sexual assault (Koss, Gidycz, and Wisniewski, 1987) but also developed a rapport with the study participants, so that these women would feel more comfortable discussing their assaults (Russell, 1984). In 1984, Diana E. H. Russell interviewed a random selection of 930 women in San Francisco, asking specifically about their experiences of sexual coercion. She found that 44 percent of these women had been victimized by an attempted or completed sexual assault. Mary Koss and her colleagues surveyed more than three thousand college women and found that 25 percent had had an experience that met the legal definition of rape or attempted rape (Koss, Gidycz, and Wisniewski, 1987). Other studies confirm that forced sexual activity is more prevalent than official reports or the NCVS would indicate, demonstrating that sexual assault is a significant problem that must be addressed (see, for example,

*This survey was formerly called the National Crime Survey (NCS).

Olday and Wesley, 1983; Kanin and Parcell, 1977; Muehlenhard and Linton, 1987).

What Is Rape?

In addition to rape prevalence, social scientists have also reexamined conventional understandings of rape. Their research has challenged the dominant cultural stereotype of the rapist as a crazed stranger, typically a black man, who violently attacks his victim in public places—dark alleys, street corners, parking lots, places where a woman is away from the protection of home, family, and friends. Traditional scholarship on rape upheld this stereotype to a large extent. Professionals and scholars studying the problem asserted that the typical rapist was a highly abnormal individual. More recently, social scientists have developed new analyses of rape and rapists. First, they contend that rape is an extension of normative sexual attitudes and relations in a society that demands and objectifies women. From this perspective, rapists are seen not as psychologically disturbed individuals but as normal men whose behavior stems from dominant cultural practices and beliefs about gender and sexuality (Brownmiller, 1975; Herman, 1984; Griffin, 1971).

Second, scholars have disputed the common view that most women are raped by strangers. Numerous studies over the past two decades have shown that women are more likely to be assaulted by men they know, including friends, acquaintances, lovers, husbands, and male relatives. In one of the best known of these studies, Mary Koss (see Koss, 1988, Chapter 6 in this volume) examined sexual victimization in a national sample of college students and found that most incidents (84 percent) involved close acquaintances or dates. Diana Russell's 1984 survey of women in San Francisco concluded that acquaintance rape was the most prevalent type of rape. She found that, whereas 55 percent of all rapes reported to the police were stranger rapes, only 17 percent of the total number of rapes (which includes the unreported rapes) were committed by men unknown to the victims. The acquaintance rapists included boyfriends, dates, friends, husbands or ex-husbands, relatives, and family friends. Researchers such as Koss, Russell, and others have drawn public attention to the problem of acquaintance rape, and have analyzed its prevalence, risk factors, causes, and long-term consequences (Lundberg-Love and Geffner, 1989; Parrot and Bechhofer, 1991).

One form of acquaintance rape that scholars have studied in detail is marital rape. Prior to the anti-rape movement of the 1970s, the law did not even recognize a husband's coerced sex with his wife as rape.

Most state legal codes defined rape as "the forcible penetration of the body of a woman who is not the wife of the perpetrator" (Russell, 1991, p. 129). Feminist activism has led to the criminalization of marital rape in most states; and researchers have broadened our understanding of the prevalence, causes, and traumatic consequences of marital rape (Finkelhor and Yllo, 1985; Frieze and Browne, 1983; Russell, 1990, Chapter 7 in this volume).

A third issue addressed by scholars is the dominant racial construction of rape. Throughout United States history, a dominant image of rape in our society has been that of a black man attacking a white woman. Contrary to this pervasive stereotype, studies have repeatedly shown that most rapes arc committed by men of the same ethnic/racial background as their victims. That is, most white women face sexual assaults by white men and most women of color are assaulted by men of color (Harlow, 1991). The image of black-on-white rape not only distorts the reality of rape but also reinforces racial and gender hierarchies in our society. It serves to stigmatize black men as typical rapists, deny the sexual violence committed by white men, and ignore completely the sexual assault of black women (Davis, 1981; Wriggins, 1983, Chapter 15 in this volume).

Why Does Rape Occur?

In order to address the problem of sexual assault, it is crucial to understand why sexual assault occurs. Traditional scholarship on rape, which was the domain of psychology and psychiatry, held that rape was committed by mentally ill men unable to control their sexual impulses (Amir, 1971). This illness was believed to be caused by a variety of factors, such as early childhood experiences (domineering mothers and passive fathers), biological conditions, or fears of sexual inadequacy (Hammer and Glueck, 1957; MacDonald, 1971). Whatever the specific cause, however, rape was seen as a sexual crime committed by a deviant individual. Because rapists were believed to be mentally ill, they were not responsible for their behavior. Thus, a women who was raped was simply the unlucky victim of a crazed individual. Influenced by feminist analyses, social scientists have challenged conventional scholarly understandings of rape by demonstrating the importance of social and cultural factors in producing sexual aggression. They argue that rape cannot be viewed simply as a product of individual pathology, but rather must be seen as a product of the patriarchal society in which it is imbedded (Brownmiller, 1975; Schwendinger and Schwendinger, 1983; Sheffield, 1984).

Scholars have investigated various ways in which our male-dominated society perpetuates sexual assault. One widely researched area is socialization. Some scholars argue that rape exists, at least in part, because of the differential socialization of men and women, whereby men are taught to be sexually aggressive, while women are taught to be passive and dependent. Men are taught not to take "no" for an answer and come to view sex as a commodity that women withhold at will (Clark and Lewis, 1977; Jackson, 1978; Sheffield, 1984). Thus, men are taught to pursue sex even when a woman says "no." The result is rape.

Another set of socialized beliefs that contributes to sexual assault are "rape myths," which are commonly held assumptions about rape that are untrue but that allow individuals to deny that forced sex is actually rape. Examples include the belief that women secretly want to be raped, or that a woman can stop a rape if she really wants to. Other myths hold the victim responsible for rape, claiming that women invite sexual assault by the clothes they wear or by their behavior toward men. Another category of rape myths further absolves the rapist from blame by stating that men cannot be expected to control their sexual impulses (see Lonsway and Fitzgerald, 1994). As Martha Burt (1980) has found, males who believe in rape myths are more likely to be sexually coercive and to rape than are men who do not hold these beliefs. Both men and women who hold these beliefs are also less sympathetic to rape victims than are those who do not believe in rape myths. These myths allow men to excuse their coercive behavior and encourage women to blame themselves for their own victimization.

Other researchers have explored whether pornography plays a role in increasing sexual aggression. Studies have found that when men are exposed to aggressive pornography (images of rape or other sexual assaults that are depicted as pleasurable to women) they show a greater acceptance of rape myths (Malamuth and Check, 1983) as well as increased aggression toward women in experimental situations (Donnerstein, 1984). Some assert that it is the violent nature of this pornography and not its sexual explicitness that promotes sexual aggression. To examine this assumption, Linz, Donnerstein, and Penrod (1984) exposed a group of men to five mainstream R-rated, sexually violent ("slasher") films over a period of five days. They found that these men became increasingly desensitized to violence and reported that the films were more enjoyable and less degrading to women as the experiment progressed. These men also were less sympathetic to the rape victim in a filmed reenactment of a rape trial than were those who had not watched the films. As a result of this type of research, many social scientists contend that sexually violent media images of women help perpetuate the attitudes that allow rape to occur.

While some scholars focus on rape myths, strict gender roles, and sexually violent images of women in the media, others emphasize that the economic inequality between men and women also facilitates rape. For instance, many women are unable to leave abusive relationships because they are economically dependent upon their partner. For these women, rape is a daily threat (Schwendinger and Schwendinger, 1983; Gottfried, 1991). Other women face sexual coercion and assault in the workplace but do not report the crime because they fear losing their jobs. Limited economic and political resources also make it difficult for women to challenge existing rape laws and improve society's treatment of rape survivors. As a result, a number of women have joined together through rape crisis centers and political organizations to effect change. In these days of governmental budget cuts, however, social service agencies are turning more and more to private funding. Those causes that can be supported through private dollars are the causes more likely to survive lean economic times. As long as women lack adequate economic resources, rape crisis centers and other rape action groups will continue to fight for survival.

Ultimately, many argue that rape will stop only when women have attained equality with men in all spheres. Until that time, men will continue to use rape to control women, and, for as long as women remain subjugated, they will be unable to challenge men's authority and power. The challenge, however, has begun; as women's groups lobby for changes in the legal system and for better treatment of rape survivors, more women refuse to be silenced, and more men understand the fear that grips their wives and daughters. While much progress has been made, we still have a long way to go. Fortunately, feminist analyses provide us with a road map for rape prevention.

Preventing Rape and Sexual Assault

Anti-rape researchers and activists have explored a range of different strategies for preventing sexual violence on individual, organizational, and structural levels. Rape crisis centers have been a major force for change as they work to empower and support rape survivors and to challenge the harsh and demeaning treatment of them by police, hospitals, and courts. Women's groups in San Francisco and Washington, DC, organized the first rape crisis centers in the early 1970s, and today such centers are found throughout the United States, in cities of all sizes and even in many rural areas. Through their efforts rape crisis centers have fundamentally altered our society's traditional response to rape and victims of rape. They address the emotional and physical needs of rape survivors, and work to change hospital, police, and legal practices regarding sexual violence. While services vary, most centers offer counseling for rape victims, their families, and friends, maintain a twenty-four-hour telephone hotline staffed by trained volunteers, teach self-defense classes, and organize support groups for rape survivors, In addition, staff and volunteers at the centers accompany survivors to the hospital for physical examinations, as well as to appointments with police and court officials. Another important goal of rape crisis centers has been to educate the broader community about the problem of sexual assault. Through their many activities, rape crisis centers have been at the forefront of the struggle against sexual violence (Matthews, 1994; Gornick, Burt, and Pittman, 1985).

One important concern of anti-rape activists and researchers has been to identify strategies that individuals can use to avoid becoming victims of sexual assault. The traditional advice given to women by experts and law enforcement officials was to avoid potentially dangerous activities such as going out alone at night, hitchhiking, inviting men to their homes, and wearing revealing clothing. In the face of an attack, women were urged to remain passive to avoid upsetting or antagonizing their assailant. In recent years, some scholars have strongly criticized this advice, arguing that it is oppressive to women, reinforces unequal power relations, and promotes a sense of fear and helplessness in women, all of which make rape more likely to happen.

An alternative approach is to empower women to avoid rape by encouraging women to know their surroundings, not to fear them, and in the face of an assault, to defend themselves against their assailants. A number of researchers have conducted empirical studies of women who have been attacked in order to determine the effectiveness of various rape-avoidance strategies (Bart and O'Brien, 1985; Ullman and Knight, 1992; Zoucha-Jensen and Coyne, 1993, Chapter 17 in this volume). Contrary to the traditional message given to women, the studies conclude that women who actively resist are more likely to avoid rape; women who remain passive are more likely to be raped. While there is no foolproof strategy for avoiding rape, these studies do indicate the importance of teaching women self-defense skills to protect themselves against an assault.

Feminist researchers and activists also have called for broad changes in the criminal justice system. Rape law and legal practice have tended to hold victims responsible for their assault and to make prosecution and conviction of rapists very difficult. As a result, many women felt that they had been raped twice—first by the assailant and then by the criminal justice system. Reformers have challenged the traditional legal response to rape in a variety of ways. They have demanded changes in the narrow legal definition of rape, which held that "a man commits rape when he engages in intercourse with a woman not his wife, by force or threat of force, against her will and without her consent" (Estrich, 1987, p. 8). Many states have broadened their definitions of rape to make wife rape illegal and to include not only forced vaginal penetration by the penis but also anal penetration and the intrusion of other objects into genital or anal openings. In addition, a number of states have adopted gender-neutral rape statutes, recognizing that both men and women can be victims of rape (Estrich, 1987; Largen, 1988).

Rape-law reformers also have called into question the "utmost resistance" standard used in rape trials, which required victims to prove that they had done everything within their physical and psychological power to resist the sexual assault. A number of states eventually altered this standard to focus on the alleged rapist's behavior and the level of force that he used, instead of the victim's behavior. Another important rape-law reform was the enactment of rape-shield laws restricting the introduction of evidence about the prior sexual behavior of rape victims. In the past, courts routinely permitted this type of evidence on the grounds that it was relevant to the central issue of consent. The assumption was that a "pure" woman was less likely to consent to sex than one who was "immoral" (Berger, Searles, and Newman, 1988; Largen, 1988; Spohn and Horney, 1992; Bohmer, 1991, Chapter 19 in this volume).

Scholars evaluating the effectiveness of rape-law reforms have come up with different conclusions. Some argue that the reforms have had limited impact on conviction rates or victims' experiences in the legal system. Others conclude that rape-law reforms have led to an increased reporting of and prosecution of sexual assaults (see Goldberg-Ambrose, 1992, for a review of these studies). Evidentiary changes in particular have encouraged more victims to work with the criminal justice system to prosecute rapists. But alone, legal reform is not enough. Studies show that juries, judges, and other court officials continue to hold distorted assumptions and attitudes about rape, a factor that interferes with the effective legal response to this crime (Largen, 1988; Estrich, 1987; LaFree, 1989).

Scholars and activists have thus sought broad cultural and structural changes, as well as legal reforms, to address the problem of rape in our society. A major effort has been to challenge prevailing "rape myths"—found not only in the courtroom but also in schools, fraternities, workplaces, and the media—that perpetuate and condone sexual assault. Activists have worked to change these beliefs by presenting educational programs about rape in high schools, colleges, churches, fraternities, businesses, and offices. Empirical studies, most of them conducted among student populations, demonstrate that rape-prevention education is successful in changing attitudes about rape among both men and women (Fonow, Richardson, and Wemmerus, 1992).

Researchers also have called for changes in traditional gender-role socialization, in which boys are raised to be aggressive and dominant and girls are raised to be passive, pleasing, and submissive. The scholarly literature shows a clear link between an adherence to these conventional sex roles and an acceptance of rape myths, particularly the tendency to blame women for rape (Check and Malamuth, 1983; Muehlenhard, Friedman, and Thomas, 1985; Burt, 1980). Changing dominant notions of childrearing and socialization practices is no easy task, but anti-rape experts urge parents and schools to avoid rigid gender-role stereotyping and, instead, to encourage characteristics of cooperation, care, independence, and self-esteem among both boys and girls.

Finally, a number of scholars contend that we must address the structural inequalities between men and women in our society if we are to end sexual violence (Sheffield, 1989; Gottfried, 1991). Women have had and continue to have less access to economic resources, education, political power, and job opportunities than men, inequities that are greatest for women of color and working-class women. This situation has made women more financially dependent on men and consequently more vulnerable to sexual coercion by men. A range of remedies have been suggested to promote women's economic independence: greater educational opportunities; vocational training; publicly financed child care; higher wages for women workers; and safe, long-term shelters with child care for women seeking to leave abusive relationships (Gottfried, 1991).

Clearly, research on rape and sexual assault has advanced greatly over the last three decades. Through these articles, we will explore in depth many of these developments. We recognize that it can be disturbing to read about a topic as painful as rape, particularly for those who have experienced sexual violence personally or have friends or family members who have been victims. Yet, it is important to confront the problem of rape intellectually in order to understand and change the forces that contribute to sexual assault. The progress made so far, at least in part, is a result of the work of social scientists and feminist researchers. We must continue the search for explanations of, and solutions to, the problem of sexual assault in the interest of creating a more humane and less violent world.

References

Amir, Menachem. *Patterns in Forcible Rape*. Chicago: University of Chicago Press, 1971.

Bachman, Ronet, and Linda E. Saltzman. *Violence against Women: Estimates from the Redesigned Survey*. Washington, DC: Bureau of Justice Statistics, U.S. Department of Justice, August 1995.

Bart, Pauline B., and Patricia H. O'Brien. *Stopping Rape: Successful Survival Strategies*. New York: Pergamon, 1985.

Berger, Ronald J., Patricia Searles, and W. Lawrence Newman. "The Dimensions of Rape Reform Legislation." *Law and Society Review* 22 (1988): 329–49.

Bohmer, Carol. "Acquaintance Rape and the Law." In *Acquaintance Rape: The Hidden Crime*, edited by Andrea Parrot and Laurie Bechhofer, 317–33. New York: John Wiley and Sons, 1991.

Brickman, Julie, and John Briere. "Incidence of Rape and Sexual Assault in an Urban Canadian Population." *International Journal of Women's Studies* 7 (1983): 195–206.

Brownmiller, Susan. *Against Our Will: Men, Women, and Rape*. New York: Simon and Schuster, 1975.

Burt, Martha R. "Cultural Myths and Support for Rape." *Journal of Personality and Social Psychology* 38 (1980): 217–30.

Check, James V. P., and Neil Malamuth. "Violent Pornography, Feminism, and Social Learning Theory." *Aggressive Behavior* 9 (1983): 106–7.

Clark, Lorenne, and Debra Lewis. *Rape: The Price of Coercive Sexuality*. Toronto: Women's Press, 1977.

Davis, Angela, ed. *Women, Race and Class*. New York: Random House, 1981.

Donnerstein, Edward. "Pornography: Its Effect on Violence against Women." In *Pornography and Sexual Aggression*, edited by Neil Malamuth and Edward Donnerstein. Orlando, FL: Academic Press, 1984.

Estrich, Susan. *Real Rape*. Cambridge, MA: Harvard University Press, 1987.

Finkelhor, David, and Kersti Yllo. *License to Rape: Sexual Abuse of Wives*. New York: Holt, Rinehart and Winston, 1985.

Fonow, Mary Margaret, Laurel Richardson, and Virginia A. Wemmerus. "Feminist Rape Education: Does it Work?" *Gender and Society* 6 (1992): 109–21.

Frieze, Irene Hanson, and Angela Browne. "Investigation into the Causes and Consequences of Marital Rape." *Signs* 8 (1983): 532–53.

Goldberg-Ambrose, Carole. "Unfinished Business in Rape Law Reform." *Journal of Social Issues* 48 (1992): 173–86.

Gornick, Janet, Martha R. Burt, and Karen J. Pittman. "Structure and Activities of Rape Crisis Centers in the 1980s." *Crime and Delinquency* 31 (1985): 247–68.

Gottfried, Heidi. "Preventing Sexual Coercion: A Feminist Agenda for Economic Change." In *Sexual Coercion: A Sourcebook on Its Nature, Causes and Prevention*, edited by Elizabeth Grauerholz and Mary A. Koralewski, 173–83. Lexington, MA: D. C. Heath, 1991.

Griffin, Susan. "Rape: The All-American Crime." *Ramparts* 10 (1971): 26–35.

Hammer, Emanuel, and Bernard Glueck. "Psychodynamic Patterns in Sex Offenders: A Four-Factor Theory." *Psychiatric Quarterly* 31 (1957): 167–73.

Harlow, Caroline Wolf. *Female Victims of Violent Crime*. Washington, DC: U.S. Department of Justice, 1991.

Herman, Dianne. "The Rape Culture." In *Women: A Feminist Perspective*, 4th edition, edited by Jo Freeman, 20–38. Mountain View, CA: Mayfield, 1984.

Jackson, Stevie. "The Social Context of Rape: Sexual Scripts and Motivation." *Women's Studies International Quarterly* 1 (1978): 27–38.

Johnson, Allen Griswold. "On the Prevalence of Rape in the United States." *Signs* 6 (1980): 136–46.

Kanin, Eugene J., and Stanley R. Parcell. "Sexual Aggression: A Second Look at the Offended Female." *Archives of Sexual Behavior* 6 (1977): 67–76.

Koss, Mary. "Hidden Rape: Sexual Aggression and Victimization in a National Sample of Students in Higher Eduction." In *Rape and Sexual Assault II*, edited by Ann Wolbert Burgess, 3–25. New York: Garland Publishing, 1988.

Koss, Mary P., Christine A. Gidycz, and Nadine Wisniewski. "The Scope of Rape: Incidence and Prevalence of Sexual Aggression and Victimization in a National Sample of Higher Education Students." *Journal of Consulting and Clinical Psychology* 55 (1987): 162–70.

LaFree, Gary. *Rape and Criminal Justice: The Social Construction of Sexual Assault*. Belmont, CA: Wadsworth, 1989.

Largen, Mary Ann. "Rape Law Reform: An Analysis." In *Rape and Sexual Assault II*, edited by Ann Wolbert Burgess, 271–92. New York: Garland Publishing, 1988.

Linz, Daniel, Edward Donnerstein, and Steven Penrod. "The Effects of Multiple Exposure of Filmed Violence against Women." *Journal of Communication* 34 (1984): 130–47.

Lonsway, Kimberly A., and Louise F. Fitzgerald. "Rape Myths: In Review." *Psychology of Women Quarterly* 18 (1994): 133–64.

Lundberg-Love, Paula, and Robert Geffner. "Date Rape: Prevalence, Risk Factors, and a Proposed Model." In *Violence in Dating Relationships*, edited by Maureen Pirog-Good and Jan Stets, 169–84. New York: Praeger, 1989.

MacDonald, John. *Rape Offenders and Their Victims*. Springfield, IL: Thomas, 1971.

Maguire, Kathleen, and Ann L. Pastore. *Sourcebook of Criminal Justice Statistics*. U.S. Department of Justice, Bureau of Justice Statistics. Washington, DC: USGPO, 1996.

Malamuth, Neil M., and James V. P. Check. "Sexual Arousal to Rape Depictions: Individual Differences." *Journal of Abnormal Psychology* 92 (1983): 436–46.

Matthews, Nancy A. *Confronting Rape: The Feminist Anti-Rape Movement and the State*. London: Routledge, 1994.

Muehlenhard, Charlene L., Debra E. Friedman, and Celeste M. Thomas. "Is Date Rape Justifiable? The Effects of Dating Activity, Who Initiated, Who Paid and Men's Attitude toward Women." *Psychology of Women Quarterly* 9 (1985): 297–310.

Muehlenhard, Charlene L., and Melaney A. Linton. "Date Rape and Sexual Aggression in Dating Situations: Incidence and Risk Factors." *Journal of Counseling Psychology* 34 (1987): 186–96.

Olday, D., and Wesley B. "Premarital Courtship Violence: A Summary Report." Unpublished manuscript. Morehead, KY: Morehead State University, 1983.

Parrot, Andrea, and Laurie Bechhofer. *Acquaintance Rape: The Hidden Crime*. New York: John Wiley and Sons, 1991.

Russell, Diana E. H. *Sexual Exploitation: Rape, Child Sexual Abuse, and Sexual Harassment*. Beverly Hills, CA: Sage Publications, 1984.

———. "Wife Rape." In *Acquaintance Rape: The Hidden Crime*, edited by Andrea Parrot and Laurie Bechhofer, 129–39. New York: John Wiley and Sons, 1991.

———. "Wife Rape and the Law." In *Rape in Marriage*. Bloomington, IN: Indiana University Press, 1990.

Schwendinger, Julia R., and Herman Schwendinger. *Rape and Inequality*. Beverly Hills, CA: Sage Publications, 1983.

Sheffield, Carole J. "Sexual Terrorism." In *Women: A Feminist Perspective*, 4th edition, edited by Jo Freeman, 3–19. Mountain View, CA: Mayfield, 1984.

Spohn, Cassia, and Julie Horney. *Rape Law Reform: A Grass Roots Revolution and Its Impact.* New York: Plenum Press, 1992.

Ullman, Sarah E., and Raymond A. Knight. "Fighting Back: Women's Resistance to Rape." *Journal of Interpersonal Violence* 7 (1992): 31–43.

Wriggins, Jennifer. "Rape, Racism, and the Law." *Harvard Women's Law Journal* 6 (1983): 103–41.

Zoucha-Jensen, Janice M., and Ann Coyne. "The Effects of Resistance Strategies on Rape." *American Journal of Public Health* 83 (1993): 163–64.

I   Speaking Out

The selections in this section give voice to women's own experiences with sexual assault. "Rape Poem," by well-known novelist Marge Piercy, describes women's fear of rape and also exposes society's treatment of the victim. In her moving essay, Andrea Benton Rushing discusses her struggles as a rape survivor, demonstrating the long-lasting effects that such an assault can have. Rushing, a professor of English at Amherst College, also analyzes the way that race affected her recovery and her reaction to the assault. Next, poet and novelist Andi Rosenthal eloquently describes her journey from rape victim to survivor. In her series of sonnets, Rosenthal focuses on the inner turmoil she felt as she first remained quiet about the incident and then struggled to speak. In the final selection, Laura Levitt, a professor of religion at Temple University, and Rabbi Sue Ann Wasserman document a healing ceremony that they composed for Laura after she was raped. The ceremony incorporates the *mikvah*, which is a traditional Jewish ritual bath, as well as selections from ancient and contemporary texts. These powerful pieces demonstrate the far-reaching effects of sexual assault and provide us with an appropriately personal backdrop against which to examine the issue of rape.

1

Rape Poem

~

Marge Piercy

There is no difference between being raped
and being pushed down a flight of cement steps
except that the wounds also bleed inside.

There is no difference between being raped
and being run over by a truck
except that afterward men ask if you enjoyed it.

There is no difference between being raped
and being bit on the ankle by a rattlesnake
except that people ask if your skirt was short
and why you were out alone anyhow.

There is no difference between being raped
and going head first through a windshield
except that afterward you are afraid
not of cars
but half the human race.

The rapist is your boyfriend's brother.
He sits beside you in the movies eating popcorn.
Rape fattens on the fantasies of the normal male
like a maggot in garbage.

From Marge Piercy, "Rape Poem," in *Circles on the Water* (New York: Alfred A. Knopf, 1982), 164–65. © 1982 by Marge Piercy. Reprinted by permission of Alfred A. Knopf.

Fear of rape is a cold wind blowing
all of the time on a woman's hunched back.
Never to stroll alone on a sand road through pine woods,
never to climb a trail across a bald
without that aluminum in the mouth
when I see a man climbing toward me.

Never to open the door to a knock
without that razor just grazing the throat.
The fear of the dark side of hedges,
the back seat of the car, the empty house
rattling keys like a snake's warning.
The fear of the smiling man
in whose pocket is a knife.
The fear of the serious man
in whose fist is locked hatred.

All it takes to cast a rapist is seeing your body
as jackhammer, as blowtorch, as adding-machine-gun.
All it takes is hating that body
your own, your self, your muscle that softens to flab.

All it takes is to push what you hate,
what you fear onto the soft alien flesh.
To bucket out invincible as a tank
armored with treads without senses
to possess and punish in one act,
to rip up pleasure, to murder those who dare
live in the leafy flesh open to love.

2

Surviving Rape: A Morning/ Mourning Ritual

~

Andrea Benton Rushing

For Frank, who asked how I endured it, and Audre, who asked me
to write about it, and those whose love leads me

> I am writing because rape is . . . I am writing to understand. I am
> writing so I won't be afraid. I am writing so I won't start crying
> again. . . . I am writing to allow myself to feel the anger. I am writ-
> ing to keep from running toward it or away from it or into anybody's
> arms. I am writing to find solutions and pass them on. I am writing
> to find a language and pass it on.
> I am writing, writing, writing, for my life.
>
> (Pearl Cleage, *Mad at Miles*, p. 5)

"DON'T MOVE!" YANKS MY EYES OPEN. Night light's off. Can't
see. Not in-the-swimming-pool-without-my-glasses can't see.
REALLY can't see. Need to get up and find out what's wrong, but
something's pressing me down. "DON'T MAKE A SOUND OR I'LL
HAVE TO HURT YOU!" The barked command's garbled. Have to
come out of this nightmare. A man's on top of me. One of his hands
pinned both of mine above my head. His breath's warm on my face,
but his jacket's cold when he pulls my robe and nightgown up, my
underpants down. Short, flabby penis. He is telling me how much I
want him, how much he satisfies me. Maybe I can go back to sleep or
pass out until it's over. . . . Suppose he can't get inside my vulva or

From Andrea Benton Rushing, "Surviving Rape: A Morning/Mourning
Ritual," in *Theorizing Black Feminisms*, ed. Stanlie M. James and Abena Busia
(London: Routledge, 1993), 127–40. Reprinted by permission of Routledge and
Andrea Benton Rushing.

ejaculate. If I make him angry, he'll cut, shoot, strangle me. Did he kill the kitten? Where are Osula and Ann?

It's been 21,900 hours, 912 days, 130 Saturday nights, 30 months, 3 years since October 16, 1988 when I was stunned awake, straddled by a man I did not know. First I think I'm nightmaring. . . . Then try to sink back under sleep's blanket and weave whatever is going on into a dream the way I do when I have to urinate or am hungry and don't want to leave the bed's womb. Then I try to pass out. Can't because I don't know what he'll do, because I am adrenalined 360 degrees opposite of relaxed. Besides, he wants me to be conscious of his omnipotence and my humiliating powerlessness. It's almost blackstrap-molasses dark. And horribly quiet.

Saying the story, I usually claim, "All I asked God for was my life. God gave me that and so much more." But there were no words in my mind when I was being raped. I chose life and did what I thought would keep me in the land of the living. My body responds to his in a vicious parody of intimacy while my brain whirls to read his mind so I can save my life by satisfying him. The sustaining, salvific prayers came from friends and ancestors on the other side of the membrane that separates the living from the dead. While I moan and whimper, some choir is singing, "I don't know where, but I know that you do. I can't see how, but I know you'll get through. God, please touch somebody right now, right now."

Will he slash my face when he's through? All he asks for is money. Not a demand. A casual request as if I'm "his woman," and he's going to run an errand. Same man who has walked through the walls of my apartment to rape me, waits, almost patiently, while I fumble through two purses for my wallet *and* he lets me take the bills out. Doesn't count the seventy dollars I hand over or mention my credit cards. He leaves the room, speaking over his shoulder, "Stay there, I'll be back," as if he were my honey getting up to fix us drinks or snacks or turn our favorite music on, as if every cell in my body wasn't trying to eject him from my life.

If you'd told me way back then that I'd still be recovering from rape now, I wouldn't have laughed in your face, but I wouldn't have believed you either. I'd faced traumas before—tenure review, major surgery, heartshattering divorce—stumbled through some and transcended others, so I expect rape to slip from me like a boiled beet's rough skin.

Since I'm living in an upscale Euro-American neighborhood, the police are as surprised—though for different reasons—as I am that the rapist was AfAm and question how I can be sure if I couldn't see him. They also wonder if I associate a smell with him. I don't, which rules out a smoker, loud cologne, and alcohol on his breath. No beard, sideburns, or goatee—though he may have a mustache. This "brother" doesn't have "good" hair, isn't balding, doesn't sport a juicy jheri-curl. He's wearing a clammy imitation leather jacket and heavyish gloves, which should have impeded unzipping his fly more than I remember them doing. He wasn't heavy on top of my 110 pounds. I don't remember feeling the scratch of his pubic hair. Does he, I wonder then and for months afterward, keep his raping ensemble in the trunk of the car? Who has he already raped? Who will he rape next?

In a clotted voice I don't recognize as mine, I talk to 911's drawling police officer who offers to stay on the phone until the patrol car arrives. Then my daughter and her best friend come in. Since they know me to be a night person, they're completely unsurprised to see me sitting at the kitchen counter at 3:30 A.M. "Mama's been raped," I blurt. "The police are on their way." At first Osula and Ann are kind of calm. When they become hysterical, I stop sobbing, have my daughter call her father, and have Ann call her mother. Get on the phone to assure both parents that I'm fine, hospital-bound for a routine check-up, but fine. And I believed I was!

The slim, short woman officer who entered the apartment first while the men hung back on the threshold has told me that I'll be asked to leave what I'm wearing at the hospital as evidence. While I write out my statement, I have Osula and Ann pack something for me to wear home and put the necessary items in a purse. As the scene-of-the-crime men go over the apartment dusting (as in grade B movies) for fingerprints they don't find, photographing the window the attacker came through and the pallet I was raped on, they speak in soft voices and wait for the detective to arrive. Osula and Ann are too traumatized to drive. So raped and night-blind (but trained to strong-Black-wonder-woman roles) I drive myself, following Detective Butler's tail lights, to a hospital I've never seen or even heard of before.

I decide to go into therapy or join a support group. Of the women I know who are rape victims and talk about it, twenty years after the attack the one who wasn't treated spews rage at the drop of a hat and, aside from going to work and visiting her large family, is a near-recluse; the one who joined a support group has kept her high-profile job and even traveled to China. Like her I have no intention of letting the rapist mangle my life.

Leaving home in September, I'd crowed to family and friends, "My daughter's off to college, and I can still touch my toes! I'm gon live like a graduate student!" After long years of being a single parent and professor, my Atlanta sabbatical (delayed a year so it will coincide with my daughter's first year away) opens another phase of my life. And I had such ambitious plans.

My loose connection with Spelman's English department includes teaching classes, grading papers, advising students, writing letters of recommendation, or going to meetings. Now I'll *finally* be able to write all day, and I have three projects at various stages of work-in-progress: *Birthmarks & Keloids* is my short story collection; "These Wild and Holy Women" is about spiritually powerful women characters in contemporary AfAm fiction; and "A Language of Their Own" is my book-to-be, about how Yoruba women's attire "speaks," what it signifies to other Yoruba and to outsiders who can read its syntax, grammar, vocabulary, cadences.

When I need a break from the rigors of writing, I'll go to AfAm bookstores, museums, art galleries, plays, dance concerts, film series, night spots. Back in a city after years in a New England university town, I'll eat soul, Ethiopian, West Indian, Japanese and Thai food; instead of driving two and half hours to get to church in Cambridge, Mass., I'll join an Atlanta Holy-Ghost-filled, political, and Afrocentric congregation; and, 48, keep an eye out for that good man who is so very hard to find, the husband for my old age.

Since I'm feeling fine (not a single bruise, broken fingernail, or out-of-place earring), it's a hassle to be in the dry cold of Clayton Hospital's air-conditioned examining room waiting the hours it takes doctors to finish treating Saturday night knife slashes and bullet gashes before one can get to me. The crisis counsellor says I seem like a woman accustomed to being in control and, since rape rendered me powerless, I may have a more difficult recovery than a more passive woman.

The next time the counsellor checks up on me, I ask what stages I can expect to go through and what I should do to recover from rape quickly and completely. Suck my teeth and groan to hear, "Each victim has to find her own way. It's hard to predict. Women mourn and mend differently." WAIT! STOP! HALT! Every six minutes some girl or woman in the USA is raped. Some recovered victim must have chronicled her journey, published her 12-step program, copywritten a recipe I can improve on. Though I scour, I never find a thing. Three years later all I can offer the next rape victim is two poems by twice-raped (!!) June Jordan. Audre Lorde's *Cancer Journals* have saved minds and lives, but there's no equivalent to guide a rape survivor. And there's no Bessie Smith, Ida Cox, Dinah Washington, Nina Simone, Koko Taylor, Sweet Honey in the Rock sound that testifies about and transcends rape's agonies.

Way down younder by myself,
and I couldn't hear nobody pray.

In movie and television versions of rape, *the* problems are that people
think you seduced the man, police are sexistly hostile, hospital staff is
icily callous, but my ordeal wasn't going that way at all. In my apartment, the Georgia police officers who look and sound like red-necks
treat me with a courtesy nothing in my childhood summers in segregated Jacksonville, Florida, or Dothan, Alabama, prepared me for. I'm
questioned gently. Did I recognize the rapist? A boyfriend? Someone
who'd stalked me? Was he a college student my daughter and her friend
knew? Did we have oral sex? Anal sex? Did he bite me? They accept
my word that I've never seen the man before and don't even ask if I
tried to fight him off. At the hospital, the in-take clerk, crisis counsellor, lab technician, nurse, doctor, billing clerk are all considerably
consoling. At the time I didn't notice, but a week later their behavior
upsets me. There is, I tell sympathizers, no plan to end rape. People
are just refining their treatment of the inevitable.

When the crisis counsellor leaves, I scan the hospital's "Recovering from Rape" brochure:

> REMEMBER. . . . You did nothing to provoke the attack. You are
> not at fault. You are the victim of a violent crime. Men do not rape
> because of sexual desire; they rape to humiliate, control, and de-
> grade. Rape is a violent assault on the body and leaves emotional
> scars which can take weeks, months, or years to resolve. Each per-
> son is unique and must work through this emotional trauma in their
> own individual way. There is no "right" or "wrong" way to deal
> with this stressful time.

The counsellor describes the hospital's exam and treatment: If
there's a chance that I might be pregnant, I'll get the morning-after
pill; had the rapist bitten me, I'd get a tetanus shot—BITTEN ME;
blood will be drawn to see if I've gotten a sexually transmitted disease, but, while waiting for the results, I'm to take antibiotics just in
case. . . . The doctor—a nurse by his side—turns off the light so his
ultraviolet lamp can look for traces of rapist's semen between my legs.
The second strange man in this long evening standing over my body,
focused on my vulva. I've neither seen nor heard about this phase of
rape's aftermath. As my nails claw the crisis counsellor's palm, I'm
glad she alerted me and glad I said yes to her hand-holding offer. Hairs
are pulled, one by one, from my head and vulva for DNA testing. After the lab technician takes my blood and gives me a Band-Aid with

Daffy Duck decorations, I collapse into snuffling tears, "I was so scared and there was no one to help me."

The sun's high by the time I finally leave the hospital. So exhausted I *know* I'll go right to sleep as soon as I get home, which isn't what happens. Kay, who has met me in the emergency room with a serene smile and steadying affirmation, alternates between soothing Osula and Ann in the waiting room and chatting with me as I'm shuttled from examining room to examining room, get a douche, Xanax for my expected anxiety, and antibiotics in case I have a sexually transmitted disease (I'm recoiling from gonorrhea and syphilis. It's weeks before herpes occurs to me. Months before AIDS seems possible). Kay assigns the girls to rid the apartment of all signs of police and rapist intrusion, but broad black scuff marks from the rapist's sneakers won't come off the white window ledge. (And, later, I refuse to have them painted over because I want to *remember* why I am suffering so.) Kay suggests a Caribbean vacation. Overhearing, Osula thinks I should spend time with family in Boston, Minneapolis, or NYC. Having just moved to Atlanta, I can't plan, much less pack for, another trip. Besides, I don't intend to let the rapist—a man whose face and name I don't know, whose unschooled and country Southern accent is all I'm sure I can recognize—make me skitter scared. As hard-headed as always, I pooh-pooh advice about getting a second-floor apartment, dog, or gun; and I resist all suggestions to go back to safe white Amherst. Not only don't I leave apartment 2401, I even sleep (sedated, the pallet moved from its rape location, and a woman friend spending the night in the living room) in the bedroom I was raped in. Four days later, I rent furniture for my garden apartment.

Throughout the sunny Sunday hours after the hospital, I notify family and friends that I've been raped, assuring them that my body is fine and that I'm exhilarated to be alive. I ask proven intercessors to help me glorify a wonderful God and, since "the prayers of the saints availeth much," to storm heaven on my behalf. That Sunday, and ever after, my candid talk about being raped surprises because people are accustomed to rape victims' shame and reticence. "But," I say over and over, "I am the victim, not the criminal."

Rape has its own shadings and nuances. Comparatively speaking, I haven't suffered all that much. I wasn't a virgin, incestuously raped, gang-raped, penetrated with a Coke bottle or a pool table's cue stick. Yes, I felt like the man had a weapon. No I didn't see a razor, knife, or gun. He didn't make me get up and have a drink with him, defecate or urinate on me. And my daughter and her friend left before he arrived and came home after he left. Being raped in the bed at 3:00 A.M., in an apartment I'd only lived in for a month, before I'd had time to get an

Atlanta social life, by a man I didn't know, got me much more sympathy than being raped by a date or husband would have.

My core is cracked when the rapist is a man my politics have taught me to call brother. Gone are slavery, Reconstruction and lynch law days when we fear white men's rape violence. Now we learn to cringe from men who look like our fathers, uncles, nephews, godsons. I have worked so hard to keep my ties to the AfAm working class I came out of: driven two and a half hours across Massachusetts for braid styles and church; maintained my ability to talk trash, dance into the wee hours, and cook our soul food; boasted "I love a cut and shoot bar." Now the class chasm has opened and I, of all people, feel muscles from my shoulders to my toes cramp in the presence of dark men whose body language, attire, or accent echo the rapist's. Ashamed of my fear, I hate the rapist for changing me.

Swaddled in shock's soft cloak, blessedly naive about the invisible wounds rape has scalded me with, I expect to take a week or two, even a month to recover. *Then*, I'll finish the tedium of settling into my Atlanta life and hunker down to the writing life I've longed for for years. If I'd known, or even suspected, the hells that lurked on the other side of shock, I would have tried to overdose, instead of just asking counsellors and psychiatrists how likely it was for rape victims to commit suicide, instead of pleading to be hospitalized until "all this" was over; instead of telling two different, but equally startled, psychiatrists, eighteen months and 700 miles apart, to "shoot me and put me out of my misery."

> A single hour in my life pulverized all my long-laid plans.
> I couldn't have lived with that knowledge.
> I'd have fallen off life's ledge.
> Or jumped.

A week after the rape, a friend and I aerobic walk in autumn's crisp sunshine. She hesitates as we start past the housing complex the police have traced the rapist's sneakered footprints to. Still-I-rise Blackwoman, I assure her than I'm just fine—and get excruciatingly crippling muscle spasms in by back almost immediately. Later that first anniversary evening, out of Xanax, unable to get D., the masseuse Kay has found for me—or E., the rape counsellor D. has referred to me—on the phone, I rely (as I've done innumerable uneventful times in the past) on the hot water bottle to loosen pain's vise. When I wake up, a patch of skin is sticking on the rubber, and I have second degree burns. On the way home from burn treatment a few days later, suffering from the loss of peripheral vision that—I later learn—often affects trauma victims, I have a car accident.

BUT I PRESS ON . . .

I give the "Writing Myself Alive" talk I've promised Spelman College, not merely so students can see and hear a woman scholar, not even so I can, for the first time in over fifteen years of college teaching, have a class that's both all female and all of African descent. It's my coming out. After years of being mother, scholar and professor, I've declared myself a writer. Daughter I call my Sun-and-moon-and-stars is a college student. I've managed to single-parent her and achieve the security of Ph.D., tenure and full professorship, and sustained a dismaying array of physical ailments. Now it's time to live *my* life, and I'm becoming less a consumer (and decoder) of other's works and more a creator of my own. "If nothing else I ever write gets published, I'll write on because I now know that my body/mind spirit will break if I don't."

Though I arrive late, contact lenses smeared, fingernail polish chipped, and in the disoriented state my sister calls "back-side-to," I manage to be on a Spelman College inaugural symposium panel on Black Women and the Intellectual/Literary Tradition the weekend Johnnetta Cole is installed, the first Africana woman ever, as president of the college. It seems like *everyone* is on campus: Beverly Guy-Sheftall and Paula Giddings, Niara Sudarkasa and Joyce Ladner, Toni Cade Bambara and Gwendolyn Brooks, Pearl Cleage and Mari Evans, Louise Meriwether and Sonia Sanchez, Byllye Avery and Pearl Primus. After a vegetarian dinner full of the kind of cultural and political talk I so miss in Amherst and came to Atlanta for, with a group of sisters I haven't seen in years, haven't ever seen all together, my energy is suddenly sucked away, and I stagger out of Sisters' chapel and slow-drive home long before the Max Roach/Maxine Roach octet has played a single note.

The morning after that heady day, too exhausted to imagine brushing my teeth much less driving from suburban College Park to Atlanta's Civic Center and sitting up through the inauguration, I begin to realize that my recovery from rape isn't going to be like gum surgery, knee surgery, or (natural childbirth) having my daughter. More like coming back from a hysterectomy—stomach muscles cut—when I'd already been weakened by years of the heavy bleeding that stains clothes, makes you carry extra tampons and pads everywhere, and has you fainting in public.

Since I'd felt so good and been so clear-headed and capable in the immediate aftermath of being raped—no signs of the physical exhaustion, disorientation, anxiety, or amnesia that, later, become my almost constant companions—I was as unprepared as everyone else when shock's soft shawl slipped from my shoulders. I thought what went wrong with rape victims was they denied being raped, but I hadn't. I'd called the police, pressed charges, been hospital-examined, begun twice-a-week rape crisis counselling, even seen the pastoral counsellor at Morehouse Medical School to talk about the politics of being raped by a "brother" and helped by Euro-Americans. In spite of my intentions and efforts, I didn't become my old self again in the weeks and then months I'd set aside for rape recovery. As the hours, days, weeks, months, years marched away from the October rape day, I came to see that I would never be my old self again. "The only thing about me that's the same," I tell those who compliment how strong my voice sounds and how well I look, "is my fingerprints." "You get better," Evelyn-the-counsellor tells me, "and, because you feel *more*, feel worse."

From a December '88 journal entry . . .

> 8:45 A.M. . . . So it was dreadful to feel my body getting tenser and tenser as I became more and more awake. Tense about what time it was. Tense about when the alarm clock would go off. Tense about what I'd eat. Tense about calling the phone company. Tense about calling Dr. D. for a Xanax refill. Tense about the car's possible problems. So I decided to give in and take an anti-anxiety pill, but then I couldn't find my pocketbook. Couldn't even find my glasses so I could look for the pocketbook. And all the while the kitten kept sneezing. I moaned for her to stop. And the sound of me mewling reminded me of the whimpering noises I made while I was being raped.

By January, still in twice-weekly rape crisis counselling, I finally dare to open a few windows in the apartment for the first time since I was raped, but being one of 3,000 people evacuated from an extremely bourgeois (the pastor drives a Jaguar) church near the beginning of Sunday service has frightened me unbearably. As I watch police dogs bomb-sniff, it feels like no place is safe. I can be hurt by someone I don't know at home in bed and in church which is, as I've said for years, where I'd rather be than any other place. At my request, E. calls a psychiatrist for me. The AfAm doctor diagnoses post-traumatic stress disorder which I thought you had to go to Vietnam to get. He prescribes Xanax for my anxiety and is surprised that I'd expected to be fully recovered from rape by now. It will, he dismays me by saying, require a year for short-term recovery and five years—FIVE!—for as close to full recovery as one gets.

By March, despite the successes I call myself having—riding MARTA public transportation and mounting a photography exhibit at

Spelman—Dr. P. stuns me by diagnosing clinical depression. (Only hearing him read the textbook definition and having him say that my progress so far reflects my disciplined willpower, persuades me.) Rape lugs me around. No sign of light at the end of the tunnel.

Rape makes me doze off at night propped up on pillows so I'll be prepared not so much "if" as "when" the rapist comes back. Lights on all over the apartment. I, nervous as my kitten, jump when she gets in or out of bed with me, and wake up almost every night at the 3:00 A.M. rape time. Raped in almost total darkness. I don't sleep soundly until dawn. And I wake up, as though demon-ridden, with crusty saliva lines around my mouth.

Before I was raped, I'd prided myself on waking up an alert that didn't need the caffeine props of coffee and tea. Afterwards, it's a daily struggle to come into consciousness and realize AGAIN that I didn't nightmare being raped. Now, as it did when I was actually being raped, my mind scrabbles for a safe place and, finding none, tries to shut off, but the strategy is no more effective than it was that gruesome night. No idea how I'll get out of bed, much less take the ten steps from the bedroom I was raped in to the bathroom I've become afraid to shower in. Grope for eyeglasses. Turn off the bedside lamp rape has made a nighttime necessity. Step over the telephone wire the newly installed burglar alarm is hooked up to. Peer blinking as I did the rape night, into the living room. Tense, heart racing, afraid.

In the western Massachusetts university town I'm on sabbatical from, my days start (weather permitting) with a mile-long up and down hill walk while the Connecticut Valley's air is dewy and still. Atlanta is much warmer than Amherst, so I'd looked forward to being outside much more and alternating bicycle rides with long walks. But family, friends, and police think the rapist stalked me, waited until I was alone and defenseless before he came through a living room window, so I'm much too frightened to leave the house and risk being raped again. Besides, though it takes me years to know this, my body's no longer mine. The rapist controls it. Moving feels like Herculean work and distracts my mind from being rape-alert.

"Did you stop and pray this morning?" a song from childhood Florida summer wonders, "as you started on your way? Did you ask God to guide you, walk beside you all the way? Did you stop and pray this morning? Did you kneel just one moment and say, 'Give me comfort for my soul on this old, rugged road?' Did you just remember to pray?" My mind's too centrifugal for prayer. Can neither sing the songs of Zion myself nor decide whether James Cleveland's gospel growl,

Aretha Franklin's sanctified melisma, or Marion William's octave-defying witness will encourage my heart, regulate my mind, relax my forehead's accordion pleats. Exhausted from my marrow on out, I'd die if I had to will air into my lungs or work to make my blood flow. Difficult to believe I can choose an ensemble, do laundry, grocery shop, or collect the mail. Impossible to see myself doing anything I came to Atlanta to do. Foolhardy to claim one day at a time. Half-hour by half-hour is all I dare.

But I *can* make a pot of tea, and focusing on that task magnetizes my mind's scattered steel filings on a north-south axis. Drop Lemon Verbena or Mello Mint tea bags into a small pot, sweeten with an exotic honey or plain white sugar, place the pot, a tall clear glass, yogurt, a spoon and a cloth napkin on a thick wooden tray and, emboldened by my success, turn off the lights that have protected me all night and open the blinds that face the thicket behind the apartment and the grass police found the rapist's footprint path on. Then nestle back under the covers. Inhaling the tea's steam relaxes me. First ("So glad I got my religion in time!"), I read *Forward Day by Day*'s meditations; half-dozen prayers from the Book of Common Prayer, and the psalm, Old Testament reading, gospel and epistle for the day. Next, notes about my health: medicine, pains and aches, mood swings, menu, exercise. Then, as an outward and visible sign that, though horribly helpless while I was raped, I can control some things, as evidence that although I have no idea when-where-why the rapist chose me, I can figure some things out, I work a *New York Times* crossword puzzle. Finally, still desperate for motives and solutions, I read a chapter or two in a mystery.

Pre-rape, I escaped into British mysteries, and my favorites all featured men who—no matter how they differed from each other—lived in worlds as far from mine as Tolkien's Middle Earth, C. S. Lewis's Narnia or Alice's Wonderland. Rolling manicured lawns, visiting cards; butlers, valets, chauffeurs, cooks and housekeepers; port, fine sherry, and dressing for dinner; Eton-Oxford-Cambridge; tea, scones and fairy cakes; witty conversations; country villages and estates; bumblingly well-intentioned vicars and earnest innkeepers; cashmere, titles, charming eccentrics. . . . Women are never raped, police don't carry guns, crimes occur offstage, and there is a logical explanation for every crime.

Raped, I'm a character in a cruder mystery. (File #88747812.) Detective C. L. Butler is in charge of the case. Now stories about British sleuths make my eyes slide off the page. "No, no, no," the gospel song insists, "They couldn't do. They didn't have the power that you needed to bring you through . . ."

Then my best friend sends me books about two new-style U.S. women detectives, Sue Grafton's California-based Kinsey Milhone and Sara Paretsky's V. I. Warshawski. Week after week I gulp, as if drowningly desperate for air, their plain-spoken stories about acid-tongued, fast-thinking, single and self-employed women who not only dare to live alone, but scoff, sneer, seethe when men try to put them in their "weaker sex" place. Parched and starved, I read and reread Sue Grafton's alphabet adventures, but Sara Paretsky's books become my favorites because her Chicago-based private investigator is even more bodacious and sassy than my pre-rape self. And, in stark contrast to television and movie renditions of women as powerless victims of men, she both withstands and metes out physical violence in every single book. Murder mysteries restore order to worlds thrown out of balance. . . . The police may never find the "brother" who raped me, and I may never get to read him the seven-foot scroll detailing *all* I've suffered since he slithered into my life.

The morning ritual comforts me. If I don't do another purposeful thing all day, I *have* accomplished something. An hour and a half after my first sip of tea, I am focused enough to turn on radio jazz and churn out the six typewritten journal pages I require of myself daily. On days when I can't do the ritual or fall asleep as soon as I've done it, I know I am, once again, nailed to the dank floor of the abyss.

By the time my lease runs out at the end of June, Atlanta's warm enough for sweet and eat-them-in-the-bathtub-juice peaches. I'm re-mastering grocery shopping and the basics of cooking. Fear has subsided enough for me to sleep with fewer lights on and ride MARTA in relative calm. Still automatically check the physique, skin color and hair-do of all the AfAm men I see to be sure they aren't the rapist returned. Carry the phone the burglar alarm's hooked up to from room to room, spend hours watching CBS soap operas and reruns of "Murder, She Wrote" and (twice a day) "Miami Vice." No longer expect my '78 Toyota to collapse around me the way my life has, leaving me clutching the steering wheel on Atlanta's maze of highways. But . . . my sabbatical has shape-shifted into sick leave, and I've filed Social Security and TIAA/CREF claims for total disability since I'm too frightened in groups of people, too easily exhausted and too amnesiac to teach.

Summer '89, back in the college town I fled to Atlanta to escape, I can't recall what's in the drawers, closets and cabinets of a house I've lived in for a decade and am astonished at how little I remember about campus buildings, college routines, colleagues' faces, names, disciplines. When the old farmhouse makes its floor-settling night noises, I panic alert. It feels like I've sunk back to the beginning of rape recovery when, the first Saturday night I spend alone a thousand miles away from the rape site, I put knives, scissors, letter openers, potato peelers and pantyhose away with the same compulsion and dismay that drove me in Atlanta. I am back in the high-walled chasm, buried alive beneath a man in a stocking cap mask, bleeding from internal wounds people can't see when they insist on how good I look and sound.

When fast-track people in Amherst ask about my time away, they expect to hear about my photography, book proposals, chapters written, contracts signed. During my nine-month Atlanta stay, I haven't written one line or edited a single page of "A Language of Their Own," "These Wild and Holy Women," or *Birthmarks & Keloids*. Reeling toward healing, I have neither organized the negatives, photographs and slides of my Nigeria research nor mastered the word processor. My Atlanta "accomplishments" are not screaming when a man next to me in church stood close enough to hold one side of the hymnal we were singing out of and sitting between the two AfAm men AAA sent to tow my car to a Toyota dealership. My writing consists of a few personal letters, two letters of recommendation composed at a hobbled snail's pace, disability claims and my journal. Each time I'm asked how Atlanta was, the scab's scraped from my scar.

ATLANTA IS WHERE RAPE TORTURED ME,
WHERE I ALMOST DIED FROM AN INVISIBLE WOUND.

Too sick to teach Fall semester, I plan to spend it in St. Croix, healing in the sea and sun, but, for the first time in eighty-two years, St. Croix is undone by a hurricane. My *second* away-from-Amherst plan in two years *pulverized*, sealing me in the tomb Amherst feels like—with no resurrection in sight. I'm Brer Rabbit. And Amherst is my tarbaby.

Winter-bare trees. Short days. Low leaden skies. Cold. Boots, mittens, scarves, thermal underwear, snow shovels and tires, antifreeze, rock salt. I cling, as though they could save me—to the covers when the alarm goes off. Regress back to daily naps and coloring books. Exhausted no matter how much I sleep. Even the tiniest task monumental. A kind of suicidal I talk myself out of over and over only by realizing that my Sun-and-moon-and-stars would be undone. For the first time since my ugly-duckling high school days, I cry in outbursts that last an hour and try to see the banked emotions through the prisms Dame Julian of Norwich and Rebecca Jackson (of Philadelphia) did.

My Amherst psychiatrist decides Tofranil isn't affecting my depression, prescribes Prozac and makes seemingly Simon Legree rules: Do not sleep in the clothes you wore all day and wear them again the next day; leave the house, even if it's only to get the mail, every day;

go, since you have friends, family and church there, to Boston as often as your scant store of energy will allow; write. When asked, my Atlanta psychiatrist said that though raped at home I'd rather be there than anywhere else because home was where I had most control and that, as a person who "lived in my mind," getting my memory back was complicated by how many things I know. "Most people only have one language to get back. You have English, French, Spanish, and smatterings of Yoruba." My Amherst psychiatrist depicts clinical depression as a cunning illness: If you've prided yourself on the regularity of your schedule, it keeps you from going to sleep at night and getting up in the morning; if you're a sensual person, desire is expunged; if you're an intellectual, depression breaks your mind.

My morning ritual is my life-jacket. Downstairs to bigger teapot, a wider range of teas and the inventiveness to combine Mellow Mint and Tropical Escape. Sliced raw ginger and—the ingredients vary daily—pounded cloves. As the weather chills, yogurt's replaced by pears, and tangerines, warmed apple cider with ginger and vinegar or warm milk with a combination of Ovaltine and Postum alternate with tea. Winter's grip tightens, and fruit gives way to seven grain, challah and anadama bread. Using the same thick circular wooden tray I had in Atlanta, I carry a cloth napkin in a wooden ring and a tall clear glass for my elixir upstairs for myself the way I'd do for an invalid friend or a luscious man. Then burrow back in bed for the morning "work" I did in Atlanta, with additions.

Leaving Georgia has meant giving up the arc of gracious women I relied on, and I miss them so. Over and over I find myself longing for the web of loving women who surrounded Audre Lorde's mastectomy recovery. Once again, as they were in my friendless adolescence, books become my best friends, and their sister-care feeds me. Before I begin each one, I just *know* reading it will gnarl me with envy and make me even more ashamed of allowing rape to derange me so completely. But I am always wrong. Quilts in *Stitching Memories*. Poetry by Lucille Clifton, and Rita Dove, *Lionheart Gal*'s collection of feisty and backative Jamaican women's testimonies . . . Toni Morrison's heartstopping *Beloved*. Alice Walker's *Living by the Word*. Toni Cade Bambara's *Salt Eaters*. . . . These women's stories aren't mine so I know there is still space for my frayed pieces of the patchwork quilt, and their sturdy and magical creations brave me to try. Some raped woman needs my witness. Not emotions recollected in elegant tranquility when I am *finally* out of the tunnel it takes all my faith to believe even exists. She needs to taste my terror, hear my gasps for life, watch me inch through brambles of despair, reaching for life and sanity with bleeding stigmata all over me.

The story of the people and the spirits, the story of earth, is the story of what moves, what moves on, what patterns, what dances, what sings, what balances, so life can be felt and known. The story of life is the story of moving. Of moving on.

Your place in the great circling spiral is to help in that story, in that work. To pass on to those who can understand what you have learned, what you know.

It is for this reason you have endured. . . .

. . . Pass it on. . . . That is the story of life. . . . Grow, move, give, move.

(Paula Gunn Allen, *The Woman Who Owned the Shadows*, p. 210)

References

Allen, Paula Gunn. 1994. *The Woman Who Owned the Shadows*. San Francisco: Aunt Lute.

Cleage, Pearl. 1990. *Mad at Miles: A Blackwoman's Guide to Truth*. Southfield, MI: Cleage Group.

3

Rape Sonnets

~

Andi Rosenthal

*On July 30, 1987, this writer was a victim of acquaintance rape.
She was seventeen years old.*

*Like many women, she chose to remain silent for a number of
reasons. After three years, however, the need to speak out slowly
and steadily began to surface. By the time these poems were written in 1991, she was sufficiently ready to tell her story.*

*These poems, which were originally published under an as-
sumed name, express the belief that victims of rape, in order to
acquit themselves of guilt and self-blame, must learn to express
themselves in a form that reaffirms their own concept of the person who existed before the event—something that is often lost when
victims lend their words and their lives to a name that is not their
own.*

*The following sequence of poems attempts to depict the slow
transition from victim to survivor.*

1. This Really Happened

Afterwards, I walk to the edge of the silent
pond, where strands of water lay entwined
in the grass. The night is warm and thick
with summer; the voices from the house, the lights
hang in the air like overripe fruit. The sounds
pervade my mouth, my skin like some sick fog,
like my tongue rotting inside my throat. The house—

Someone is playing music, and the sound
has burned my eyes. I am the only dead thing here,
kneeling beside the water's edge without a mouth
to pray, without hands to clasp or implore, without
the eyes that mutely screamed, and were ignored.
A swan glides, rageless, through my reflection.
Blood trickles down my thigh, and the party goes on.

2. After the Silence

The truth grows inside me like a thicket
of wild fruit, boundless, with its branches
that twist about my bones and make me small,
and later, the harvest of rotten fruit,
swollen and reeking in that sacred space
below my throat. It rages over this
interminable ground, its leaves
grow false and jaded, ageless and insane.
Yet telling, as I see the terrible flowers
burst forth with measured honey, drop by jewelled drop
brimming with deliberate grace, I know—
I sell these stems for absolution, but
not even the blade of self-inflicted ignorance
can suffuse the silence of my torn roots.

3. Given Names

Can you see where I end and she begins
within that printed page? I feel as if
a puppeteer who drinks too much has painted
a new face for me. It's hers, the name
they gave me when I told about the blood.
Now there are words. They do not belong
to me. They are suspended from someone
else's name with strings. I wonder why
they think they are protecting me from
the people who will look at me and know.
I don't need names to tell them; no amount
of paint will ever hide the bruises on my
mouth. I am the smiling mask, the dead doll.
Behold, she is the handmaid of the truth.

4. The First Love

When I was a girl, I counted candles in church
behind the altar when I should have been praying.
Those jewelled sentinels were silent and still,

at the feet of the Virgin Mother—guardians;
Yet even a child's whisper could distract them.

The first time, you lit a candle before love.
One light, constant. There were no words.
I was not a virgin, and I didn't know how to pray.

I should have learned the lesson of the lights.
Now there is only darkness without words. I wanted
so much to give myself that way, but could not,
because the light inside me was taken in whispers.
You cannot give fire back to ashes.
There is no place for light here, and nothing is sacred.

5. A Girl's Garden—Revisited

When shall we plant, beloved? I have found
my garden grown with longing. Have you tried
the rusted doorknob on the old green shed
where rakes and seeds are kept? It makes a sound
like turtle bones.

        O, love, and all around
are layers of broken leaves. The grass is dead
below; above, the maple tree has died.

We wed our withered blossoms to the ground
expecting them to grow. We never know
the pull of dark sweet earth upon our hands,
under our fingernails.

        My love, the night
is thick with angels flying bright and slow.
They scatter seedlings over barren lands
and souls bereft of earth air water light.

4

Mikvah Ceremony for Laura

~

Laura Levitt
Sue Ann Wasserman

LAURA: The ceremony that follows was put together for me by my friend and my rabbi Sue Ann Wasserman after my rape in November 1989. The ceremony marks my particular experience and desire to heal. It is a ritual that speaks to the specific place I had come to in my healing on November 24, 1989. I went to the *mikvah*[1] with Sue Ann and my mother a few days after my first period after the rape. It was the day after Thanksgiving during my parents' first visit. It was erev Shabbat. Since November I have had other ways of marking time since the rape. My body has overcome a multitude of diseases punctuated by visits to doctors. This has been ongoing. I just took my second HIV test.[2] I have had to wait over six months for definitive results. Although I have maintained my professional life from the beginning, both teaching and studying, it has taken much time to recover other aspects of my life. I have slowly resumed my fantasy life and sex life, but I still long for a time when I will be able to live alone again.

SUE ANN: Although I grew up in a religious Reform Jewish home, *mikvah* was not a part of my background. I became interested in *mikvah* and the laws of family purity[3] while in rabbinic school. My interest stemmed from my need and desire to find parts of my tradition that spoke to me as a woman. I read and wrote and thought about *mikvah* as a woman's ritual both past and present. My practical knowledge of

From Laura Levitt and Sue Ann Wasserman, "*Mikvah* Ceremony for Laura," in *Four Centuries of Jewish Women's Spirituality*, ed. Ellen M. Umansky and Dianne Ashton (Boston: Beacon Press, 1992), 321–26. Reprinted by permission of Laura Levitt and Sue Ann Wasserman.

mikvah has come through my work with people who are converting to Judaism. I became convinced of its power to provide a meeting place for people and God, through listening to my students speak about their experience and how significant the *mikvah* was as a conclusion to their formal study for conversion.[4]

LAURA: Healing is a process. This *mikvah* ceremony is distinct in that it represents one of the few ways that I have been able to attend to my spiritual as well as my physical and emotional healing. Sharing this ceremony with other Jewish women is part of this healing. It is a way for me to give something of myself to other Jewish women, especially those who have been sexually abused. I want them to know that they are not alone. I also want them to know that there is a place for us and even our most painful experiences to be commemorated in Jewish community/ies.

My body was violated by rape. The *mikvah* offered me a place to acknowledge both that violation and my desire to heal. My need for ritual was very real. I needed to do something concrete to express my psychic and physical pain as a Jewish woman among other Jewish women I am close to.

For me, healing is not simply a return to some "wholeness" in the past; it is an experience of growth and change. Healing is the careful rebuilding of a life in the present that does not deny what has happened.

SUE ANN: When Laura was raped, I wanted to find a way to support her as her friend. As a rabbi, I needed to find a way for Judaism to respond to her. The *mikvah* seemed to be the most appropriate ritual for several reasons. (1) It was predominantly our foremothers' ritual. (2) It requires the whole body. (3) Its waters flow in and out—representing continuity and process. (4) Its waters symbolically flow from Eden, a place of wholeness. (5) The natural waters remind us of the constant intermingling presence of the Creator in our own lives. (6) Finally, water itself is cleansing, supportive, and life sustaining.

The task then was to find words that would give this ancient ritual meaning in the context of Laura's experience. I drew on the sources at hand and included my own words as well as asking Laura to bring whatever readings she thought would be healing for her.

LAURA: The poems I chose to read during the *mikvah* ceremony reflect these feelings. Like the narrator in Irena Klepfisz's "Di rayze aheym" (The journey home),[5] I too wanted to return "home" but knew that the home I knew before the rape was no longer accessible to me. Nevertheless, I still needed a home. Healing has meant that I have had to rebuild a new life where I can attend to my scars while also experiencing joy again. I have had to rebuild my life "even from a broken web."[6] These words, the poetry of contemporary Jewish women, have helped me articulate some of these feelings, but to speak them at the *mikvah* made them physically tangible.

Historically, the *mikvah* is a sacred space for Jewish women and our bodies. Through this ceremony, I was able to enter into that tradition. Sue Ann helped me reconstitute this place to attend to my own physical needs for healing. In a steamy room overlooking a pool of running water in a synagogue in Atlanta, we recited these words and I entered the water. In so doing, the violation of my Jewish female body was attended to. It was neither silenced nor ignored.

SUE ANN: We stood together at the *mikvah*, the three of us [Sue Ann, Laura, and Laura's mother], reading a liturgy that had been created in a day, to prepare us to perform a ritual that has existed for centuries. It was a powerful and empowering experience, but it was only a first step in the creation of a new liturgy that will speak to those who seek healing after a rape or any form of sexual abuse.

"*Mikvah* Ceremony for Laura"

SUE ANN: According to the Talmud, the ultimate source of all water is the river that emerged from Eden. By immersing ourselves in the *mikvah*, we participate in the wholeness of Eden. Natural water is required for a *mikvah* because water is a symbol of the life forces of the universe. Fundamentally, *mikvah* is not about "uncleanliness" but about human encounters with the power of the holy.[7]

To be read around by paragraph:
"In our tradition, water has always played a pivotal role. There is something elemental about it. Before the world was created, there existed the presence of God hovering over the surface of the water.

When, in the times of Noah, God wished to make a new beginning of life on earth, the fountains of the deep were opened and waters came forth, returning the earth to its pristine beginnings.

Our patriarchs and matriarchs met at the well, for the source of water was the center of community life. Thus the well, the source of water, marked the promise of new beginnings in their lives.

Water is also a sign of redemption in our People's history. It was the waters of the Red Sea that parted and allowed us to go forth from bondage into freedom.

Water is also a symbol of sustenance. Miriam, the sister of Moses, was deemed to be so righteous that during her lifetime, when the Israelites wandered in the wilderness, God caused a well, Miriam's well it was called, to accompany the people and sustain them with water."[8]

LAURA: "Anger and tenderness: my selves.
And now I can believe they breathe in me
as angels, not polarities.
Anger and tenderness: the spider's genius
to spin and weave in the same action
from her own body, anywhere—
even from a broken web."[9]

(*Laura reads*)
"Di rayze aheym" (The journey home), by Irena Klepfisz[10]

SUE ANN: This ceremony is to help bring closure to your physical healing and cleansing. Your physical injuries are fading. You've done much cleaning; your apartment, your body, with soaps and masks, and miraculously your body has cleansed itself through menstruation.

This ceremony is also an attempt to help you begin the spiritual and emotional healing you must do. I see these *mikvah* waters as symbolic of two things. First, the tears you have yet to cry. Perhaps being surrounded by them from the outside will release them from the inside. Second, we do not sink in water but rather are buoyed up by it. It supports us gently. This is like your community of friends and family who have kept you afloat and sustained you. We, like the waters, are messengers of the Shechinah.[11] The Divine Presence is made present in your life through our loving and embracing arms and through the warm caress of these living waters.

LAURA: Now, as I immerse myself, I begin a new cycle in my life. May my entry into the waters of the *mikvah* strengthen me for the journey that lies ahead.[12]

"Water is God's gift to living souls,
to cleanse us, to purify us,
to sustain us and renew us."[13]

SUE ANN: "May the God whom we call Mikveh Yisrael, and God who is the source of living waters, be with you now and always."[14]

Immersion and then recite:

*Baruch ata Adonai Eloheynu Melech Ha-olam asher kid'shanu,
bemitzvotav vitsivanu al ha'tevilah.*

Blessed are You, Adonai, God of all creation, who sanctifies us with
your commandments and commanded us concerning immersion.

Immersion and then recite:

*Baruch ata Adonai Eloheynu Melech Ha-olam she-hehiyanu vihigianu
vikiamanu lazman hazeh.*

Blessed are You, Adonai, God of all creation, who kept us alive and
preserved us and enabled us to reach this season.

Immersion for a third and final time.

*Following the immersion
Read around by stanzas:*

"God give us the strength
   to transcend setbacks and pain
   to put our difficulties into perspective

God give us the strength
   to fight against all forms of injustice,
   whether they be subtle or easily apparent

God give us the strength
   to take the path less traveled
      and more disturbing

God give us the strength
   to persevere
   to reach out to those in need—
      may we abandon none of your creations

May we never become callous or apathetic because
   of our own disappointments

May our personal pain never be used as
   an excuse to stop heeding your call

God give us the strength
   to continually strive to do more

Let us always strive to give, even if we,
   ourselves, feel alone or impoverished

For we must always strive to reach beyond
      ourselves."[15]

Notes

1. *Mikvah* has many meanings in Hebrew. It is a confluence of water, a reservoir, a pool, or a ritual bath. *Mikvah* is also understood to be a source of hope and trust, another name for God. The *mikvah* ceremony refers to the ritual of immersion in such a place for purposes of ritual purification. According to halakhah, Jewish law, the ritual of immersion is required for conversion to Judaism, but it is most commonly associated with "laws of family purity." Within monogamous heterosexual Jewish marriages, "as menstruation begins, a married couple halts all erotic activities. A minimum of five days are considered menstrual, then seven 'clean' days are observed with the same restrictions. After nightfall of the seventh day, the woman bathes herself . . . and immerses herself in a special pool built to exacting specifications" (Susan Weidman Schneider, *Jewish and Female: A Guide and Sourcebook for Today's Jewish Woman* [New York: Touchstone, 1985], 204; see pp. 203–13 for an extended discussion of the ritual and its revival).

2. HIV, the human immunodeficiency virus, is believed to be the cause of AIDS, acquired immunodeficiency syndrome. HIV is a blood-borne virus transmitted through the exchange of bodily fluids.

3. See n. 1 above.

4. *Mikvah* is a part of the traditional conversion process. To convert to Judaism one must engage in formal study of the tradition and, having done so for a significant period of time, must agree to take on the obligations of the tradition. According to *halakhah*, the ceremony that marks this transition is *mikvah*. Immersion concretizes the transformation that has already been achieved through study and obligation. In Reform Judaism, ritual immersion is an optional part of the conversion process.

5. Melanie Kaye/Kantrowitz and Irena Klepfisz, eds., *The Tribe of Dina: A Jewish Women's Anthology* (Montpelier, Vt: Sinister Wisdom 29/30, 1986), 49–52.

6. Adrienne Rich, *A Wild Patience Has Taken Me This Far: Poems, 1978–1981* (New York: Norton, 1981), 9.

7. Anita Diamant, *The New Jewish Wedding* (New York: Summit, 1985), 151.

8. Jeffrey Perry-Marx, "A Ceremony of Tevilih," unpublished manuscript used in a Senior Rabbinic workshop on Outreach given by Rabbi Nina Mizrachi at Hebrew Union College-Jewish Institute for Religion, New York, spring 1987.

9. Rich, *A Wild Patience*, 9.

10. Kaye/Kantrowitz and Klepfisz, eds., *The Tribe of Dina*, 49–52.

11. The Shechinah is the Divine Presence in the world, the in-dwelling or immanent presence of God. Jewish mystical literature describes this presence as female. In the mystical tradition, the Shechinah is the feminine principle of God to be found in the world.

12. From "A Bridal Mikvah Ceremony," written by Barbara Rossman Penzener and Amy Zwiback-Levenson, in Diamant, *The New Jewish Wedding*, 157–58.

13. Ibid.

14. Perry-Marx, "A Ceremony of Tevilih."

15. This prayer was written by Angela Graboys and Laura Rappaport. It is found in a daily service they edited, "ROW Service," an unpublished manuscript,

Cincinnati, Hebrew Union College-Jewish Institute of Religion. ROW is an organization for women rabbinical students at Hebrew Union College-Jewish Institute of Religion in Cincinnati.

II   Defining the Problem

Each of the articles in this section in some way challenges conventional definitions of rape and urges us to reexamine understandings of rape in light of social science research. Psychologist Patricia Donat and historian John D'Emilio outline the changing definitions of rape in "A Feminist Redefinition of Rape and Sexual Assault: Historical Foundations and Change." By examining societal definitions of rape from colonial times until the present, Donat and D'Emilio argue that prevailing conceptions of rape affect society's treatment of rape and rape victims. They also explore in depth the impact that the feminist movement has had on beliefs about sexual assault, stating that we must continue to educate men and to empower women if we are to prevent rape.

One significant change in the understanding of rape occurred when researchers began to recognize that large numbers of women are assaulted by men they know. Psychologist Mary Koss, a professor of public health at the University of Arizona, Tucson, discusses this phenomenon of "acquaintance rape" in "Hidden Rape: Sexual Aggression and Victimization in a National Sample of Students in Higher Education." Here, Koss questions the prevalent statistics gathered by official agencies and asserts that rape is actually more widespread than these statistics would indicate. Koss finds in her large-scale survey of college students that a number of women are assaulted by acquaintances, but they do not define their experience as rape, due to the prevailing cultural belief that rape is a crime committed by a stranger. Koss concludes that official reports of rape vastly underestimate the actual number of rapes, because many women assaulted by acquaintances do not report the crime to the police.

In "Wife Rape and the Law," Diana Russell, a psychologist at Mills College in Oakland, California, investigates marital rape and focuses upon the changes in rape laws that have eliminated the so-called "marital privilege," whereby a man could not be charged with raping his wife. As Russell notes, sex within marriage has historically been viewed as a man's legal right. As a result, wives who have experienced coercive sex have not been considered rape victims. Society's failure to recognize these incidents as rape makes it difficult for married women who have been sexually assaulted to define their experiences. Thus,

Russell identifies wife rape as another area that must be addressed if we are to reach an accurate understanding of sexual assault.

Finally, standard definitions of rape often ignore the fact that males may also be victims of sexual assault. Psychiatrists Gillian Mezey and Michael King explore this little-researched topic in "The Effects of Sexual Assault on Men: A Survey of Twenty-two Victims." They find that male victims of sexual assault suffer many of the same reactions as do female victims. Like women, many men react to rape with passive submission, fearing that a strong response may provoke the assailant's wrath. Mezey and King note that male victims often feel responsible for the assault and berate themselves for their failure to defend themselves more strongly. Also, like female rape survivors, most men in Mezey and King's survey knew the man who had assaulted them. The authors argue that because male rape falls outside the standard definition of rape, these victims suffer great social stigma that can be reduced only when definitions of rape are changed to include men as well as women.

5

A Feminist Redefinition of
Rape and Sexual Assault:
Historical Foundations and Change

~

Patricia L. N. Donat
John D'Emilio

THE ISSUES OF RAPE AND sexual assault have been major concerns of
the feminist movement since its revival in the late 1960s. Because
of the work of feminists, the contemporary understanding of rape and
sexual assault, and the social response to sexual violence, have under-
gone significant revision. This paper examines the feminist response
to traditional conceptualizations of rape and the impact it has had. It
begins by presenting some historical background to set a context for
understanding more recent events.

The Colonial Era

During the colonial period, settlers in the English colonies were influenced strongly by the church, which prescribed the behavior of its
congregation. The family was defined as the central unit in society
and sex roles were differentiated rigidly. Men were dominant and
women were submissive. The woman was regarded "not as a person
. . . but as a sexual 'type'—an inferior, a receptacle . . . or a simple
answer to his needs" (Koehler, 1980, p. 93). Sexuality was channeled
into marriage for the procreation of legitimate offspring. Nonmarital

From Patricia L. N. Donat and John D'Emilio, "A Feminist Redefinition of
Rape and Sexual Assault: Historical Foundations and Change," *Journal of Social
Issues* 48, no. 1 (1992): 9–22. © 1992 by the Society for the Psychological Study
of Social Issues. Reprinted by permission of the Society for the Psychological
Study of Social Issues.

sexual intercourse was immoral, an offense against both family and community (D'Emilio and Freedman, 1988).

In order to regulate deviance, the church, courts, and community joined to monitor private sexual behavior and to limit sexual expression to marriage. Colonial society held the entire community responsible for upholding morality, and sexual crimes were punished severely. Women bore the heaviest responsibility for regulating premarital sexual contact. "Church and society dealt more harshly with women . . . [because] female chastity and fidelity assured men of the legitimacy of their children" (D'Emilio and Freedman, 1988). The integrity of the family was critical to the development of community and was guarded with care. For men, the integrity of the family rested on female purity and monogamy.

A woman's value within society was based on her ability to marry and to produce legitimate heirs. The ability to attract a spouse was influenced by the woman's perceived purity. The rape of a virgin was considered a crime against the father of the raped woman rather than against the woman herself. A raped woman could not expect to marry into a respectable family and might very well remain the economic liability of the father.

During the colonial period, the rape cases most likely to come to court were those in which the perpetrator was from a lower social class than the victim or in which the victim was a married woman who physically resisted. "When men of the lower order raped women of a higher social standing, they threatened the prerogatives of other men" (Lindemann, 1984, p. 81).

Women were dependent on the courts and community (i.e., men) for their protection. In order to ensure her safety, a woman who was sexually attacked needed to comply with male standards for her behavior by proving her nonconsent through physical and verbal resistance, and through immediate disclosure of the attack to both family and neighbors. Proof of nonconsent was necessary to verify that the woman had not voluntarily engaged in sexual acts outside of marriage. If a woman could not prove nonconsent, she might be punished for the assault (D'Emilio and Freedman, 1988). Rape was therefore "an expression of male control over women, regulated by law in a way that serves the men who hold political power more than it protects women" (Lindemann, 1984, p. 81).

The 19th Century

Toward the end of the 18th century, sexual meanings began to change. Sexuality no longer was tied so closely to reproductive intentions, and more emphasis was placed on courtship and individual choice rather than on community and family control. The subsequent decline in traditional church and state regulation of morality loosened constraints on nonmarital sex.

During the 19th century, young women from the countryside and from immigrant families began to enter the paid work force and earn their livings outside the family household. Patriarchal controls over women's time, behavior, and sexuality weakened (Stansell, 1986). With increased freedom, however, also came increased vulnerability. Previously, "courtship was one part of a system of barter between the sexes, in which a woman traded sexual favors for a man's promise to marry. Premarital intercourse then became a token of betrothal" (Stansell, 1986, p. 87). Women, however, no longer could assume that pregnancy would lead to marriage.

Female virtue continued to be important for finding a spouse. In the 19th century women were viewed as pure and virtuous by nature, and as disinterested in sex. Women of all classes were expected to use their natural purity and superior morality to control men's innate lust. The impure woman threatened the delicate moral balance and suggested the "social disintegration that sexuality symbolized" (Freedman, 1981, p. 20). A woman who engaged in sexual intercourse, even against her will, was considered to be depraved—a "fallen" woman—and was often blamed for the man's crime and socially stigmatized as a result of the attack. "As woman falls from a higher point of perfection, so she sinks to a profounder depth of misery than man" (Freedman, 1981, p. 18).

The 20th Century

During the 20th century, the writings of Sigmund Freud and other psychologists and sexologists provided the foundation for reconceptualizing sexual behavior and categorizing sexual deviations. One emerging concern was an interest in understanding the causes of sexual aggression. Many hypotheses were developed, but most theories included the belief that rape was a perversion and that rapists were mentally ill (Amir, 1971). One theory of sexual aggression suggested that the rapist's behavior was the result of socialization by a strong maternal figure and a weak paternal figure. Another theory proposed that the rapist's behavior was the result of a defective superego that left the individual unable to control his sexual and aggressive impulses. Therefore, the rapist was considered to have a "character disorder" and was classified as a "sick" individual. Other theories to explain the rapist's behavior included castration fears, feelings of sexual inferiority and inadequacy, homosexual tendencies, organic factors, and mental deficiencies (Amir, 1971). All of these theories reduced the rapist's responsibility for his actions since he was considered unable to control his pathological impulses. In other words, rape was reconceptualized from the perpetrator's point of view. The focus was on understanding the plight of the man, not the woman. Her victimization was simply a by-product of his pathology.

During the 1930s, the public increasingly became interested in sex crimes committed by men against women. In 1937, the New York Times created a new index category of sex crimes, which included 143 articles published that year (Freedman, 1989). Due to the influence of psychoanalytic theories, sex offenders began to be considered more as deviants than as criminals. Between 1935 and 1965, several state commissions to investigate sex crimes were formed; in many places, authority for the treatment and rehabilitation of the sex offender shifted away from the penal system and toward the mental health system (Freedman, 1989). Psychiatrists began to carry more influence concerning treatment of the sex offender. The label "sexual psychopath" was used to describe the violent male offender who was unable to control his sexual impulses and attacked the object of his frustrated desires. Thus rape was conceptualized primarily as an act of sex rather than an act of violence.

As awareness of sex crimes increased, public concern also escalated. Several "sex psychopath laws" were passed that permitted offenders to receive indefinite commitment to state mental hospitals rather than jail sentences. This law reform, initiated by male legislators, was opposed by many women who endorsed stronger criminal penalties for rape and sexual assault. Although sexual psychopath laws were promoted as a measure to protect women, in reality these laws often resulted in White men being labeled as mentally ill and sent to state hospitals, and Black men being found guilty of a crime and sent to jail (Freedman, 1989).

Racial Aspects of Rape

In addition to oppressing women, rape served as a method of racial control. The sexual assault of minority women maintained the supremacy of White men. The experience of the Black female victim was virtually ignored. White men used

> women as verbs with which to communicate with one another (rape being a means of communicating defeat to the men of a conquered tribe). . . . Rape sent a message to black men, but more centrally, it

expressed male sexual attitudes in a culture both racist and patriarchal. (Hall, 1983, p. 322)

In the post-Reconstruction South, White men used the myth of the Black man as sexually uncontrollable and as a threat to all White women as an excuse for violence toward Black men and as a means to control women through fear. Black men who were accused of sexually attacking White women received the harshest penalties. A Black man convicted of rape often was executed or castrated (D'Emilio and Freedman, 1988; Jordan, 1968). In the 1930s the Association of Southern Women for the Prevention of Lynching stated that the traditions of chivalry and lynching were a form of sexual and racial intimidation rather than protection.

> Lynching, it proclaimed, far from offering a shield against sexual assault, served as a weapon of both racial and sexual terror, planting fear in women's minds and dependency in their hearts. It thrust them in the role of personal property or sexual objects, ever threatened by black men's lust, ever in need of white men's protection. (Hall, 1983, p. 339)

The myth of the Black rapist still lingers in more severe sentencing penalties for Black offenders (Hall, 1983). Thus, rape and its legal treatment can be seen as the ultimate demonstration of power in a racist and patriarchal society.

Perceptions of the Rape Victim

In addition to changes in the conceptualization of male offenders, society's perception of the victim's role in the assault also changed during the 20th century. As female nature became sexualized and female desire for sexuality legitimated, rape became redefined as "not only a male psychological aberration, but also an act in which women . . . contributed to their victimization" (Freedman, 1989, p. 211). Many people became skeptical that a woman could be raped if she did not consent. A well-known attorney once began a rape trial by placing a Coke bottle on a table, spinning it, and demonstrating to the jury his difficulty in forcing a pencil into the opening (Margolin, 1972). The implication was that a woman would be able to fend off a man attempting to rape her (Schwendinger and Schwendinger, 1983). Therefore, if a woman was raped, she must have "asked for it."

Laws requiring physical evidence of penetration, the need for corroboration, and allowing testimony about the victim's sexual history in court trials had the effect of placing the victim on trial. In addition, juries often still received the traditional instruction that an accusation of rape "is one which is easily made and, once made, difficult to defend against, even if the person accused is innocent" (Berger, 1977, p. 10) The jury was cautioned to be suspicious of the victim's testimony, much more so than in other criminal cases. As a result, prosecution rates for rape remained low.

> In 1972, 3,562 rapes were reported in Chicago, 833 arrests were made, 23 defendants pleaded guilty: and 8 were found guilty and sentenced after a trial . . . fewer than 1 percent of rapes resulted in jail sentences. (Deckard, 1983, p. 433)

The Feminist Redefinition of Sexual Assault

During the 1960s, increasing numbers of women were employed. As the decade began, approximately 36% of women worked outside the home; by its end, over 50% of women were in the paid labor force (Deckard, 1983). Although women's presence in the public sphere was increasing, they rarely held decision- and policymaking positions.

With women's increasing involvement in activities outside the home, the opportunity for a woman to be victimized increased (Gardner, 1980). A few men viewed women's newfound assertiveness and involvement in the public sphere as an attack on traditional roles and a defiance of chivalry. To such men, the woman who did not conform to traditional roles was relegated to the role of the "loose woman" and was not entitled to protection under the traditional guidelines for male-female relationships (Griffin, 1971). The following description of rape in the 19th century still applied:

> sexual assault could be conceived of . . . as an exploitation of women's presumed dependence on men. If a woman had herself violated patriarchal norms by straying out of her dependent position— if she had fought off her attacker, asserted her rights alone in court, or behaved in too self-reliant a manner more generally—the term "rape" no longer applied, no matter how forceful the attack visited on her. (Arnold, 1989, p. 49)

Societal definitions of rape demanded adherence to traditionally defined feminine roles and behaviors. The implicit warning to women was to behave (e.g., accept traditional feminine roles) or to suffer the consequence—rape.

Women, however, began to resist traditional definitions of appropriate feminine behavior and expressed their dissatisfaction. Betty

Friedan (1963), in *The Feminine Mystique*, and the National Organization for Women (NOW), founded in 1966, expressed women's changing views and interest in public reform. Women's liberationists also began to work toward changing social policies. A process called consciousness raising was used in informal women's groups to begin to empower women and to help them identify sources of sisterhood and oppression. As women began to meet, they realized that individual concerns (e.g., sexual harassment, fear of walking the streets at night) were widely shared. As a result, many women questioned the reasons for their oppression, and they began to recognize that "the personal is political." The dilemmas women were experiencing were not idiosyncratic, but were constructed socially as a result of the hierarchical gender system in our culture (D'Emilio and Freedman, 1988). Kate Millet (1970) in her landmark book, *Sexual Politics*, concluded that within our patriarchal system, force takes "a form of violence particularly sexual in nature and realized most completely in the act of rape" (p. 69).

During the 1970s, rape became an important issue within the feminist movement. Sexual assault was redefined from the victim's perspective. A woman's victimization was an "experience of helplessness and loss of control, the sense of one's self as an object of rage" (Hall, 1983, p. 342). The act of rape was seen not as an end in itself, but as a means of enforcing gender roles in society and maintaining the hierarchy in which men retained control. Feminists refuted the long-held belief that rapists were men who were helplessly controlled by their overwhelming sexual impulses. Rape was recognized as an act of violence, *not* of sex as psychoanalytic theorists had previously held. Rape was a form of domination and control, a weapon used to enforce women's subordinate role to men.

In 1971, an article by Susan Griffin described rape as the "all-American crime." She reported that "forcible rape is the most frequently committed violent crime in America today," and emphasized that all women are victims even if they are not the direct targets of the attack because "rape and the fear of rape are a daily part of every woman's consciousness" (p. 27). She held that women's behavior is shaped by their fear of attack, and as a result, women's movements are restricted. They fear to live alone, walk outside at night, smile at strangers, and leave their windows open. Psychological research has found that women's perceptions of their vulnerability to attack and their fear of being a victim of a violent crime are related to the amount of precautionary behaviors in which they engage. Women, especially those unsure of their ability to protect themselves physically, engage in isolating behavior, such as not going out at night or visiting friends (Riger and

Gordon, 1981). This limits women's opportunities to be active participants in the public sphere.

The first rape crisis center was founded in Washington, DC, in 1972, and the number of centers has increased steadily since that time (Deckard, 1983). Now there are more than 550 rape crisis centers across the country, some helping as many as 1,100 victims annually (King and Webb, 1981). Rape crisis centers and rape hotlines provide valuable assistance to victims of sexual assault and rape. Victims are provided with information and escorted to the police station and the hospital, and volunteers serve as advocates for the victim after the attack. Many of these centers also have educational programs in the community to help dispel rape myths and change public attitudes about rape (Deckard, 1983). Cuts in governmental funding during the Reagan administration, however, have resulted in the closing of some centers, and in an increased need for volunteers and private funding.

Susan Brownmiller (1975), in her bestselling book, *Against Our Will: Men, Women, and Rape*, reaffirmed the relationship between sexual aggression and women's fear, defining rape as "a conscious process of intimidation by which all men keep all women in a state of fear" (p. 5). Her book was crucial in the definition of rape from a feminist perspective. Brownmiller's analysis formed the foundation for numerous theoretical papers and psychological research. Her book detailed the evolution of rape in our culture and the role it has played throughout history.

Brownmiller began her analysis by considering biology. Women are physiologially vulnerable to sexual attack, and once "men discovered that they could rape, they proceeded to do it" (1975, p. 6). Rape served a critical function of domination and intimidation in primitive societies. "His forcible entry into her body, despite her physical protestations and struggle, became the vehicle of his victorious conquest over her being, the ultimate test of his superior strength, the triumph of his manhood" (p. 5). Rape, therefore, was a purposeful act of control. In some cases, rape was an act of manhood, a rite of passage, or a form of male bonding. This male bonding, on occasion, is exhibited in the form of gang rape. Examining gang rape, Brownmiller concluded that " 'sharing the girl among us fellows' strengthens the notion of group masculinity and power" (p. 28). This bond between men results from their "contempt for women" and thrives in a culture of "forced and exaggerated male/female polarities" (p. 211). . . .

As public discourse on sexual violence continued, it became increasingly evident that rapists were not only strangers behind bushes, but also might be dates, acquaintances, neighbors, husbands, friends, and relatives. Feminists made the case that every man is a potential rapist and all women are potential victims. Due to this reconceptualization, date rape became an area of concern. In 1972, *Ms.* magazine discussed the issue of date rape on college campuses across the country. Initial research indicated that rape between acquaintances was much more common than previously believed. Kanin and Parcell (1977) found that approximately 83% of college women had experienced male sexual aggression while dating. Research a decade later confirmed this incidence rate. Koss, Gidycz, and Wisniewski (1987) found that 27.5% of college women reported being victims of rape or attempted rape; 53.7% of women, including those who reported being raped, had experienced some form of unwanted sexual contact and/or sexually assaultive behavior. These results suggest that sexually aggressive behavior is experienced by the majority of women in "normal" dating relationships. This high incidence rate gives credence to the feminist conceptualiza-tion of rape as being supported by our culture.

Psychological Research on Rape

The views of feminists, in particular the work of Susan Brownmiller, sparked research within psychology to examine the "rape-supportive culture" that provides the context for sexual assault. Researchers made empirical studies of feminist ideas and combined these feminist views into a theoretical framework to understand and predict sexual aggression. Martha Burt (1980) hypothesized that our culture and the status of women within that culture play a significant role in the attitudes toward sexual violence held by persons, particularly rapists. She hypothesized that myths about rape (e.g., "women ask for it") might act as releasers or facilitators of sexual aggression. These rape myths were proposed as part of a larger attitudinal structure that serves to facilitate sexually aggressive acts in our culture. Attitudinal factors that were found by Burt to predict rape-supportive myths were (a) sex role stereotyping, (b) adversarial sexual beliefs, and (c) acceptance of interpersonal violence.

Sex role stereotyping refers to the appropriateness of familial, work, and social roles being based on the sex of the individual being considered (e.g., "It is acceptable for a woman to have a career, but marriage and family should come first"; Burt, 1980, p. 222). Adversarial sexual beliefs refers to the view that male-female relationships are naturally filled with conflict and competition (e.g., "Most women are sly and manipulating when they are out to attract a man"—p. 222). Acceptance of interpersonal violence refers to the belief that violence is an appropriate way of interacting with others, particularly in male-female relationships (e.g., "Sometimes the only way to get a cold woman turned on is to use force"—p. 222). These attitudes were studied by researchers (Burt and Albin, 1981; Check and Malamuth, 1983; Malamuth, 1983) as a means to understand sexual aggression using a feminist framework.

Koss, Leonard, Beezley, and Oros (1985) developed a theoretical model for characterizing nonstranger sexual aggression that incorporated Burt's findings and feminist views. They proposed a social control/social conflict model of date rape:

> Culturally transmitted assumptions about men, women, violence, sexuality, and myths about rape constitute a rape-supportive belief system. Furthermore, stratified systems such as the American dating situation may legitimate the use of force by those in power and weaken resistance of the less powerful. Finally, acquisition of stereotyped myths about rape may result in a failure to label as rape sexual aggression that occurs in dating situations. (Koss et al., 1985, p. 982)

This view of a culturally based belief system that perpetuates violence against women and oppresses women has been endorsed by several feminist writers (Brownmiller, 1975; Griffin, 1971; Johnson, 1980).

Rape Within the Legal System

In the colonial period, the law conceptualized rape as the violation of a man's property. It was a man's personal privilege to have access to a woman's body. Feminist theorists have rejected traditional legal conceptualizations, which often blame the woman for her own victimization, and have refuted rape myths that women enjoy being raped, and ask and deserve to be raped by dressing provocatively. They refuse to allow women to be blamed for their own victimization. Instead, blame is placed squarely on the attacker.

Feminists have lobbied for changes in rape legislation. Previous laws considered rape an all-or-nothing crime, in which convicted offenders received sentences that ranged from 5 years to life depending on the particular state's statutes. Maximum sentences of 30–50 years in prison were not uncommon for convicted rapists (Babcock, Freedman, Norton, and Ross, 1975). Prior to the 1972 case of *Furman v. Georgia*, which "invalidated arbitrary capital punishment laws, sixteen states permitted imposition of death for rape" (Berger, 1977, p. 8). Some writers hypothesized that the severe penalties for rape may have discouraged juries from convicting a defendant because of a "perceived sense of disproportion between culpability and the prescribed sentence" (Andenaes, 1966, p. 970). Now most states have revised their laws to include several levels of sexual assault with a broader range of penalties. A perpetrator may be charged with first-, second-, or third-degree rape, with each charge varying in the maximum sentence following conviction. First-degree rape is defined as forced sexual intercourse under aggravated circumstances. Second-degree rape is described as forced sexual intercourse. Third-degree rape is defined as nonconsensual intercourse or intercourse with threat to self or property. This calibrated system of offenses and penalties has increased conviction rates, and may therefore enhance the effectiveness of prosecution as a deterrent (Andenaes, 1966, p. 970).

In addition, the criterion of force was determined in the past by examining the victim's behavior rather than the offender's behavior. In the 1970s, women in New York needed the corroboration of a witness who saw or heard the assault to verify that it had indeed been rape, and that the woman has resisted the attack. In addition, some states viewed "no resistance" as consensual intercourse, and required the victim to have verbally said "no" or forcibly resisted or screamed (Margolin, 1972). Unless the woman exhibited these behaviors, the man's behavior was not considered rape.

In 1974, Michigan passed the first comprehensive rape reform legislation in the country (Loh, 1981). Since that time, most states have enacted similar changes. These reforms have focused on the perpetrator's behavior (e.g., use of physical force or threat of force) as the legal criterion rather than the victim's behavior alone. The context of the assault and the interaction between the victim and assailant are becoming increasingly important. . . .

Criticism of Radical Feminist Reconceptualizations

Some feminists have criticized Brownmiller's (1975) conceptualization of rape. Rather than placing all the blame on women as in the past, Brownmiller counterblamed, condemning all men for their innate violence (Benjamin, 1983). In addition, radical feminists have ignored the "history of women's resistance to oppression" and focused on sexuality itself as the enemy—"an unchanging, aggressive male sexuality of which women have been eternally the victims" (Arnold, 1989, p. 36). Brownmiller's book also has been faulted as "supporting a notion of universal patriarchy and timeless sexual victimization; it leaves no room for understanding the reasons for women's collaboration, their own sources of power, . . . the class and racial differences in their experience of discrimination and sexual danger" (Hall, 1983, p. 341). The radical feminist view also focuses exclusively on the negative.

Some writers believe that in order for feminism to persist, women must use their own strength as an energy source for reform.

> Social movements, feminism included, move toward a vision; they cannot operate solely on fear. It is not enough to move women away from danger and oppression; it is necessary to move toward something: toward pleasure, agency, self-definition. Feminism must increase women's pleasure and joy, not just decrease our misery. (Vance, 1984, p. 24)

Areas of Action and Change: Then and Now

Education is still needed to help change society's attitudes about rape, In the recent past, women have been the target for increased awareness, but now men also are being included in the process of consciousness raising (Walsh, 1990). "The anti-rape movement must not limit itself to training women to avoid rape or depending on imprisonment as a deterrent, but must aim its attention at changing the behavior and attitudes of men" (Hall, 1983, p. 346). For example, the University of Florida has introduced a program called FARE (Fraternity Acquaintance Rape Education) to educate men in fraternities and on athletic teams (Walsh, 1990).

Education of women also is needed to empower them to action. In our culture, women are socialized to be submissive, but some feminists have challenged this role. "To be submissive is to defer to masculine strength; is to lack muscular development or any interest in defending oneself" (Griffin, 1971, p. 33). Women can take courses in self-defense to strengthen their bodies, and to gain the ability and the confidence to defend themselves should they be attacked. Ann Sheldon (1972) felt this solution to rape was inescapable: "There is no other way except resistance to be free" (p. 23).

Feminists clearly have made a major difference in the way sexual assault and rape are understood in our culture. Yet considering the long historical tradition of women bearing the guilt for sexual victimization, it is not surprising that much still needs to change. Over 15 years ago, Brownmiller called for action, saying, "the purpose in this book has been to give rape its history. Now we must deny it a future" (1975, p. 454). That need is still true today.

References

Amir, M. (1971). *Patterns in forcible rape.* Chicago: University of Chicago Press.

Andenaes, J. (1966). The general prevention effects of punishment. *Pennsylvania Law Review, 114*, 949–983.

Arnold, M. H. (1989). The life of a citizen in the hands of a woman: Sexual assault in New York City, 1790–1820. In K. Peiss and C. Simmons (Eds.), *Passion and power: Sexuality in history* (pp. 35–56). Philadelphia, PA: Temple University Press.

Babcock B., Freedman, A., Norton, D., and Ross, S. (1975). *Sex discrimination and the law*. Boston: Little, Brown.

Benjamin, J. (1983). Master and slave: The fantasy of erotic domination. In A. Snitow, C. Stansell, and S. Thompson (Eds.), *Powers of desire: The politics of sexuality* (pp. 280–299). New York: Monthly Review Press.

Berger, V. (1977). Man's trial, woman's tribulation: Rape cases in the courtroom. *Columbia Law Review, 77*, 1–101.

Box, S. (1983). *Power, crime, and mystification*. London: Tavistock.

Brownmiller, S. (1975). *Against our will: Men, women and rape*. Toronto: Bantam.

Burt, M. R. (1980). Cultural myths and supports for rape. *Journal of Personality and Social Psychology, 38*, 217–230.

Burt, M. R., and Albin, R. S. (1981). Rape myths, rape definitions, and probability of conviction. *Journal of Applied Social Psychology, 11*, 212–230.

Check, J. V. P., and Malamuth, N. M. (1983). Sex role stereotyping and reactions to depictions of stranger versus acquaintance rape. *Journal of Personality and Social Psychology, 45*, 344–356.

Deckard, B. S. (1983). *The woman's movement: Political, socioeconomic, and psychological issues* (3rd ed.). New York: Harper & Row.

D'Emilio, J., and Freedman, E. B. (1988). *Intimate matters: A history of sexuality in America*. New York: Harper & Row.

Freedman, E. B. (1981). *Their sisters' keepers: Women's prison reform in America, 1893–1930*. Ann Arbor: University of Michigan Press.

Freedman, E. B. (1989). Uncontrolled desires: The response to the sexual psychopath, 1920–1960. In K. Peiss and C. Simmons (Eds.), *Passion and power: Sexuality in history* (pp. 199–225). Philadelphia, PA: Temple University Press.

Friedan, B. (1963). *The feminine mystique*. New York: Dell.

Gardner, T. A. (1980). Racism in pornography and the women's movement. In L. Lederer (Ed.), *Take back the night: Women on pornography* (pp. 105–14). New York: Morrow.

Griffin, S. (1971). Rape: The all-American crime. *Ramparts, 10*, 26–35.

Groth, A., and Birnbaum, H. (1979). *Men who rape: The psychology of the offender*. New York: Plenum.

Hall, J. D. (1983). The mind that burns in each body: Women, rape, and racial violence. In A. Snitow, C. Stansell, and S. Thompson (Eds.), *Powers of desire: The politics of sexuality* (pp. 328–349). New York: Monthly Review Press.

Johnson, A. G. (1980). On the prevalence of rape in the United States. *Signs: Journal of Women in Culture and Society*, 6, 136–146.

Jordan, W. D. (1968). *White over Black: American attitudes toward the Negro*. Chapel Hill: University of North Carolina Press.

Jozsa, B., and Jozsa, M. (1980). Dirty books, dirty films, and dirty data. In L. Lederer (Ed.), *Take back the night: Women on pornography* (pp. 204–217). New York: Morrow.

Kanin, E. J., and Parcell, S. R. (1977). Sexual aggression: A second look at the offended female. *Archives of Sexual Behavior*, 6, 67–76.

King, H. E., and Webb, C. (1981). Rape crisis centers: Progress and problems. *Journal of Social Issues,* 37(4), 93–104.

Koehler, L. (1980). *A search for power: The "weaker sex" in seventeenth-century New England*. Urbana: University of Illinois Press.

Koss, M. P., Gidycz, C. A., and Wisniewski, N. (1987). The scope of rape: Incidence and prevalence of sexual aggression and victimization in a national sample of higher education students. *Journal of Consulting and Clinical Psychology*, 55, 162–170.

Koss, M. P., Leonard, K. E., Beezley, D. A., and Oros, C. J. (1985). Non-stranger sexual aggression: A discriminant analysis of the psychological characteristics of undetected offenders. *Sex Roles*, 12, 981–992.

Lindemann, B. S. (1984). "To ravish and carnally know": Rape in eighteenth-century Massachusetts. *Signs: Journal of Women in Culture and Society*, 10, 63–82.

Loh, W. D. (1981). Q: What has reform of rape legislation wrought? A: Truth in criminal labelling. *Journal of Social Issues*, 37(4), 28–52.

Malamuth, N. M. (1983). Factors associated with rape as predictors of laboratory aggression against women. *Journal of Personality and Social Psychology*, 45, 432–442.

Margolin, D. (1972). Rape: The facts. *Women: A Journal of Liberation*, 3, 19–22.

Millet, K. (1970). *Sexual politics*. New York: Avon.

Morgan, R. (1980). Theory and practice: Pornography and rape. In L. Lederer (Ed.), *Take back the night: Women on pornography* (pp. 134–140). New York: Morrow.

Read, D. (1989). (De)constructing pornography: Feminisms in conflict. In K. Peiss and C. Simmons (Eds.), *Passion and power: Sexuality in history* (pp. 277–292). Philadelphia, PA: Temple University Press.

Riger, S., and Gordon, M. T. (1981). The fear of rape: A study in social control. *Journal of Social Issues*, 37(4), 71–92.

Schwendinger, J. R., and Schwendinger, H. (1983). *Rape and inequality*. Beverly Hills, CA: Sage.

Sheldon, A. (1972). Rape: The solution. *Women: A Journal of Liberation*, 3, 23.

Stansell, C. (1986). *City of women: Sex and class in New York, 1789–1860*. New York: Alfred A. Knopf.

Vance, C. S. (1984). Pleasure and danger: Toward a politics of sexuality. In C. Vance (Ed.), *Pleasure and danger: Exploring female sexuality* (pp. 1–27). Boston: Routledge and Kegan Paul.

Walsh, C. (1990, April). *FARE: Fraternity acquaintance rape education*. Paper presented at the Southeastern Psychological Association meeting, Atlanta.

Warshaw, R. (1988). *I never called it rape*. New York: Harper and Row.

6

Hidden Rape: Sexual Aggression and Victimization in a National Sample of Students in Higher Education

~

Mary P. Koss

"You better not never tell nobody but God. It'd kill your mammy."

(Walker 1982, 1)

O FFICIALLY, 87,340 RAPES OCCURRED IN 1985 (Federal Bureau of In- vestigation [FBI] 1986). However, this number greatly underesti- mates the true scope of rape since it includes only instances that were reported to the police. Because many victims never tell even their clos- est friends and family about their rape (Koss 1985), it is unrealistic to expect that they would report the crime to the police. Government es- timates suggest that for every rape reported to police, 3–10 rapes are not reported (Law Enforcement Assistance Administration [LEAA] 1975).

Victimization studies such as the annual National Crime Survey (NCS) are the major avenue through which the full extent of crime is estimated (e.g., Bureau of Justice Statistics [BJS] 1984). In these stud- ies, the residents of a standard sampling area are asked to indicate those crimes of which they or any other household members have been victims during the previous six months. The survey results are then

From Mary P. Koss, "Hidden Rape: Sexual Aggression and Victimization in a National Sample of Students in Higher Education," in *Rape and Sexual Assault II*, ed. Ann Wolbert Burgess (New York: Garland Publishing, 1988), 3–25. © 1988 by Garland Publishing. Reprinted by permission of Garland Publishing.

compared to the number of reported crimes in the area, and the rate of unreported crime is estimated. On the basis of such research, the authors of the NCS have observed rape is an infrequent crime (LEAA 1974, 12) and is the most rare of NCS measured violent offenses (BJS 1984, 5). Women's chances of being raped have been described as a small fraction of 1% (Katz and Mazur 1979).

However, the accuracy of these conclusions and the validity of the research on which they are based must be examined closely, as the perceived severity of rape influences the social and economic priority it is accorded.

Several features of the NCS approach (e.g., BJS 1984) may lead to underreporting of rape, including the use of a screening question that requires the subject to infer the focus of inquiry, the use of questions about rape that are embedded in a context of violent crime, and the assumption that the term *rape* is used by victims of sexual assault to conceptualize their experiences.

In an effort to extend previous research on rape (e.g., Koss and Oros 1982; Koss 1985) to a national sample, the *Ms*. Magazine Project on Campus Sexual Assault was undertaken. Because the FBI definition of rape (used in victimization studies such as the NCS) limits the crime to female victims (BJS 1984) and because women represent virtually 100% of reported rape victims (LEAA 1975), the project focused on women victims and male perpetrators.

Previous Research

Several recently reported estimates of the prevalence of sexual victimization have been reported that were based on studies designed specifically to gauge the extent of sexual assault. Kilpatrick and colleagues (Kilpatrick, Veronen, and Best 1984; Kilpatrick et al. 1985) conducted a victimization survey via telephone of 2,004 randomly selected female residents of Charleston County, South Carolina. In their sample, 14.5% of the women disclosed one or more attempted or completed sexual assault experiences, including 5% who had been victims of rape and 4% who had been victims of attempted rape. Of the women who had been raped, only 29% reported their assault to police. Russell found that 24% of a probability sample of 930 adult women residents of San Francisco described experiences that involved "forced intercourse or intercourse obtained by physical threat(s) or intercourse completed when the woman was drugged, unconscious, asleep, or otherwise totally helpless and unable to consent" (Russell 1984, 35). Only 9.5% of these women reported their experience to police.

Many studies of the prevalence of rape and lesser forms of sexual aggression have involved college students however. There are scientific as well as pragmatic reasons to study this group. College students are a high risk group for rape because they are in the same age range as the bulk of rape victims and offenders. The victimization rate for females peaks in the 16–19-year age group, and the second highest rate occurs in the 20–24-year age group. These rates are approximately four times higher than the mean for all women (BJS 1984). In addition, 47% of all alleged rapists who are arrested are individuals under age 25 (FBI 1985). Approximately 25% of all persons age 18–24 are attending school (U.S. Bureau of the Census 1980). Finally, a substantial proportion of rape prevention efforts take place under the auspices of educational institutions and are targeted at students.

Kanin and his associates (Kanin 1957; Kirkpatrick and Kanin 1957; Kanin and Parcell 1977) found that 20–25% of college women reported forceful attempts by their dates at sexual intercourse during which the women ended up screaming, fighting, crying, or pleading and that 26% of college men reported making a forceful attempt at sexual intercourse that caused observable distress and offense in the woman. Rapaport and Burkhart (1984) reported that 15% of a sample of college men acknowledged that they had obtained sexual intercourse against their dates' will. Koss and colleagues (Koss 1985; Koss and Oros 1982; Koss et al. 1985) administered the self-report sexual experiences survey to a sample of 2,016 female and 1,846 male Midwestern university students. They found that 13% of the women experienced a victimization that involved sexual intercourse as a result of actual force or threat of harm; and 4.6% of the men admitted perpetrating an act of sexual aggression that met legal definitions of rape.

All of these prevalence studies suggest that rape is far more extensive than reported in official statistics. However, reported prevalence rates for rape vary from 5% (Kilpatrick et al. 1985) to 20–25% (Kanin 1957; Russell 1984). Unfortunately these different figures are not easy to reconcile as the studies involved both relatively small and geographically diverse samples and different data collection techniques.

Methods

The *Ms.* Magazine Project on Campus Sexual Assault involved administration of a self-report questionnaire to a sample of 6,159 students enrolled in 32 institutions of higher education across the United States. The following is an overview of the project's methodology, described more fully elsewhere (Koss, Gidycz, and Wisniewski 1987).

Sampling Procedures

The sampling goals of the project were to represent the universe of the U.S. college student population. No sample design could be expected to result in a purely random or representative sample, as the subject of rape is sufficiently controversial that some schools targeted by a systematic sampling plan can be expected to refuse to participate.

On the basis of enrollment-characteristics data maintained by the U.S. Department of Education (Office of Civil Rights 1980), the nation's 3,269 higher education institutions were sorted by location into ten regions (i.e., Alaska, Hawaii, New England, Mideast, Great Lakes, Plains states, Southeast, Southwest, Rocky Mountain, and West). Within each region, institutions were placed into homogeneous clusters according to five criteria: (1) location inside or outside a standard metropolitan statistical area (SMSA) of certain sizes; (2) enrollment of minority students above or below the national mean percentage; (3) control of the institution by private secular, private religious, or public authority; (4) type of institution, including university, other four-year college, two-year junior college, and technical/vocational institution; and (5) total enrollment within three levels. Every xth cluster was sampled according to the proportion of total enrollment accounted for by the region. Replacements were sought from among other schools in the homogenous cluster if the original school proved uncooperative.

The amount of time required to obtain a sample of cooperating institutions was extended; some schools required 15 months to arrive at a final decision. During that period, 93 schools were contacted and 32 institutional participants were obtained. Of the institutions, 19 were first choices; the remaining 13 were solicited from among 43 replacements. The institutional participants were guaranteed anonymity.

A random selection process based on each institution's catalogue of course offerings was used to choose target classes and alternates. The questionnaire was administered in classroom settings by one of eight postmaster's level psychologists: the two men and six women used a prepared script and were trained to handle potential untoward effects of participation. The anonymous questionnaire was accompanied by a cover sheet that contained all the elements of informed consent. Only 91 persons (1.5%) indicated that they did not wish to participate.

Subjects

The final sample consisted of 6,159 students: 3,187 females and 2,972 males. The female participants were characterized as follows: Mean age = 21.4 years; 85% single, 11% married, and 4% divorced;

86% white, 7% black, 3% Hispanic, 3% Asian, and 1% native American; and 39% Catholic, 38% Protestant, 4% Jewish, and 20% other or no religion. The male participants were characterized as follows: mean age = 21.0 years; 90% single, 9% married, 1% divorced; 86% white, 6% black, 3% Hispanic, 4% Asian, and 1% native American; and 40% Catholic, 34% Protestant, 5% Jewish, and 22% other or no religion.

Because of the assumptions on which the sampling plan was based and the hesitancy of many institutions to participate, the sample is not completely representative. Four variables were examined to determine the sample's representativeness: (1) institution location, (2) institution region, (3) subject ethnicity, and (4) subject income. Region in which the institutions were located was the only variable on which significant discrepancy was noted. The regional disproportion is unimportant in many respects, as even without extensive sampling in the West, the individual participants in the sample were still reflective of national enrollment in terms of ethnicity and family income. Nevertheless, for purposes of calculating prevalence data, weighting factors were used.

Survey Instrument

The data on the incidence and prevalence of sexual aggression were obtained through the use of the ten-item sexual experiences survey (Koss and Oros 1982; Koss and Gidycz 1985). This survey is a self-report instrument designed to reflect various degrees of sexual aggression and victimization. During survey administration, separate wordings were used for women and for men. The text of all ten items (female wording) can be found in table 1. Descriptive data were obtained through the use of closed-ended questions administered subsequent to the survey. The survey booklet instructed all respondents who described any level of experience with sexual aggression or victimization to turn to a section of questions about the characteristics of the most serious incident in which they were involved.

Many investigators have questioned the validity of self-reported sexual behavior. The accuracy and truthfulness of self-reports on the sexual experiences survey have been investigated (Koss and Gidycz 1985), and significant correlations were found between a woman's level of victimization based on self-report and her level of victimization based on responses related to an interviewer several months later ($r = .73, p < .001$). Most important, only 3% of the women (2/68) who reported experiences that met legal definitions of rape were judged to have misinterpreted questions or to have given answers that appeared to be false. Men's levels of aggression as described on self-report and reported to an interviewer were also significantly correlated ($r = .61$, $p < .001$).

A further validity study was conducted in conjunction with the *Ms.* project. Because previous work had raised more questions about the validity of males' responses than about females' responses, male students were selected as subjects. The sexual experiences survey items were administered both by self-report and by one-to-one interview on the same occasion and in one setting. The interviewer was a fully trained, licensed, and experienced male Ph.D. clinical psychologist. Subjects were 15 male volunteers, identified by first name only, recruited through newspaper advertisements on the campus of a major university. Participants gave their self-reports first and then were interviewed individually. The results indicated that 14 of the participants (93%) gave the same responses to the survey items on self-report and in the interviews.

Table 1. Frequencies of Individual Sexual Experiences Reported by Postsecondary Students: Prevalence since Age 14

				Sex		
Sexual Behavior		Women			Men	
	%	M	SD	%	M	SD
1. Have you given in to sex play (fondling, kissing, or petting, but not intercourse) when you didn't want to because you were overwhelmed by a man's continual arguments and pressure?	44	3.2	1.5	19	2.9	1.5
2. Have you had sex play (fondling, kissing, or petting, but not intercourse) when you didn't want to because a man used his position of authority (boss, teacher, camp counselor, supervisor) to make you?	5	2.7	1.7	1	2.5	1.5
3. Have you had sex play (fondling, kissing, or petting, but not intercourse) when you didn't want to because a man threatened or used some degree of physical force (twisting your arm, holding you down, etc.) to make you?	13	2.1	1.5	2	2.3	1.5
4. Have you had a man attempt sexual intercourse (get on top, attempt to						

insert his penis) when you didn't want to by threatening or using some degree of force (twisting your arm, holding you down, etc.), but intercourse *did not* occur? 15 2.0 1.4 2 2.0 1.2

5. Have you had a man attempt sexual intercourse (get on top, attempt to insert his penis) when you didn't want to by giving you alcohol or drugs, but intercourse *did not* occur? 12 2.0 1.4 5 2.2 1.4

6. Have you given into sexual intercourse when you didn't want to because you were overwhelmed by a man's continual arguments and pressure? 25 2.9 1.6 10 2.4 1.4

7. Have you had sexual intercourse when you didn't want to because a man used his position of authority (boss, teacher, camp counselor, supervisor) to make you? 2 2.5 1.7 1 2.0 1.4

8. Have you had sexual intercourse when you didn't want to because a man gave you alcohol or drugs? 8 2.2 1.5 4 2.5 1.5

9. Have you had sexual intercourse when you didn't want to because a man threatened or used some degree of physical force (twisting your arm, holding you down, etc.) to make you? 9 2.2 1.5 1 2.3 1.5

10. Have you had sexual acts (anal or oral intercourse or penetration by objects other than the penis) when you didn't want to because a man threatened or used some degree of physical force (twisting your arm, holding you down, etc.) to make you? 6 2.2 1.6 1 2.5 1.5

Notes: The sample size was 3,187 women and 2,972 men. All questions were prefaced with instructions to refer to experiences "from age 14 on." Sexual intercourse was defined as "penetration of a woman's vagina, no matter how slightly, by a man's penis. Ejaculation is not required." [M = mean; SD = standard deviation]

Scoring Procedures

The groups labeled rape ("yes" responses to items 8, 9, and/or 10 and any lower-numbered items) and attempted rape ("yes" responses to items 4 and/or 5 but not to any higher-numbered items) included individuals whose experiences met broad legal definitions of these crimes. The legal definition of rape in Ohio (Ohio Revised Code 1980, 2907.01A,2907.02), similar to many states, is the following:

> Vaginal intercourse between male and female, and anal intercourse, fellatio, and cunnilingus between persons regardless of sex. Penetration, however slight, is sufficient to complete vaginal or anal intercourse. . . . No person shall engage in sexual conduct with another person . . . when any of the following apply: (1) the offender purposely compels the other person to submit by force or threat of force, (2) for the purpose of preventing resistance the offender substantially impairs the other person's judgment or control by administering any drug or intoxicant to the other person.

The group labeled sexual coercion ("yes" responses to items 6 and/or 7 but not to any higher-numbered items) included subjects who engaged in/experienced sexual intercourse subsequent to the use of menacing verbal pressure or misuse of authority. No threats of force or direct physical force were used. The group labeled sexual contact ("yes" responses to items 1, 2, and/or 3 but not to any higher-numbered items) consisted of individuals who had engaged in/experienced sexual behavior (such as fondling or kissing) that did not involve attempted penetration, subsequent to the use of menacing verbal pressure, misuse of authority, threats of harm, or actual physical force.

Results

Prevalence of Sexual Aggression/Victimization

Prevalence rates indicate the total number of persons who report experiences, with sexual aggression or victimization during a specified time period, which in this study was since the age of 14. The unweighted response frequencies for each item of the Sexual Experiences Survey are presented in table 1. The frequencies of victimization ranged from 44% (women who reported having experienced unwanted sexual contact subsequent to coercion) to 2% (women who reported having experienced unwanted sexual intercourse subsequent to the offender's misuse of authority). The frequency with which men reported having perpetrated each form of sexual aggression ranged from the 19% who said that they had obtained sexual contact through the use of coercion to the 1% who indicated that they had obtained oral or anal penetration through the use of force. Those respondents who had engaged in/experienced sexually aggressive acts indicated that each act had occurred a mean of 2.0–3.2 times since age 14.

However, the data on the individual sexually aggressive acts are difficult to interpret, because persons may have engaged in/experienced several different sexually aggressive acts. Therefore, respondents were classified according to the highest degree of sexual victimization/aggression they reported (see table 2). With weighted data correcting for regional disproportions, 46.3% of women respondents revealed no experiences whatsoever with sexual victimization, while 53.7% of women respondents indicated some form of sexual victimization. The most serious sexual victimization ever experienced was sexual contact for 14.4% of the women, sexual coercion for 11.9% of the women, attempted rape for 12.1% of the women, and rape for 15.4% of the women. Weighted data for males indicated that 74.8% of men had engaged in no forms of sexual aggression, whereas 25.1% of the men revealed involvement in some form of sexual aggression. The most extreme level of sexual aggression perpetrated was sexual contact for 10.2% of the men, sexual coercion for 7.2% of the men, attempted rape for 3.3% of the men, and rape for 4.4% of the men. Examination of these figures reveals that the effect of weighting was minimal and tended to reduce slightly the prevalence of the most serious acts of sexual aggression. . . .

Table 2. Prevalence Rates for Five Levels of Sexual Aggression and Sexual Victimization

| | *Sex* | | | |
| *Sexual Aggression/Victimization (Highest Level Reported)* | *Women (%)* | | *Men (%)* | |
	Weighted	*Unweighted*	*Weighted*	*Unweighted*
No sexual aggression/victimization	46.3	45.6	74.8	75.6
Sexual contact	14.4	14.9	10.2	9.8
Sexual coercion	11.9	11.6	7.2	6.9
Attempted rape	12.1	12.1	3.3	3.2
Rape	15.4	15.8	4.4	4.6

Notes: The sample size was 3,187 women and 2,972 men. Prevalence rates include sexual experiences since age 14.

Incidence of Sexual Aggression/Victimization

Incidence rates indicate how many new episodes of an event occurred during a specific time period. In this study, respondents were asked to indicate how many times during the previous year they had engaged in/experienced each item listed in the survey. To improve recall, the question referred to the previous academic year from September to September, time boundaries that are meaningful to students. Some subjects reported multiple episodes of sexual aggression/victimization during the previous year. Therefore, the incidence of sexual aggression/victimization was calculated two ways. First, the number of people who reported one or more episodes during the year was determined. Second, the total number of sexually aggressive incidents that were reported by women and by men was calculated.

The incidence rate for rape during a 12-month period was found to be 353 rapes involving 207 different women in a population of 3,187 women. Comparable figures for the other levels of sexual victimization were 533 attempted rapes (323 victims), 837 episodes of sexual coercion (366 victims), and 2,024 experiences of unwanted sexual contact (886 victims). The incidence data for the individual items used to calculate these rates are found in table 3.

Table 3. Frequencies of Individual Sexual Experiences Reported by Postsecondary Student: One-Year Incidence

	Sex			
Sexual Experience	*Women*		*Men*	
	Victims	*Incidents*	*Perpetrators*	*Incidents*
Sexual contact by verbal coercion	725	1,716	321	732
Sexual contact by misuse of authority	50	97	23	55
Sexual contact by threat or force	111	211	30	67
Attempted intercourse by force	180	297	33	52
Attempted intercourse by alcohol/drugs	143	236	72	115
Intercourse by verbal coercion	353	816	156	291
Intercourse by misuse of authority	13	21	11	20
Intercourse by alcohol/drugs	91	159	57	103
Intercourse by threat or force	63	98	20	36
Oral/anal penetration by threat or force	53	96	19	48

Note: The sample size was 3,187 women and 2,972 men.

Incidence rates for the sexual aggression admitted by men also were calculated. Responses to the three items that characterize rape for the 12-month period preceding the survey indicate that 187 rapes were perpetrated by 96 different men. Comparable incidence rates during a 12-month period for the other levels of sexual aggression were 167 attempted rapes (105 perpetrators), 854 episodes of unwanted sexual contact (374 perpetrators), and 311 situations of sexual coercion (167 perpetrators). The incidence data for the individual items that were used to calculate these rates also are presented in table 3.

From these data, victimization rates can be calculated. If the total number of all the women who during the previous year reported a sexual experience that met legal definitions of rape and attempted rape is divided by two (to obtain a six-month basis) and set to a base of number of 1,000 women (instead of the 3,187 women actually surveyed), the victimization rate for the surveyed population of women was 83/1,000 women during a six-month period. However, the FBI definition of rape (i.e., forcible vaginal intercourse with a female against consent by force or threat of force, including attempts) on which the NCS is based is narrower than the state laws (i.e., oral, anal, or vaginal intercourse or penetration by objects against consent through threat, force, or intentional incapacitation of the victim via drugs) on which the groupings in this study were based (BJS 1984). Therefore, the victimization rate was also calculated in conformance with the FBI definition. Elimination of all incidents except those that involved actual or attempted vaginal sexual intercourse through force or threat of harm resulted in a victimization rate of 38/1,000 women during a six-month period.

Perpetration rates were also determined using data from the male subjects. When all unwanted oral, anal, and vaginal intercourse attempts and completions were included in the calculations, a perpetration rate of 34/1,000 men was obtained. Use of the FBI definition resulted in a perpetration rate of 9/1,000 college men during a six-month period.

Descriptive Profile of Sexual Aggression/Victimization

To develop a profile of the sexual aggression/victimization experiences that were reported by postsecondary students, researchers used inferential statistics descriptively.

WOMEN'S VANTAGE POINT—Women were asked detailed questions about the most serious victimization, if any, that they had experienced since the age of 14. . . . From this data, the following profile of the rapes reported by women students emerge. (All items were scored on a 1 [not at all] to 5 [very much] scale unless otherwise indicated.) The victimizations happened 1–2 years ago when the women were 18–19 years old (M = 18.5); 95% of the assaults involved one offender only; 84% involved an offender who was known to the victim; 57% of offenders were dates. The rapes happened primarily off campus (86%), equally as often in the man's house or car as in the woman's house or car. Most offenders (73%) were thought to be drinking or using drugs at the time of the assault, while the victim admitted using intoxicants in 55% of the episodes. Prior mutual intimacy had occurred with the offender to the level of petting above the waist (M = 3.52 on a 1–6 scale). However, the victims believed that they had made their nonconsent to have sexual intercourse "quite" clear (M = 4.05). Typically, the victim perceived that the offender used "quite a bit" of force (M = 3.88), which involved twisting her arm or holding her down. Only 9% of the rapes involved hitting or beating, and only 5% involved weapons. Women rated their amount of resistance as moderate (M = 3.80). Forms of resistance used by many rape victims included reasoning (84%) and physically struggling (70%). Many women (41%) were virgins at the time of their rape. During the rape, victims felt scared (M = 3.66), angry (M = 3.97), and depressed (M = 3.93). Rape victims felt somewhat responsible (M = 2.80) for what had happened, but believed that the man was much more responsible (M = 4.29).

Almost half of victimized women (42%) told no one about their assault. Just 8% of the victims who told anyone reported to police (equivalent to 5% of all rape victims), and only 8% of the victims who told anyone visited a crisis center (again equivalent to 5% of all rape victims). Those who reported to police rated the reaction they received as "not at all supportive" (M = 1.02). On the other hand, family (M = 3.70) and campus agency (M = 4.00) reaction were seen as supportive.

Surprisingly, 42% of the women indicated that they had sex again with the offender on a later occasion, but it is not known if this was forced or voluntary; most relationships (87%) did eventually break up subsequent to the victimization. Many rape victims (41%) stated that they expected a similar assault to happen again in the future, and only 27% of the women whose experience met legal definitions of rape labeled themselves as rape victims.

Although these analyses demonstrated statistically significant differences between the situational characteristics of the rapes reported by women compared with the lesser degrees of sexual victimization, the effect sizes of these differences were generally small. Thus, the descriptive profile of the rapes reported by college women is applicable to a great extent to the lesser degrees of sexual victimization as well. With the effect sizes for guidance, the following large and important differences between rapes and other forms of sexual victimization can be noted. Rapes were less likely to involve dating partners than other forms of sexual victimization. While 70–86% of lesser forms of victimization involved dating couples, only 57% of the rapes did.

Men who raped were perceived by the victims as more often drinking (73%) than men who engaged in lesser degrees of sexual aggression (35–64%). Rapes, as well as attempted rapes, were more violent. More than half of rape victims (64%) and attempted rape victims (41%) reported that the offender used actual violence, such as holding them down, while fewer than 10% of other victims reported actual force. Likewise, the use of physical resistance was reported by many more victims of rape (70%) and attempted rape (52%) than by victims of lesser degrees of sexual assault (26–33%). Finally, rape victims (27%) were much more likely than any other group (1–3%) to see their experience as a rape.

MEN'S VANTAGE POINT—Men were asked detailed questions about the most serious sexual aggression, if any, that they had perpetrated since the age of 14. . . . With this data, characteristics of the rapes perpetrated by college men can be determined. The rapes happened one to two years ago when the men were 18–19 years old (M = 18.5); 84% of the assaults involved one offender only; 84% involved an offender who was known to the victim; 61% of offenders were dates. The rapes happened primarily off campus (86%), equally as often in the man's house or car as in the woman's house or car. Most men who raped (74%) said they were drinking or using drugs at the time of the assault, and most (75%) perceived that their victims were using intoxicants as well. Men believed that mutual intimacy had occurred with the victim to the level of petting below the waist (M = 4.37), and they felt that the victims' nonconsent to have sexual intercourse was "not at all" clear (M = 1.80).

Typically, men who raped perceived that they were "somewhat" forceful (M = 2.85) and admitted twisting the victim's arm or holding her down. Only 3% of the perpetrators of rape said that they hit or beat the victim, and only 4% used weapons. They perceived victims' resistance as minimal (M = 1.83). Forms of resistance that assailants observed included reasoning, which was used by 36% of the rape victims, and physically struggling, which was used by 12%. Few men (12%) were virgins at the time they forced a woman to have sexual intercourse.

During the assault, offenders felt minimal negative emotions, including feeling scared (M = 1.52), angry (M = 1.45), or depressed (M = 1.59). Instead, perpetrators of rape were more likely to feel proud (M = 2.27). Although they felt mildly responsible (M = 2.43) for what had happened, rapists believed that the woman was equally or more responsible (M = 2.85). Half of the men who reported an act that met legal definitions of rape (54%) told no one at all about their assault, and only 2% of them were reported to police by the victim. Among the men, 55% indicated that after the assault they had had sex with the victim again, but it is not known if this was forced or voluntary. A substantial number of men who raped (47%) stated that they expected to engage in a similar assault at some point. Most men (88%) who reported an assault that met legal definitions of rape were adamant that their behavior was definitely not rape.

Although these analyses demonstrated statistically significant differences between the assault characteristics reported by men who raped compared with men who perpetrated lesser degrees of sexual aggression, the effect sizes of these differences were generally small. Thus, the descriptive profile of the rapes reported by male college students generally is applicable to the lesser degrees of sexual aggression as well. With the effect sizes for guidance, the following large and important differences between rapes and other forms of sexual aggression can be noted. Men who raped were more often drinking (74%) than men who engaged in lesser degrees of sexual aggression (33–67%). They perceived that the victim was more often drinking (75%) than was perceived by men who perpetrated lesser degrees of sexual aggression (31–65%). Men who reported behavior that met legal definitions of rape were less likely to be virgins at the time of their assault (12%) than other sexually aggressive men (24–48%). Men who perpetrated rape and sexual coercion were more likely to have sex with the victim again (64% and 55% respectively) than other perpetrators (32–37%). In addition, men who raped reported sexual intercourse with a larger number of partners since the assaultive episode than was reported by less sexually aggressive men.

Discussion

In this study, behaviorally specific items regarding rape and lesser forms of sexual aggression/victimization were presented in a noncrime context to an approximately representative national sample of college students. The results indicate that 15.4% of women reported experiencing and 4.4% of men reported perpetrating, since the age of 14, an act that met legal definitions of rape. Because virtually none of these victims or perpetrators had been involved in the criminal justice system, their experiences qualify as "hidden rape," which is not reflected in official crime statistics such as the *Uniform Crime Reports* (e.g., FBI 1985).

As mentioned earlier, a victimization rate for women of 38/1,000 was calculated. This rate is 10–15 times greater than rates based on the NCS (BJS 1984), which are 3.9/1,000 for women age 16–19 and 2.5/1,000 for women age 20–24. Even men's rate of admitting to raping (9/1,000) is two to three times greater than NCS estimates of the high risk of rape for women between the ages of 16–24. At least among students in higher education, it appears that official surveys (such as the NCS) fail to describe the full extent of sexual victimization.

However, NCS rates are based on representative samples of all persons in the U.S. in the 16–24-year-old group, whereas the present sample represents only the 25% of persons age 18–24 who attend college. Using other available data for guidance, one can speculate how the victimization rates among postsecondary students might compare with the rates among nonstudents in the same age group. Although the data do not suggest a direct relationship between level of education and rape victimization rates, the rates are related to family income. Thus, nonstudents, who are likely to come from poorer families than students enrolled in higher education, might show even higher incidence rates than those found in the study sample. However, only when empirical data on young persons not attending school become available can the victimization rates reported in the NCS for persons age 18–24 be fully analyzed.

The characteristics of the rapes described by study respondents differ from the characteristics of rapes described by official statistics (e.g., BJS 1984). For example, 60–75% of the rapes reported in the NCS by women age 16–24 involved strangers, and 27% involved multiple offenders (i.e., group rapes). Study respondents, most of whom were between the ages of 18–24, did report stranger rapes (16%) and group rapes (5%), but the vast majority of incidents were individual assaults (95%) that involved close acquaintances or dates (84%).

The differences between the kinds of rape described in official reports and in this study suggest that it is episodes of intimate violence that differentiate between the results. Either the wording of screening questions or the overall crime context-questioning of the NCS may fail to elicit from respondents the large number of sexual victimizations that involve close acquaintances.

The findings of this study demonstrate that men to not admit enough sexual aggression to account for the number of victimizations reported by women. Specifically, 54% of women claimed to be sexually victimized, but only 25% of men admitted any degree of sexually aggressive behavior. However, the number of times that men admitted perpetrating each aggressive act is virtually identical to the number of times women reported experiencing each act. Thus, the results fail to support notions that a few sexually active men could account for the victimization of a sizable number of women. Clearly, some of the victimizations reported by college women occurred in earlier years and were not perpetrated by the men who were surveyed. In addition, some recent victimizations may have involved community members who were not attending college. Future research must determine the extent to which these explanations account for the sizable difference in rates.

The data on validity suggest that those sexual experiences reported by the women did, in fact, occur, while additional relevant sexual experiences may not have been reported by men. Men may not be intentionally withholding information, but rather may be perceiving and conceptualizing potentially relevant sexual experiences in a way that was not elicited by the wording of the sexual experiences survey. Scully and Marolla (1982) studied incarcerated rapists who denied that the incident for which they were convicted was a rape. Many of these men, although they used physical force and injured their victims, saw their behavior as congruent with consensual sexual activity. It may be that some men fail to perceive accurately the degree of force and coerciveness that was involved in a particular sexual encounter or to interpret correctly a woman's consent or resistance.

This hypothesis is supported by the descriptive differences between men's and women's perceptions of the rape incidents. Although there were many points of agreement between men and women (e.g., the proportion of incidents that involved alcohol and the relationship of victim and offender), victims saw their nonconsent as clearer and occurring after less consensual intimacy than offenders. Victims perceived their own resistance and the man's violence as much more extreme than the offenders did. Future research might compare consent, violence, and resistance attributions among sexually aggressive and sexually nonaggressive men. If differences were found, the line of inquiry would lead to a new focus for rape prevention programs—educating vulnerable men to perceive accurately and communicate clearly.

The results of the study have additional implications for clinical treatment and research. The extent of sexual victimization uncovered by the national survey suggests that clinicians should consider including questions about unwanted sexual activity in routine intake interviewing of women clients and that they more frequently should consider sexual victimization among the possible etiological factors that could be linked to presenting symptoms. Of course, the study sample consisted of students, whereas many psychotherapy seekers are adults. However, it is not unusual for symptoms of post-traumatic stress disorder, which victims of rape may experience, to emerge months or even years after the trauma (American Psychiatric Association 1980).

For researchers, these results in combination with the work of others begin to describe the full extent of rape and suggest how reported statistics on rape reflect only those rapes reported to police (i.e., 5%), rapes acknowledged as rape by the victim (i.e., 27%), and those for which victim assistance services are sought (i.e., 5%), rather than reflecting rapes that have not been revealed (i.e., 42%). Future research must address the traumatic cognitive and symptomatic impact of rape on victims who do not report, confide in significant others, seek services, or even identify as victims. It is possible that the quality of many women's lives is reduced by the effects of encapsulated, hidden sexual victimization and the victims' subsequent accommodation to the experience through beliefs and behavior (Koss and Burkhart 1986).

Statistically significant regional and ethnic differences in the prevalence of sexual aggression/victimization were found. Unfortunately, the meaning of these results cannot be fully interpreted, as ethnicity and region were confounded (i.e., minority students are not distributed randomly across the regions of the country). However, effect sizes calculated on the variables of region and ethnicity indicate that their impact on the prevalence rates is small. In the future, researchers will need to analyze the effect of ethnicity by controlling for region (and vice versa). As a result, other data available on the subjects, including personality characteristics, values, beliefs, and current behavior, can be used to attempt to account for any remaining differences.

Overall, the prevalence rates for sexual victimization/aggression were robust and did not vary extensively from large to small schools; across types of institutions; or among urban areas, medium-sized cities, and rural areas. The ubiquity of sexual aggression and victimization supports Johnson's observation that "the locus of violence rests squarely in the middle of what our culture defines as 'normal' interaction between men and women" (Johnson 1980, 146). As the editors of the *Morbidity and Mortality Weekly Report*, issued by the Centers for Disease Control in Atlanta, have noted, there is an ". . . increasing awareness in the public health community that violence is a serious public health problem and that nonfatal interpersonal violence has far-reaching consequences in terms of morbidity and quality of life" (Centers for Disease Control 1985, 739). Future research needs to devote attention to the preconditions that foster sexual violence.

Within the rape epidemiology literature are studies that have differed in methodology and have reported varying prevalence rates. Although the *Ms.* project involved a set of self-report questions whose validity and reliability have been evaluated, each data-collection method has advantages and disadvantages and cannot be fully assessed without reference to the special requirements of the topic of inquiry, the target population, and practical and financial limitations. Future epidemiological research must define how much variation in rates is due to the method of data collection or the screening question format and how much is due to sample differences. Nevertheless, the most important conclusion suggested by this entire line of research is that rape is much more prevalent than official statistics suggest.

References

American Psychiatric Association. 1980. *Diagnostic and statistical manual of mental disorders.* 3rd ed. Washington, D.C.: American Psychiatric Association.

Bureau of Justice Statistics. 1984. *Criminal victimization in the United States, 1982.* Washington, D.C.: U.S. Department of Justice.

Centers for Disease Control. 1985. Adolescent sex offenders—Vermont, 1984. *Morbidity and Mortality Weekly Report* 34: 738–741.

Cohen, J. 1977. *Statistical power analysis for the behavioral sciences.* rev. ed. New York: Academic Press.

Federal Bureau of Investigation. 1986. *Uniform crime reports.* Washington, D.C.: U.S. Department of Justice.

Johnson, A. G. 1980. On the prevalence of rape in the United States. *Signs: Journal of Women in Culture and Society* 6: 136–46.

Kanin, E. J. 1957. Male aggression in dating-courtship relations. *American Journal of Sociology* 63: 197–204.

Kanin, E. J., and S. R. Parcell. 1977. Sexual aggression: A second look at the offended female. *Archives of Sexual Behavior* 6: 67–76.

Katz, S., and M. A. Mazur. 1979. *Understanding the rape victim: A synthesis of research findings.* New York: John Wiley and Sons.

Kilpatrick, D. G., L. J. Veronen, and C. L. Best. 1984. Factors predicting psychological distress among rape victims. In *Trauma and its wake: The study and treatment of post-traumatic stress disorder*, ed. C. R. Figley, 113–41. New York: Brunner/Mazel.

Kilpatrick, D. G., et al. 1985. Mental health correlates of criminal victimization: A random community survey. *Journal of Consulting and Clinical Psychology* 53: 866–73.

Kirkpatrick, C., and E. J. Kanin. 1957. Male sexual aggression on a university campus. *American Sociological Review* 22: 52–58.

Koss, M. P. 1985. The hidden rape victim: Personality, attitudinal, and situational characteristics. *Psychology of Women Quarterly* 9: 193–212.

Koss, M. P., and B. R. Burkhart. 1986. Clinical treatment of rape. Under review.

Koss, M. P., and C. A. Gidycz. 1985 Sexual Experiences Survey: Reliability and validity. *Journal of Consulting and Clinical Psychology* 53: 422–23.

Koss, M. P., and C. J. Oros. 1982. Sexual Experiences Survey: A research instrument investigating sexual aggression and victimization. *Journal of Consulting and Clinical Psychology* 50: 455–57.

Koss, M. P., C. J. Gidycz, and N. Wisniewski. 1987. The scope of rape: Sexual aggression and victimization in a national sample of students in higher education. *Journal of Consulting and Clinical Psychology* 55: 152–70.

Koss, M. P., et al. 1985. Nonstranger sexual aggression: A discriminant analysis of the psychological characteristics of undetected offenders. *Sex Roles* 12: 981–92.

Law Enforcement Assistance Administration. 1974. *Crimes and victims: A report on the Dayton-San Jose pilot survey of victimization.* Washington, D.C.: National Criminal Justice Information and Statistics Service.

———. 1975. *Criminal victimization surveys in 13 American cities.* Washington, D.C.: U.S. Government Printing Office.

Office of Civil Rights. 1980. *Fall enrollment and compliance report of institutions of higher education.* Washington, D.C.: U.S. Department of Education.

Ohio Revised Code. 1980. 2907.01A, 2907.02.

Rapaport, K., and B. R. Burkhart. 1984. Personality and attitudinal characteristics of sexually coercive college males. *Journal of Abnormal Psychology* 93: 216–221.

Russell, D. E. H. 1984. *Sexual exploitation: Rape, child sexual abuse, and sexual harassment.* Beverly Hills, Calif.: Sage Publications.

Scully, D., and J. Marolla. 1982. Convicted rapists' construction of reality: The denial of rape. Paper presented at meeting of American Sociological Association, September, San Francisco.

U.S. Bureau of the Census. 1980. *Current population reports, 1980–1981.* Washington, D.C.: U.S. Government Printing Office.

Walker, A. 1982. *The Color Purple.* New York: Harcourt Brace Jovanovich.

7

Wife Rape and the Law

~

Diana E. H. Russell

I can not say that I think you very generous to the Ladies, for whilst you are proclaiming peace and good will to men, Emancipating all Nations, you insist upon retaining an absolute power over Wives. But you must remember that Arbitrary power is like most other things which are very hard, very liable to be broken. . . .

> —Abigail Adams to John Adams, 1776, *Familiar Letters of John Adams and His Wife, Abigail Adams, During the Revolution*, ed. Charles Francis Adams, 1876

The marriage license [is] a raping license.

> —David Finkelhor and Kersti Yllo, "Forced Sex in Marriage," 1980

THE LAWS RELATING TO RAPE in most states of this nation, and in most countries of the world, include what is commonly referred to as "the marital rape exemption." These laws usually define rape as *the forcible penetration of the body of a woman, not the wife of the perpetrator*, and so according to them, rape in marriage is a legal impossibility.

The origin of this exemption is invariably traced to a pronouncement by Matthew Hale, Chief Justice in England in the 17th century. As published in *History of the Pleas of the Crown* in 1736 it reads as follows:

> But the husband cannot be guilty of a rape committed by himself upon his lawful wife, for by their mutual matrimonial consent and

From Diana E. H. Russell, "Wife Rape and the Law," in *Rape in Marriage*, rev. ed. (Bloomington: Indiana University Press, 1990), 17–26, 387–88. Reprinted by permission of Indiana University Press.

contract the wife hath given up herself in this kind unto the husband which she cannot retract.

The rationale behind the rule seems to have been the idea that "marriage, with the promise to obey, implied the right to sexual intercourse with the wife upon all occasions."[1] This idea, in turn, rested upon the notion that women were the property of their husbands, and procreation was the sole purpose of marriage.[2] Though Hale offered no legal authority in support of his opinion, case law in the United States "indicates an unquestioning acceptance of the Hale *dictum*, almost as if the courts were incapable of conceiving other resolutions of the issue."[3] Even the knowledge that Hale "made a name for himself by presiding over 'witch' trials and leading juries to convictions over enormous odds" does not seem to have made any dent in the credibility of this 17th century misogynist.[4]

The women's movement was very successful in drawing public attention to the issue of rape in the early 1970s, and equally successful in pressuring for changes in the laws pertaining to extramarital rape. For example, almost every state had passed some form of rape reform legislation by 1980.[5] Common reforms include limiting the cross-examination of the victim about her sexual history, disallowing what used to be a routine cautionary instruction given by the judge to the jury that rape is an easy charge to make but a difficult one to defend against, redefining rape to acknowledge that males as well as females can be victimized, and including forced oral or anal penetration in the definition of rape. However, these reforms did not sail through the state legislative bodies; rather they came after a considerable grass-roots lobbying effort by a coalition of feminists and law and order groups.[6] The slow progress in the passage of rape reform legislation has been compared by Hubert Feild and Leigh Bienen with the rapid and enthusiastic enactment of legislation against the exploitation of children in the pornography industry in 1978.[7]

There seems to have been an even greater reluctance to change laws condoning wife rape. One explanation for this is that "the matter may be too close for personal comfort for the well-placed, married males who make up the vast majority of the membership of American state legislatures. It may take only a little imagination for them to create a scenario in which, in their worst forebodings, they are cast as the protagonist in a Kafka-like performance."[8] Some of the arguments that have greeted legislative efforts to outlaw rape in marriage give strong support to this thesis. The following are examples of such arguments described as "typical" by the National Center on Women and Family Law:

"The State of Florida has absolutely no business intervening into the sexual relationship between a husband and a wife. . . . We don't need Florida invading the sanctity and intimacy of a relationship." (Rep. Tom Bush, May 29, 1980)

"[T]he Bible doesn't give the state permission anywhere in that Book for the state to be in your bedroom, and that is just exactly what this bill has gone to. It's meddling in your bedroom; the State of Florida, as an entity, deciding what you can do and what you can't do." (Rep. John Mica, May 29, 1980)

"But if you can't rape your wife, who can you rape?" (California State Senator Bob Wilson, addressing a group of women lobbyists, spring 1979).[9]

The Rideout Case in Oregon

The spousal immunity clause was deleted from Oregon's rape statute in 1977. A year later in that state, John Rideout was indicted for raping his wife, Greta, and he thus became the first husband charged with marital rape while still living with his wife to be criminally prosecuted. Although there have been several other cases of husbands charged with rape in various states since then, the Rideout case is best known, or more accurately, most notorious. Despite the fact that the publicity about this case was often critical of Greta Rideout and the fact that a husband could be accused of raping his wife, it has done more than any other to raise consciousness about the issue of wife rape. The case was described in the media of the time:[10]

> A twenty-three-year-old woman who'd been physically and psychologically abused by her husband for over two years, [Greta Rideout] found that as soon as she quit submitting to his desires, her husband's sexual aggression became so violent she could label it nothing less than rape. . . .
>
> She had met John Rideout four years ago (in 1974) in Portland. . . . Before they were married (shortly after their two-and-a-half-year-old daughter, Jenny, was born), Greta said he'd slapped her face and "demolished" the house they were living in. She left him then—the first of three times.
>
> "Two months after we were married, he began the mental abuse—calling me a dumb bitch, accusing me of being with someone else," she said, "but I was trying to deal with it. I wanted the marriage to work out, for better or worse. And believe me, most of it was worse."
>
> Slowly she began to see a change taking place. The first time he gave her a black eye was a year and a half ago (in 1976). Aggressive sex, too, began to be a part of the pattern, according to Greta. "He

was highly obsessed with sex; he wanted it two or three times a day. No matter what I gave him, he was never totally satisfied."

What seemed to give him the most pleasure, she reflected, was the violent sex which became a once-a-week occurrence. "And the more riled I got, the more he seemed to enjoy it."

Like most battered women, Greta Rideout had been afraid to fight back. The relationship became one of "love-hate, love-hate." John even threatened to sexually manipulate their daughter and told his wife he would show Jenny "what sex is all about" when she became an adolescent. . . .

She left him for the third time in July but returned for the same reason she had done so before. She couldn't support her daughter on the part-time minimum wages of her cashier's job or on welfare. She said she considered leaving Jenny with friends while she got on her feet financially, but thought John would accuse her of abandoning the child and try to take Jenny from her. Many of their arguments had been over money; John's work as a gas station attendant plus her meager wages "barely covered essentials," she said.

When she returned for the last time, her plan was to save up enough money to be able to leave for good.

"Before this point I had submitted. Now I was swimming to the surface to get out of the gutter, and he knew it. He saw the strength rising in me. . . ." It was around this time that his violence toward her seemed to intensify. "At times I'd be laying watching TV, and he'd walk up and kick me. I started feeling, God, he's weird." But he told her, "You're my wife; I can do what I want."

"He was in love with me when I was weak, but when I showed any strength, he hated my guts," she recalled. At the same time, she now realizes, he both loathed and was excited by strong women.

"He would see pretty women, strong career women, on TV or in magazines, and they seemed 'prudish' to him. He'd get worked up and say, 'Jeez, I'd like to rape that bitch's ass.' "

On October 10 (1978), John and Greta had an argument over money. He'd quit his job to return to school on the GI Bill and she thought he was squandering money at bars, playing pool—and not attending classes. She ran away from him, but he chased her, locked her in the apartment and started demanding sex. When she refused, he beat her until finally, she testified in court, she submitted for fear he would break her jaw.

John Rideout and his attorney never denied that he beat her that day, or that they had sexual intercourse. Their marriage had a pattern of fight, make up, and make love, the men said. (By the time their fights were over, said Greta, she often just submitted to sex. On the day of the rape, she said she was "totally repulsed" by the idea of having sex with John.)

Greta's rape story was confirmed by the doctor who examined her afterward and the Crisis Center worker who'd answered her call.

"She was so scared that I was shaking; she had me scared to death," remembered volunteer Wanda Monthey.[11]

On December 27, 1978, John Rideout was acquitted of the charge of first degree rape of his wife by a jury of eight women and four men.

On January 6, 1979, less than two weeks after John was found not guilty, the Rideouts announced their reconciliation. Their faces beamed out from the pages of newspapers across the nation. "The law is right," John Rideout was quoted as saying. "It's a hard thing for a person like me to come back and say he believes the law is right when the law was used on me."

In March 1979, the couple separated again. Greta was quoted as saying, "I was going to go mad if I stayed there any longer. He has some pretty wild ideas about marriage." She added, "He also said that the things he told me about women's rights after the trial were wrong." Jean Christensen, Greta's attorney, obtained a divorce for her. Greta resumed her maiden name.

A few months later, John Rideout was back in court. On September 4, 1979, he pled guilty to a charge of criminal trespass for breaking into his ex-wife's home on August 27. He was given a nine-month suspended jail sentence, put on two years' probation, and required to pay $15 for the door he damaged and to submit to psychiatric evaluation. In February of this year, John Rideout was sentenced once again to nine months in jail for harassing his ex-wife; probation would be considered if Rideout consented to mental counseling.

Rideout's continuing attacks upon his ex-wife [after the rape trial] did not receive the sensational headlines that had attended the trial and reconciliation, so people still remember the Rideouts when they announced they were back together. Reporter Rae Nadler, writing in the *Hartford Courant*, described them at the time: "They posed together, a handsome couple, while the headlines declared 'Rideouts Will Ride It Out.' The world grinned and shook its head."

The reconciliation of John and Greta Rideout, though brief, was seen as confirmation by those who opposed the striking out of the marital exemption in Oregon's rape laws, that the state had no business meddling in the private affairs of married couples. And it was received as a blow to those who favored the legal reform and/or who believed Greta's story of wife rape. It was seen to demonstrate that, though she had been raped, it could not have been that upsetting an experience or she would not have become reconciled with her husband. But such a conclusion shows little understanding of the dynamics of relationships, particularly those in which women are being battered; for Greta was not just a victim of wife rape, she was a battered wife as well.

The issues of battered women and rape victims emerged as public concerns at different times and have developed in this and other countries as if they were two totally different problems. Separate literatures have developed around each, different institutions have been developed for handling them, and different people have been attracted to working with either rape victims or battered women, each often remaining quite ignorant of the other problem.

The Rideout case is one of many in which it is impossible to separate these two forms of male violence. But although ongoing intimate heterosexual relationships that are violent often involve both rape and beating, it is also important to recognize that the issues of wife rape and wife beating can be quite separate in many marriages, and that wife rape is not merely one more abuse suffered by the already battered woman.

Marital Rape Legislation and Court Decisions: The Contemporary Scene in the United States

In July 1980 only Oregon, Nebraska, and New Jersey had completely abolished the marital rape exemption, and California, Delaware, Hawaii, Minnesota, and Iowa had partially stricken it. Nine years later in July 1989, husbands can be prosecuted for raping their wives in forty-two states, the District of Columbia, and on all federal land. This represents an extraordinary achievement on the part of many feminists and their allies who have had to work very hard to break through the resistance on the part of mostly male legislators. These forty-two states are listed in the two left-hand columns of the chart below.

The sixteen states in the far left column of the chart are those that no longer permit a marital rape exemption. This is to say that wife rape is a crime in these states, regardless of whether the couple lives together or apart.

In the twenty-six states in the middle column of the chart, husbands can be prosecuted for raping their wives in some circumstances, but they are totally exempt from prosecution in others that are prosecutable for non-marital rape. For example, in some states, so-called lower degrees of rape are not considered crimes in cases of wife rape: for instance, rape imposed by force but without the wife's suffering additional degrees of violence such as kidnapping or being threatened with a weapon; and non-forceful rape that is imposed when the woman is unable to consent because she is unconscious, drugged, asleep, ill, or physically or mentally helpless is some other way. . . .

In the eight remaining states (those on the far right of the chart), wife rape is not a crime. If a husband rapes his wife when they are living apart or have obtained a legal separation, or when one of the parties has filed for a divorce or for an order of protection, the couple is defined as unmarried for the purposes of prosecution. As marital rape expert Laura X states: "The seventeenth century legal definition of 'married' (i.e., a wife gives up her right to consent) is thus reinforced in these states."[12]

Table 1. State Law Chart*

Husbands Can Be Prosecuted for Raping Their Wives		*Husbands Cannot Be Prosecuted Unless Couple Living Apart or Legally Separated or Filed for Divorce or Order of Protection*
No Exemptions	*Some Exemptions*	
N = 16	N = 26	N = 8
Alabama	Arizona	Kentucky
Alaska	California	Missouri
Arkansas	Connecticut	New Mexico
Colorado	Delaware	North Carolina
Florida	Hawaii	Oklahoma
Georgia	Idaho	South Carolina
Indiana	Illinois	South Dakota
Maine	Iowa	Utah
Massachusetts	Kansas	
Nebraska	Louisiana	
New Jersey	Maryland	
New York	Michigan	
North Dakota	Minnesota	
Oregon	Mississippi	
Vermont	Montana	
Wisconsin	Nevada	
(District of Columbia,	New Hampshire	
and federal lands in	Ohio	
any state)	Pennsylvania	
	Rhode Island	
	Tennessee	
	Texas	
	Virginia	
	Washington	
	West Virginia	
	Wyoming	

*This is an adaptation of an updated chart prepared by the National Clearinghouse on Marital and Date Rape, Berkeley, California, January 1990.

She goes on to point out that the husband in these eight states can continue to rape his wife until she takes action; the burden is on her to leave him or to file for divorce—sometimes life-threatening steps for her to initiate—instead of it being the state's responsibility to remove him from her, and from society, for raping her.[13]

The National Clearinghouse on Marital and Date Rape is the only source for national statistics on the outcome of wife rape cases that have been reported to the police. The Clearinghouse staff followed up information obtained from a newspaper clipping service and a vast network of contacts at rape crisis centers and battered women's shelters, with phone calls to the prosecutors, court officials, attorneys, and journalists—in short, anyone who could supply them with further information about the outcome of the cases they had learned about. Unfortunately, the Clearinghouse data cover only the period 1978 (after the acquittal of John Rideout) to 1985, when lack of funding prevented the continuation of this project. Although it can be assumed that their method of acquiring information did not enable the staff to draw up a complete compendium of all the wife rape cases reported in the United States between 1978 and 1985, it is nevertheless the most complete data available on the outcome of wife rape cases.

An adapted version of the National Clearinghouse's table on arrest, prosecution, and conviction statistics for marital rapists appears below.

Table 2. Outcome of Wife Rape Cases Reported to the Police: 1978–1985

Outcome	Number of Cases
Husband Arrested	210
Charge Dropped	48
Case Still Pending (as of 1985)	44
Prosecution Ended with Acquittal	14
Prosecution Ended with Conviction	*104*
Total Prosecuted Cases	*118*
Convictions as a Percentage of Prosecuted Cases	88%

The 88 percent conviction rate for victims of wife rape whose reports to the police resulted in arrest is strikingly high. It is considerably higher than many people either anticipated or currently realize. It is also significantly higher than the conviction rate for *non*-marital rapes. This is surprising because it is generally true that the more intimate the relationship between the victim and the rapist, the less likely are reporting, arrest, and conviction.[14]

One reason for the high conviction rate for wife rape is probably that—contrary to the fears of many legislators—the wives who charge their husbands with rape have often been subjected to particularly brutal and/or deviant experiences. The thousands of women who are raped by their husbands in more "ordinary" ways, without the employment of tire irons, dogs, strangulation, or death threats, are simply not reporting their experiences to the police. And it is doubtful that the vast majority ever will. Given the continuing misogyny of the legal and law enforcement systems, we should not delude ourselves that this is a problem that will be solved by having every victim of wife rape report her attack to the police.

I believe that the next steps in the campaign for the rights of wife rape victims (and all married women are potential wife rape victims) are for concerned women and men to mobilize for the pursuit of the following goals:

1. The criminalization of wife rape in the eight holdout states that have so far been unwilling to institute this reform.
2. The passing of laws in the twenty-six states which still treat some forms of rape by husbands as non-criminal, the implicit assumption being that wife rape is less serious than rape by other perpetrators.

    Feminist legal theorists, such as Joanne Schulman (formerly the staff attorney of the National Center on Women and Family Law), Sarah Wunsch and Anne Simon (formerly at the Center for Constitutional Rights), have noted that proposed marital rape laws are often butchered by amendments before becoming law. This is what has happened in twenty-six states. In contrast, the highest courts in several states have simply struck down the marital rape exemption as an unconstitutional denial of equal protection for wives. Because the rape of unmarried women is considered a crime, some of them have argued that equity requires that it also be so for married women. The courts have not followed the practice of many legislatures in maintaining that wife rape is different from rape by other perpetrators.

    These feminist attorneys therefore have proposed that the wives in the thirty-four states that either do not have a law against wife rape or that do not have a satisfactory law, should organize a class action suit in each of these states to have the exemptions struck down by the courts as unconstitutional.
3. Courts can also strike down the exemptions for husbands as unconstitutional if they agree, as in *Liberta* (New York),[15] with Friend of the Court briefs requesting such a decision.
4. Wives who reside in states where wife rape is still legal can sue their husbands for damages in civil court, as pioneering rape law analyst Camille Le Grand proposed in the seventies.

However, she also pointed out that it would be easier to sue one's husband civilly in a state where wife rape was taken seriously enough to be considered criminal.

On the other hand, it is equally important for all of us to recognize that wife rape is not a problem that will ever be solved by turning to the law. As long as men are the ones to make and implement the laws, there will be no justice for women. Taking their husbands to court is not an option that many wives will consider, for economic, social and psychological reasons. In addition, many women realize that the system is unlikely to be fair to them. For some it would also be highly dangerous to report sexual assault by their husbands because of the vindictive and sometimes lethal violence to which they might then be subjected.

The solution to the problem of wife rape starts with breaking silence about it. Women must realize that rape in marriage is common, but illegal, and married women need to know that they have a *right* to decline their husbands' sexual advances whenever they want to. For these goals to be achieved, feminists—particularly those who work in battered women's shelters and rape crisis centers—must acknowledge the significance and seriousness of wife rape in the United States, and place it on their agenda of issues that must be confronted and remedied. Service workers must extend their services to the victims of wife rape, and include wife rape in their efforts to educate the community. These are some of the first steps toward creating new norms for men's behavior in marriage. New remedies will emerge once these norms have been established. This may involve publicly shaming men, as the Chinese battered wives did in their "speak bitterness" sessions after the Communist revolution. Whatever the method, one thing is clear. True gender equality in and outside of marriage is necessary before all wives will be free from the risk of rape by their husbands.

Notes

1. Hubert S. Feild and Leigh B. Bienen, *Jurors and Rape: A Study in Psychology and Law* (Lexington, Mass.: D.C. Heath and Company, 1980), p. 163.
2. Ibid.
3. Gilbert Geis speculates that Hale was in fact probably reflecting even earlier standards. "Rape-in-Marriage: Law and Law Reform in England, the United States, and Sweden," *Adelaide Law Review*, Vol. 6, No. 2 (June 1978), p. 285. For two excellent in-depth discussions of the validity or lack thereof of the Hale doctrine, see "The Marital Rape Exemption," *New York University Law Review*, Vol. 52 (May 1977), and Dennis Drucker, "The Common Law Does Not Support a Marital Exemption for Forcible Rape," *Women's Rights Law Reporter*, Vol. 5 (1979).

4. Geis, "Rape-in-Marriage," p. 286.

5. Feild and Bienen, *Jurors and Rape*, p. 153.

6. Ibid., p. 153,

7. Ibid.

8. Geis, "Rape-in-Marriage," p. 294.

9. Joanne Schulman, "The Marital Rape Exemption in the Criminal Law," *Clearinghouse Review*, Vol. 14, No. 6 (October 1980).

10. The first portion of the account is excerpted from an article by Michelle Celarier, "I Kept Thinking Maybe I Could Help Him," *In These Times* (January 10–16, 1979).

11. The remainder of this account of the Rideout case is excerpted from an article by Moira K. Griffin, "In 44 States, It's Legal to Rape Your Wife," *Student Lawyer*, Vol. 9, No. 1 (September 1980).

12. National Clearinghouse on Marital and Date Rape, State Law Chart. Unpublished sheet, updated January 1, 1990.

13. Ibid.

14. Diana E. H. Russell, *Sexual Exploitation: Rape, Child Sexual Abuse, and Workplace Harassment* (Beverly Hills, California: Sage Publications, 1984).

15. Sarah Wunsch of the Center for Constitutional Rights has summarized the significance of the 1984 New York State Court of Appeals' case called *People of the State of New York v. Mario Liberta* in a pamphlet first published in July 1986. The Court of Appeals demolished "the excuses for not having laws to protect women against marital rape" by offering the following arguments:

Marriage does not give a husband a right to forced sex; rape is not part of the marriage contract. While it is understood that sex is a part of marriage, a woman has no "duty" to provide sex on demand whenever and in whatever way the husband desires it; and often, rape has nothing to do with sex.

Accusing angry wives of making up charges of rape is just another example of discrimination against women. In states where marital rape is treated as rape, there is no evidence that wives are making up charges. In fact, rape is one of the most underreported of all crimes.

Just because a crime may be hard to prove in some cases doesn't mean that prosecutors should be unable to ever present such a case. Actually, there is a high conviction rate in marital rape cases that have gone to trial.

Marital privacy is meant to protect the privacy of husbands and wives to engage in activities they both agree to; it is not a shield for violent, brutal acts.

Making marital rape a crime does not make it harder to keep a marriage going. By making rape in marriage a crime, some rapes can be prevented and the institution of marriage may be strengthened by the respect for women it conveys (*Stopping Sexual Assault in Marriage: A Guide for Women, Counselors and Advocates*, 1986, pp. 8–9).

8

The Effects of Sexual Assault
on Men: A Survey of
Twenty-two Victims

~

Gillian Mezey
Michael King

Introduction

V ERY LITTLE WORK HAS BEEN DONE on the effects of forcible sexual
assault on men. One possible reason may be that it is not recognized as a distinct entity within the 1976 Sexual Offences (Amendment) Act but is included with other consensual and nonconsensual
acts of buggery on both women and men. This has obvious implications in reporting and public awareness (Mezey & King, 1987). The
term "rape" specifies forcible vaginal penetration. Male sexual assault
has been regarded as an aberration of institutional life where the sex
object of choice is unavailable (Sagarin, 1976). There has been little
recognition that it may also be a problem in the wider community.

Contrary to popular belief, rape is predominantly an assertion of
power and aggression rather than an expression of sexual need (Groth
et al., 1977). There is no information in the UK regarding the nature
and extent of male sexual assault and the effects on victims. We would
hypothesize that men can be forcibly sexually assaulted, that most do
not report the crime and that the effects on them may have parallels
with the rape trauma syndrome described in female victims (Burgess
& Holmstrom, 1974).

From Gillian Mezey and Michael King, "The Effects of Sexual Assault on
Men: A Survey of 22 Victims," *Psychological Medicine* 19 (1989): 205–9. Reprinted by permission of Cambridge University Press and Gillian Mezey.

Method

Several national daily newspapers and gay periodicals publicized our study, concluding their articles with a request for adult males who had been sexually assaulted to contact us for the purposes of research. Respondents were asked to complete an extensive questionnaire covering demographic information, circumstances of the assault, post-assault reactions including reporting and past and present psychological health. All subjects were also asked to attend for a semi-structured interview conducted by either G.M. or M.K. The purpose of this interview was to verify and expand on the information already gained by questionnaire. Although respondents were advised that the study was primarily for research purposes, advice on referral and treatment was given where appropriate.

Results

Response to the Study

Twenty-eight men from all over the UK contacted us. In addition, we received one anonymous letter and one from a correspondent who described an assault on a friend. The latter two, as well as several miscellaneous letters, could not be included in the study.

Of the 28 potential subjects, three had been assaulted under the age of 16 years and thus were excluded from the analysis. Questionnaires were sent to the remaining 25 subjects, three of whom did not reply despite several reminders. Thus, 22 subjects completed the questionnaires and of these eight attended for interview. Fourteen subjects were not interviewed for the following reasons: one had died before interview was possible, four did not reply to our request for interview, and three agreed but then failed to attend. Only six refused interview, of whom in two cases their distance from London appeared to be a deterrent factor.

Many of those who were interviewed expressed apprehension that their accounts would not be taken seriously. However, several subjects appeared to derive relief from describing their experiences, in some cases for the first time. The results to be presented concern all subjects (22) completing questionnaires.

Demographic Characteristics

All the victims were white and in only one case was the assailant black. Mean age at time of the attack was 26.3 years. with a range of 16–82 years. Almost all victims and assailants were urban dwellers.

Previous Assault

Ten subjects described themselves as homosexual, four as bisexual and eight as heterosexual at the time of assault. Eleven assailants were described by their victims as homosexual, three as heterosexual and three as bisexual. In five cases, including one gang rape, the sexuality of the assailants was not clear.

Relationship between Victim and Offender

Four victims were attacked by complete strangers. The level of acquaintance in the remaining 18 consisted of a lover or ex-lover of the victim in three cases, a family member in one, that of a well-established acquaintance in six, a brief acquaintance (a few hours) in five and a sexual "pickup" in three. In seven cases the assailant was in a position of trust or authority over the victim. For example, one heterosexual man was assaulted by a priest whom he had viewed as a confidant and one married bisexual man was assaulted by a man who had advertised himself as a counsellor for married homosexual men.

Circumstances of the Attack

Place and time of each assault are shown in Table 1. The attack was carried out by more than one assailant in four cases, numbers of assailants ranging from 4 to 8. A weapon (a knife and a tree branch) was used in two cases. In 13 cases victims reported that their assailants had been drinking alcohol prior to the assault. However, in a further five cases use of alcohol by the assailant could not be clearly established. Eight of the victims had used alcohol, although in only one case did this appear to play a major role in incapacitating the victim.

Table 1. Place and Time of Assault

Place of Attack		*Time of Attack*		
Out of doors	6	Weekday	7 A.M. to 12 midnight	7
Victim's residence	5		12 midnight to 7 A.M.	5
Assailant's residence	9	Weekend	7 A.M. to 12 midnight	7
Neutral territory	2		12 midnight to 7 A.M.	3
Total	22	Total		22

Nature of the Attack

Seventeen men were the victims of forced anal intercourse and three of attempted anal intercourse. In addition, 11 victims were subjected to multiple types of assault such as being urinated on and forced to perform fellatio. In five cases assailants masturbated their victims, three of whom ejaculated. These victims expressed profound disgust and confusion at responding in this way.

Five men sought medical help for their injuries. Ten others received injuries but did not seek medical attention. The remaining victims were not physically harmed.

Responses to the Attack

During the Assault—Twelve subjects believed their lives were in danger during the attack. Only eight were able to offer any active physical resistance although 12 tried to dissuade their assailant. Two subjects appeared to offer no resistance at all. Feelings during the attack were predominately those of intense fear, unreality and anger, accompanied by somatic manifestations such as nausea.

Reaction following the Assault—Principal reactions to the assault are shown in Table 2. In all cases, the assault was reported as having had a major detrimental effect on their lives. Most men (13) did not report the assault to anyone in the immediate aftermath and six had never disclosed the assault prior to the research. Failure to report was a consequence of the stigma, fear of rejection or disbelief they anticipated. Victims were even more reluctant to report to the police for these reasons as well as out of a perception of the police as antihomosexual. Only two victims reported to the police and both instances resulted in court proceedings. One was heterosexual and the other concealed his homosexuality despite repeatedly being challenged on this issue by police and the courts.

Table 2. Principal Long-term Reactions to the Assault

Psychological	*Behavioral*
Increased sense of vulnerability (5)	Security precautions (5)
Increased anger/irritability (5)	Sexual dysfunction (11)
Conflicted sexual orientation (6)	Rape-related phobias (11)
Loss of self-respect/damaged self-image (7)	
Emotional distancing (8)	

Figures in parentheses refer to number of subjects. Total number = 22.

Sexual dysfunction was almost a universal theme, as was interference in the ability to form close, trusting relationships. Sexual difficulties ranged from that of complete inactivity for long periods to sexual promiscuity (two men) or even difficulties during the sexual act, such as fear of re-creating the assault either as victim or assailant. One heterosexual man commented: "One fear . . . was that I might make someone do something against their will, that is, become an unintentional rapist." Several men questioned their sexual orientation or its relevance to the assault. Many subjects referred to the humiliation and stigma involved, often citing this as a barrier to disclosing the attack to others.

There was a wide range of distressing and disabling symptoms often experienced for years afterwards. Of those interviewed (eight), the time since the assault ranged from 2 to 44 years, five of whom had been assaulted within the previous 7 years. None of these men on clinical criteria showed any evidence of a formal psychiatric disorder. Two victims had attempted suicide subsequently and one victim committed suicide two years after the assault. The latter had refused to be interviewed, but was receiving help from a local counsellor. Twelve subjects received psychiatric treatment at some point after the assault, of whom four had also consulted a psychiatrist previously. It would appear that in the two subjects who revealed the assault to their psychiatrist, the response was at best unsympathetic and at worst judgmental, as exemplified in the case of one heterosexual victim: 'I was politely disbelieved and urged to come to terms with the homosexual side of myself.' Behavioral changes, including particularly phobic avoidance and increased consumption of alcohol, were also prominent. Three men increased their use of prescribed drugs, four increased alcohol consumption and a further four men reported an increase in both.

Two subjects reported no psychological aftereffects.

Discussion

The greatest difficulty of this study was in persuading men who had been sexually assaulted to come forward. It is possible that those who volunteered were most distressed and most in need of help. In addition, information given in the newspapers on the possible effects of sexual assaults on males may have influenced the reports of the more suggestible subjects. Despite this, our findings indicate that men can be victims of serious sexual assault outside an institutional setting. Many of the characteristics of the victims, their reactions and the nature of the assaults have parallels with those described in female victims (Burgess & Holmstrom, 1974; Mezey & Taylor, 1988). Ironically, the politicization of rape as a feminist issue may contribute to the isolation and suffering experienced by the male victim.

Failure to report to the police is an even greater problem for male victims of sexual assault than for females. The police are gradually changing their policies toward the investigation and management of female victims. They also need to be aware that male victims exist and that their perceived antihomosexual public image deters many from coming forward.

In contrast to American reports the majority of assailants were homosexual (Groth & Burgess, 1980). Homosexual or bisexual men also predominated among the victims. Explanations for this pattern might be as follows: first, advertising in the gay press for subjects may have led to a sampling bias. Second, in some cases homosexual victims had placed themselves at risk by seeking casual sexual encounters (cruising). These victims might fear that their lack of judgment implied responsibility for the attack being placed on them rather than on the assailant. Many female victims are accused of precipitating assaults and their evidence is discredited in a similar manner (Adler, 1987). Third, homosexuals are more vulnerable to personal victimization of all kinds (West, 1985), and it was our impression that in certain cases the sexual assault represented an extension of "queer bashing."

As is the case for female victims, only a very few conformed to the stereotype of sudden, unprovoked attack by complete strangers in a public place (Katz & Mazur, 1979). However, unlike rape attacks on women, which mainly take place at weekends between midnight and 7 A.M., the timing of these assaults fitted no particular pattern. The temporal clustering of sexual assaults on women may represent a degree of sexual opportunism in terms of women who are seen out late at night, in social situations and possibly drinking, becoming misidentified as legitimate sexual targets.

In some cases, no overt violence was used but the assailant exploited a position of trust to gain a psychological advantage over his victim. The response of the majority of men was one of helplessness and passive submission to the attack engendered by an overwhelming sense of fear and disbelief. Although it is often assumed that men are able to defend themselves, our findings demonstrate that, like women, men react to extreme personal threat with frozen helplessness (Symonds, 1975). An extreme form of loss of control is demonstrated by those victims who were physiologically aroused while being terrorized. This would accord with other finding which suggest that sexual arousal may be provoked by extreme anxiety (Redmond et al., 1983).

These assaults had considerable impact on victims' sexual identity. One heterosexual victim commented: "Something very dirty has happened to you that nobody believes can happen—if you let it happen you must be queer, if you're not a queer it can't have happened." The fact that a man can be overpowered and penetrated makes him less of a man. This may have already been a point of ambivalence for homosexual victims, and for heterosexual victims, challenged a fundamental belief about their role as active initiators of sexual activity. Interestingly, homophobia was found as a reaction among homosexual as well as heterosexual victims.

Psychiatrists need to be aware of sexual assault as a possible antecedent of psychiatric symptoms in men, as well as patients' reluctance to disclose this spontaneously. Psychiatrists should be asking their patients of either sex about previous sexual assault as part of their routine assessment. Finally, given the prevalence of suicidal ideation together with one completed suicide, the suicidal potential of male victims should not be underestimated.

This study does not provide information on the natural history of men's reaction to sexual assault, which can only be revealed by prospective studies. More definitive epidemiological work needs to be done before the full extent of this problem will be recognized.

Our thanks go to the subjects of this study for their courage and openness in taking part.

References

Adler, Z. (1987). *Rape on Trial*. Routledge & Kegan Paul: London.

Burgess, A. W. & Holmstrom, L. L. (1974). Rape trauma syndrome. *American Journal of Psychiatry* 131. 981–987.

Groth, A. N. & Burgess, A. W. (1980). Male rape: offenders and victims. *American Journal of Psychiatry* 137. 806–810

Groth, A. N., Burgess, A. W. & Holmstrom, L. L. (1977). Rape: power, anger and sexuality. *American Journal of Psychiatry* 134. 1239–1243.

Katz, S. & Mazur, M. (1979). *Understanding the Rape Victim: A Synthesis of Research Findings*. John Wiley: New York.

Mezey, G. & King, M. (1987). Male victims of sexual assault. *Medicine, Science and the Law* 27. 122–124.

Mezey, G. & Taylor, P. (1988). Psychological reactions of women who have been raped: a descriptive and comparative study. *British Journal of Psychiatry* 152. 330–339.

Redmond, D., Kosten, T. R. & Reiser, M. (1983). Spontaneous ejaculation associated with anxiety: psychophysiological considerations. *American Journal of Psychiatry* 140. 1163–1166.

Sagarin, E. (1976). Prison homosexuality and its effect on post-prison sexual behavior. *Psychiatry* 39. 245–257.

Sexual Offences (Amendment) Act 1976. Section 2.

Symonds, M. (1975). Victims of violence. *American Journal of Psychoanalysis* 35. 19–26.

West, D. J. (1985). *Sexual Victimisation*. Gower: London.

III   Why Rape Happens

One of the central questions in the scholarly literature on sexual assault is why does rape occur. A number of scholars in various social science disciplines have researched this topic and most conclude that there is not a single factor that "causes" rape, but that there are a number of factors that combine to make it more likely to occur.

Feminist scholars offer an important analysis of rape, contending that rape is a product of our patriarchal system. According to this analysis, rape is the result of certain cultural conditions that promote violence against women. Peggy Reeves Sanday, an anthropologist at the University of Pennsylvania, examines this view in "The Socio-Cultural Context of Rape: A Cross-Cultural Study." Sanday finds that rape was either rare or nonexistent in a number of the 156 tribal societies that she studied and that the rape-free societies were very different from those in which rape was prevalent. Rape-prevalent societies were characterized by an ideology of male dominance and by high levels of interpersonal violence, while rape-free societies were characterized by greater sexual equality and respect for women and their activities. Sanday concludes that men are not naturally sexually aggressive but, instead, cultural conditions in certain societies promote male sexual aggression.

Diana Scully and Joseph Marolla, sociologists at Virginia Commonwealth University, also attribute rape to socio-cultural factors in " 'Riding the Bull at Gilley's': Convicted Rapists Describe the Rewards of Rape." In their interviews with convicted rapists, Scully and Marolla find that many of these men perceived sexual violence to be rewarding and did not believe that they would be punished for their behavior. Some men raped in order to punish a particular woman, or symbolically to punish all women. Others gained sexual pleasure from the assault and viewed rape as their "right." Scully and Marolla argue that these rapists were not pathological men but were simply expressing extreme forms of widely held beliefs about women.

In "Rape Myths," Martha Burt, a social psychologist at The Urban Institute, explores how culturally supported attitudes promote sexually coercive behavior. Rape myths are widely held false beliefs about rape that serve to absolve the rapist from culpability and encourage women to blame themselves for their own assault. Burt found that men who believe in rape myths are more likely to be sexually coercive, and that both men and women who hold these beliefs are less sympathetic to rape victims than those who do not believe in rape myths. These myths help silence rape victims and control all women, thus allowing rape to continue.

While researchers usually explain the causes of rape from either a socio-cultural or a psychological perspective, David Lisak, a psychologist at the University of Massachusetts, Boston, combines these two approaches in "Sexual Aggression, Masculinity, and Fathers." He argues that both cultural and individual psychological factors produce the predisposition to rape. Lisak's interviews with a sample of male college students reveal clear differences in the types of relationships that rapists and non-rapists had with their parents, particularly with their fathers. Those who had committed rape had had poor relationships with their fathers, who had been physically and emotionally unavailable and, in some cases, abusive toward their sons. The non-rapists, on the other hand, were much more likely to report close, warm relationships with their fathers. Drawing on Nancy Chodorow's work, Lisak argues that father-distant child rearing, which he sees as a product of patriarchal culture, has harmful psychological consequences by promoting feelings of aggression and hostility toward women. One step in addressing the problem of rape, Lisak concludes, is to change our society's child-rearing practices so that both mothers and fathers share equally in this important activity.

9

The Socio-Cultural Context
of Rape: A Cross-Cultural Study

~

Peggy Reeves Sanday

I N HER COMPREHENSIVE AND IMPORTANT analysis of rape, Susan
Brownmiller says that "when men discovered that they could rape,
they proceeded to do it" and that "from prehistoric times to the present
rape has played a critical function" (1975, p. 14–15). The critical function to which Brownmiller refers has been "to keep all women in a
constant state of intimidation, forever conscious of the knowledge that
the biological tool must be held in awe for it may turn to weapon with
sudden swiftness born of harmful intent" (1975, p. 209).

Brownmiller's attribution of violence to males and victimization
to females strums a common theme in Western social commentary on
the nature of human nature. Most of the popularizers of this theme
present what amounts to a socio-biological view of human behavior
which traces war, violence, and now rape to the violent landscape of
our primitive ancestors, where, early on, the male tendency in these
directions became genetically programmed in the fight for survival of
the fittest. Human (viz. male) nature is conceived as an ever-present
struggle to overcome baser impulses bequeathed by "apish" ancestors. (For examples of this general theme, see Ardrey, 1966; Lorenz,
1966; Tiger, 1969.)

The research described in the present paper departs from the familiar assumption that male nature is programmed for rape, and begins with another familiar, albeit less popular, assumption that human

From Peggy Reeves Sanday, "The Socio-Cultural Context of Rape: A Cross-
Cultural Study," *Journal of Social Issues* 37, no. 4 (1981): 5–7, 9–18, 22–27.
© 1992 by the Society for the Psychological Study of Social Issues. Reprinted by
permission of the Society for the Psychological Study of Social Issues.

sexual behavior, though based in a biological need, "is rather a socio-logical and cultural force than a mere bodily relation of two individu-als" (Malinowski, 1929, p. xxiii). With this assumption in mind, what follows is an examination of the socio-cultural context of sexual as-sault and an attempt to interpret its meaning. By understanding the meaning of rape, we can then make conjectures as to its function. Is it, as Susan Brownmiller suggests, an act that keeps all women in a con-stant state of intimidation, or is it an act that illuminates a larger so-cial scenario?

This paper examines the incidence, meaning, and function of rape in tribal societies. Two general hypotheses guided the research: first, the incidence of rape varies cross culturally; second, a high incidence of rape is embedded in a distinguishably different cultural configura-tion than a low incidence of rape. Using a standard cross-cultural sample of 156 tribal societies, the general objectives of the paper are:

1. to provide a descriptive profile of "rape-prone" and "rape-free" societies;
2. to present an analysis of the attitudes, motivations, and socio-cultural factors related to the incidence of rape.

Description of the Evidence

In most societies for which information on rape was available, rape is an act in which a male or group of males sexually assaulted a woman. In a few cases, descriptions of women sexually assaulting a male or homosexual rape are reported. This study, however, was oriented ex-clusively to the analysis of rape committed by males against women.

The standard cross-cultural sample published by Murdock and White (1969) formed the basis for this research. This sample offers to scholars a representative sample of the world's known and well-described societies. The complete sample consists of 186 societies, each "pinpointed" to an identifiable sub-group of the society in ques-tion at a specific point in time. The time period for the sample societ-ies ranges from 1750 B.C. (Babylonians) to the late 1960s. The societies included in the standard sample are distributed relatively equally among the following six major regions of the world: Sub-Saharan Africa, Circum-Mediterranean, East Eurasia, Insular Pacific, North America, South and Central America.

This analysis of rape was part of a larger study on the origins of sexual inequality (see Sanday, 1981). Due to the amount of missing information on the variables included in this larger study, thirty of the standard sample societies were excluded, reducing the final sample size to 156. Since many of the variables included in the larger study were pertinent to the analysis of the socio-cultural context of rape, the same sample was employed here.

The information for coding the variables came from codes published in the journal *Ethnology*; library materials; and the Human Relations Area Files. The data obtained from the latter two sources were coded by graduate students in anthropology at the University of Pennsylvania using codes developed by me on one-third of the standard sample societies. When the coding was completed, a random sample of societies was selected for checking. The percentage of items on which codes and checkers agreed averaged 88% of the 21 variables checked for each society. Disagreements were resolved either by myself or still another coder after rechecking the material. . . .

Table 1. Cross-Cultural Incidence of Rape

Sanday Code	*No. and % of Societies*	
Incidence of Rape (RA4)-	*N*	*%*
1. *Rape Free.* Rape is reported as rare or absent.	45	47%
2. Rape is reported as present, no report of frequency, or suggestion that rape is not atypical.	33	35%
3. *Rape Prone.* Rape is an accepted practice used to punish women, as part of a ceremony, or is *clearly* an act of moderate to high frequency carried out against own women or women of other societies.	17	18%
Total	95	100%

Profiles of "Rape-Prone" Societies

In this study a "rape-prone" society was defined as one in which the incidence of rape is high, rape is a ceremonial act, or rape is an act by which men punish or threaten women.

An example of a "rape-prone" society is offered by Robert LeVine's (1959) description of sexual offenses among the Gusii of southwestern Kenya. In the European legal system which administers justice in the District where the Gusii live, a heterosexual assault is classified as rape when a medical examination indicates that the hymen of the alleged victim was recently penetrated by the use of painful force. When medical evidence is unobtainable, the case is classified as "indecent assault." Most cases are of the latter kind. The Gusii do not distinguish between rape and indecent assault. They use the following expressions to refer to heterosexual assault: "to fight" (a girl or woman); "to stamp on" (a girl or woman); "to spoil" (a girl or woman); "to engage in illicit intercourse." All of these acts are considered illicit by the Gusii. LeVine uses the term rape "to mean the culturally disvalued use of coercion by a male to achieve the submission of a female to sexual intercourse" (1959, p. 965).

Based on court records for 1955 and 1956 LeVine estimates that the annual rate of rape is 47.2 per 100,000 population. LeVine believes that this figure grossly underestimates the Gusii rape rate. During the same period the annual rape rate in urban areas of the United States was 13.85 per 100,000 (13,1 for rural area). Thus the rate of Gusii rape is extraordinarily high.

Normal heterosexual intercourse between Gusii males and females is conceived as an act in which a man overcomes the resistance of a woman and causes her pain. When a bride is unable to walk after her wedding night, the groom is considered by his friends "a real man" and he is able to boast of his exploits, particularly if he has been able to make her cry. Older women contribute to the groom's desire to hurt his new wife. These women insult the groom, saying:

> "You are not strong, you can't do anything to our daughter. When you slept with her you didn't do it like a man. You have a small penis which can do nothing. You should grab our daughter and she should be hurt and scream—then you're a man" (LeVine, 1959, p. 969).

The groom answers boastfully:

> "I am a man! If you were to see my penis you would run away. When I grabbed her she screamed. I am not a man to be joked with. Didn't she tell you? She cried—ask her!" (LeVine, 1959, p. 969).

Thus, as LeVine says (1959, p. 971), "legitimate heterosexual encounters among the Gusii are aggressive contests, involving force and pain-inflicting behavior." Under circumstances that are not legitimate, heterosexual encounters are classified as rape when the girl chooses to report the act.

LeVine estimates that the typical Gusii rape is committed by an unmarried young man on an unmarried female of a different clan. He distinguishes between three types of rape: rape resulting from seduction, premeditated sexual assault, and abduction (1959).

Given the hostile nature of Gusii sexuality, seduction classifies as rape when a Gusii female chooses to bring the act to the attention of the public. Premarital sex is forbidden, but this does not stop Gusii boys from trying to entice girls to intercourse. The standard pose of the Gusii girl is reluctance, which means that it is difficult for the boy to interpret her attitude as being either willing or unwilling. Misunderstandings between girl and boy can be due to the eagerness of the boy and his inability to perceive the girl's cues of genuine rejection, or to the girl's failure to make the signs of refusal in unequivocal fashion. The boy may discover the girl's unwillingness only after he has forced himself on her.

Fear of discovery may turn a willing girl into one who cries rape. If a couple engaging in intercourse out of doors is discovered, the girl may decide to save her reputation by crying out that she was being raped. Rape may also occur in cases when a girl has encouraged a young man to present her with gifts, but then denies him sexual intercourse. If the girl happens to be married, she rejects the boy's advances because she is afraid of supernatural sanctions against adultery. Out of frustration, the boy (who may not know that the girl is married) may resort to rape and she reports the deed.

In some cases one or more boys may attack a single girl in premeditated sexual assault. The boys may beat the girl badly and tear her clothing. Sometimes the girl is dragged off to the hut of one of them and forced into coitus. After being held for a couple of days the girl is freed. In these cases rupture of the hymen and other signs of attack are usually present.

The third type of rape occurs in the context of wife abduction. When a Gusii man is unable to present the bridewealth necessary for a normal marriage and cannot persuade a girl to elope, he may abduct a girl from a different clan. The man's friends will be enlisted to carry out the abduction. The young men are frequently rough on the girl, beating her and tearing her clothes. When she arrives at the home of the would-be lover, he attempts to persuade her to remain with him until bridewealth can be raised. Her refusal is ignored and the wedding night sexual contest is performed with the clansmen helping in overcoming her resistance.

Of these three types of rape, the first and third are unlawful versions of legitimate patterns. Seduction is accepted when kept within the bounds of discretion. Abduction is an imitation of traditional wedding procedures. Abduction lacks only the legitimizing bridewealth and the consent of the bride and her parents. In both of these cases LeVine says, "there is a close parallel between the criminal act and the law-abiding culture pattern to which it is related." Seduction and abduction classify as rape when the girl chooses to report the incident.

Data collected from the standard cross-cultural sample allow us to place the hostility characterizing Gusii heterosexual behavior in cross-cultural perspective. Broude and Greene (1976), who published codes for twenty sexual practices, find that male sexual advances are occasionally or typically hostile in one-quarter (26%) of the societies for which information was available. They found that males were typically forward in verbal (not physical) sexual overtures in forty percent of the societies, that females solicited or desired physical aggression in male sexual overtures in eleven percent of the societies, and that males did not make sexual overtures or were diffident or shy in twenty-three percent of the societies.

Examination of a variety of "rape-prone" societies shows that the Gusii pattern of rape is found elsewhere but that it is by no means the only pattern which can be observed. For example, in several societies the act of rape occurs to signal readiness for marriage and is a ceremonial act. Since this act signifies male domination of female genitals, its occurrence was treated as a diagnostic criterion for classification as "rape-prone."

Among the Kikuyu of East Africa it is reported that in former times, as part of initiation, every boy was expected to perform the act of ceremonial rape called *Kuihaka muunya* (to smear oneself with salt earth) in order to prove his manhood. It was thought that until a boy had performed the act of rape he could not have lawful intercourse with a Kikuyu woman and hence could not marry. During the initiation period boys would wander the countryside in bands of up to 100 in number. The object of each band was to find a woman on whom to commit the rape. The ideal woman was one from an enemy tribe who was married. In practice it appears that the ceremonial rape consisted of nothing more than masturbatory ejaculation on the woman's body or in her presence. Immediately after the act the boy was able to throw away the paraphernalia which marked him with the status of neophyte (Lambert, 1956).

Rape marks a girl as marriageable among the Arunta of Australia. At age 14 or 15 the Arunta girl is taken out into the bush by a group of men for the vulva cutting ceremony. A designated man cuts the girl's vulva after which she is gang raped by a group of men which does not include her future husband. When the ceremony is concluded the girl is taken to her husband and from then on no one else has the right of access to her (Spencer & Gillen, 1927).

In other rape-prone societies, rape is explicitly linked to the control of women and to male dominance. Among the Northern Saulteaux the assumption of male dominance is clearly expressed in the expectation that a man's potential sexual rights over the woman he chooses must be respected. A woman who turns a man down too abruptly insults him and invites aggression. There is a Northern Saulteaux tale about a girl who was considered too proud because she refused to marry. Accordingly, a group of medicine men lured her out into the bush where she was raped by each in turn (Hallowell, 1955). Such tales provide women with a fairly good idea of how they should behave in relation to men.

The attitude that women are "open" for sexual assault is frequently found in the societies of the Insular Pacific. For example, in the Marshall Islands one finds the belief that "every woman is like a passage." Just as every canoe is permitted to sail from the open sea into the lagoon through the passage, so every man is permitted to have intercourse with every woman (except those who are excluded on account of blood kinship). A trader, well acquainted with the language and customs of one group of Marshall Islanders, reported the following incident. One day while standing at the trading post he saw 20 young men enter the bushes, one after another. Following the same path, he discovered a young girl stretched out on the ground, rigid and unconscious. When he accused the young men of cruel treatment they replied: "It is customary here for every young man to have intercourse with every girl" (Erdland, 1914, p. 98–99).

In tropical forest societies of South America and in Highland New Guinea it is fairly frequent to find the threat of rape used to keep women from the men's houses or from viewing male sacred objects. For example, Shavante women were strictly forbidden to observe male sacred ceremonies. Women caught peeking are threatened with manhandling, rape, and disfigurement (Maybury-Lewis, 1967).

Perhaps the best-known example of rape used to keep women away from male ritual objects is found in the description of the Mundurucu, a society well known to anthropologists due to the work of Robert and Yolanda Murphy. The Mundurucu believe that there was a time when women ruled and sex roles were reversed with the exception that women could not hunt. During that time, it is said, women were the sexual aggressors and men were sexually submissive and did women's work. Women controlled the "sacred trumpets" (the symbols of power) and the men's houses. The trumpets are believed to contain the spirits of the ancestors who demand ritual offering of meat. Since women did not hunt and could not make these offerings, men were able to take the trumpets from them, thereby establishing male dominance. The trumpets are secured in special chambers within the men's houses and no woman can see them under penalty of gang rape. Such a threat is necessary because men believe that women will attempt to seize from the men the power they once had. Gang rape is also the means by which men punish sexually "wanton" women (Murphy & Murphy, 1974).

Another expression of male sexual aggressiveness, which is classified as rape in this study, is the practice of sexually assaulting enemy women during warfare. The Yanomamo, described by Napoleon

Chagnon and Marvin Harris, are infamous for their brutality toward women. The Yanomamo, according to Harris (1977), "practice an especially brutal form of male supremacy involving polygyny, frequent wife beating, and gang rape of captured enemy women." The Yanomamo, Harris says, "regard fights over women as the primary causes of their wars" (1977, p. 69). Groups raid each other for wives in an area where marriageable women are in short supply due to the practice of female infanticide. The number of marriageable women is also affected by the desire on the part of successful warriors to have several wives to mark their superior status as "fierce men." A shortage of women for wives also motivates Azande (Africa) warfare. Enemy women were taken by Azande soldiers as wives. Evan-Pritchard calls these women "slaves of war" and says that they were "not regarded very differently from ordinary wives, their main disability being that they had no family or close kin to turn to in times of trouble" (1971, p. 251). The absence of close kin, of course, made these women more subservient and dependent on their husbands.

Another source on the Azande discusses how the act of rape when committed against an Azande woman is treated. If the woman is not married, this source reports, the act is not treated as seriously. If the woman is married, the rapist can be put to death by the husband. If the rapist is allowed to live, he may be judged guilty of adultery and asked to pay the chief 20 knives (the commonly used currency in marriage exchanges) and deliver a wife to the wronged husband. This source indicates that the rape of woman is not permitted but the punishments are established, suggesting that rape is a frequent occurrence (Lagae, 1926).

Among some American Indian buffalo hunters, it is not uncommon to read that rape is used as a means to punish adultery. There is a practice among the Cheyenne of the Great Plains known as "to put a woman on the prairie." This means that the outraged husband of an adulterous woman invites all the unmarried members of his military society to feast on the prairie where they each rape the woman (Hoebel, 1960). Among the Omaha, a woman with no immediate kin who commits adultery may be gang raped and abandoned by her husband (Dorsey, 1884). Mead reports that the Omaha considered a "bad woman" fair game for any man. No discipline, no set of standards, other than to be cautious of an avenging father or brother and to observe the rule of exogamy, Mead says, kept young men from regarding rape as a great adventure. Young Omaha men, members of the Antler society, would prey upon divorced women or women considered loose (Mead, 1932).

Summarizing, a rape-prone society, as defined here, is one in which sexual assault by men of women is either culturally allowable or, largely overlooked. Several themes interlink the above descriptions. In all, men are posed as a social group against women. Entry into the adult male or female group is marked in some cases by rituals that include rape. In other cases, rape preserves the ceremonial integrity of the male group and signifies its status vis-à-vis women. The theme of women as property is suggested when the aggrieved husband is compensated for the rape of his wife by another man, or when an adulterous woman is gang raped by her husband and his unmarried compatriots. In these latter cases, the theme of the dominant male group is joined with a system of economic exchange in which men act as exchange agents and women comprise the medium of exchange. This is not to say that rape exists in all societies in which there is ceremonial induction into manhood, male secret societies, or compensation for adultery. For further illumination of the socio-cultural context of rape we can turn to examination of rape-free societies.

Profiles of "Rape-Free" Societies

"Rape-free" societies are defined as those where the act of rape is either infrequent or does not occur. Forty-seven percent of the societies for which information on the incidence or presence of rape was available (see Table 2) were classified in the "rape-free" category. Societies were classified in this category on the basis of the following kinds of statements found in the sources used for the sample societies.

Among the Taureg of the Sahara, for example, it is said that "rape does not exist, and when a woman refuses a man, he never insists nor will he show himself jealous of a more successful comrade" (Blanguernon, 1955, p. 134). Among the Pygmies of the Ituri forest in Africa, while a boy may rip off a girl's outer bark cloth, if he can catch her, he may never have intercourse with her without her permission. Turnbull (1965), an anthropologist who lived for some time among the Pygmies and became closely identified with them, reports that he knew of no cases of rape. Among the Jivaro of South America rape is not recognized as such, and informants could recall no case of a woman violently resisting sexual intercourse. They say that a man would never commit such an act if the woman resisted, because she would tell her family and they would punish him. Among the Nkundo Mongo of Africa it is said that rape in the true sense of the word—that is, the abuse of a woman by the use of violence—is most unusual. If a woman does not consent, the angry seducer leaves her, often insulting her to the best of his ability. Rape is also unheard of among the Lakhers, and in several villages the anthropologist was told that there had never been a case of rape.

Other examples of statements leading to the classification of "rape-free" are listed as follows:

> Cuna (South America), "Homosexuality is rare, as is rape. Both . . . are regarded as sins, punishable by God" (Stout, 1947, p. 39).

> Khalka Mongols (Outer Mongolia), "I put this question to several well-informed Mongols:—what punishment is here imposed for ràpe? . . . one well-educated lama said frankly: "We have no crimes of this nature here. Our women never resist." (Maiskii, 1921, p. 98).

> Gond (India), "It is considered very wrong to force a girl to act against her will. Such cases of ghotul-rape are not common. . . . If then a boy forces a girl against her will, and the others hear of it, he is fined" (Elwin, 1947, p. 656).

The above quotes may obscure the actual incidence of rape. Such quotes, leading to the classification of societies as "rape-free," achieve greater validity when placed within the context of other information describing heterosexual interaction.

There is considerable difference in the character of heterosexual interaction in societies classified as "rape-prone" when compared with those classified as "rape-free." In "rape-free" societies women are treated with considerable respect, and prestige is attached to female reproductive and productive roles. Interpersonal violence is minimized, and a people's attitude regarding the natural environment is one of reverence rather than one of exploitation. Turnbull's description of the Mbuti Pygmies, of the Ituri forest in Africa, provides a prototypical profile of a "rape-free" society (1965).

Violence between the sexes, or between anybody, is virtually absent among the net hunting Mbuti Pygmies when they are in their forest environment. The Mbuti attitude toward the forest is reflective of their attitude toward each other. The forest is addressed as "father," "mother," "lover," and "friend." The Mbuti say that forest is everything—the provider of food, shelter, warmth, clothing, and affection. Each person and animal is endowed with some spiritual power which "derives from a single source whose physical manifestation is the forest itself." The ease of the Mbuti relationship to their environment is reflected in the relationship between the sexes. There is little division of labor by sex. The hunt is frequently a joint effort. A man is not ashamed to pick mushrooms and nuts if he finds them, or to wash and clean a baby. In general, leadership is minimal and there is no attempt to control, or to dominate, either the geographical or human environment. Decision making is by common consent; men and women have equal say because hunting and gathering are both important to the economy. The forest is the only recognized authority of last resort. In decision making, diversity of opinion may be expressed, but prolonged disagreement is considered to be "noise" and offensive to the forest. If husband and wife disagree, the whole camp may act to mute their antagonism, lest the disagreement become too disruptive to the social unit (see Turnbull, 1965).

The essential details of Turnbull's idyllic description of the Mbuti are repeated in other "rape-free" societies. The one outstanding feature of these societies is the ceremonial importance of women and the respect accorded the contribution women make to social continuity, a respect which places men and women in relatively balanced power spheres. This respect is clearly present among the Mbuti and in more complex "rape-free" societies.

In the West African kingdom of Ashanti, for example, it is believed that only women can contribute to future generations. Ashanti women say:

> I am the mother of man. . . . I alone can transmit the blood to a king.
> . . . If my sex die in the clan then that very clan becomes extinct, for
> be there one, or one thousand male members left, not one can trans-
> mit the blood, and the life of the clan becomes measured on this
> earth by the span of a man's life (Rattray, 1923, p. 79).

The importance of the feminine attributes of growth and reproduction are found in Ashanti religion and ritual. Priestesses participate with priests in all major rituals. The Ashanti creation story emphasizes the complementarity and inseparability of male and female. The main female deity, the Earth Goddess, is believed to be the receptacle of past and future generations as well as the source of food and water (Rattray, 1923, 1927). The sacred linkage of earth-female-blood makes the act of rape incongruous in Ashanti culture. Only one incident of rape is reported by the main ethnographer of the Ashanti. In this case the man involved was condemned to death (Rattray, 1927, p. 211).

In sum, rape-free societies are characterized by sexual equality and the notion that the sexes are complementary. Though the sexes may not perform the same duties or have the same rights or privileges, each is indispensable to the activities of the other (see Sanday, 1981 for examples of sexual equality). The key to understanding the relative absence of rape in rape-free as opposed to rape-prone societies is the importance, which in some cases is sacred, attached to the contribution women make to social continuity.

Socio-Cultural Correlates of Rape

Four general hypotheses are suggested by the work of LeVine, Brownmiller, Abrahamsen, Wolfgang, and Amir. These hypotheses are:

1. Sexual repression is related to the incidence of rape;
2. intergroup and interpersonal violence is enacted in male sexual violence;
3. the character of parent-child relations is enacted in male sexual violence;
4. rape is an expression of a social ideology of male dominance.

These hypotheses were tested by collecting data on: variables relating to child rearing; behavior indicating sexual repression; interpersonal and intergroup violence; sexual separation; glorification of the male role and an undervaluation of the female role.

The relevant variables are listed in Table 2 along with the correlation of each with the incidence of rape. The correlations presented in Table 2 support all but the first of the general hypotheses listed above. There is no significant correlation between variables measuring sexual repression and the incidence of rape. Admittedly, however, sexual repression is very difficult to measure. The variables presented in Table 2 may not, in fact, be related to sexual abstinence. These variables are: length of the post-partum sex taboo (a variable which indicates how long the mother abstains from sexual intercourse after the birth of a child); attitude toward premarital sex (a variable which ranges between the disapproval and approval of premarital sex); age at marriage for males; and the number of taboos reflecting male avoidance of female sexuality.

Table 2. Correlates of Rape

Variables Related to Sexual Repression	*Correlation with Incidence of Rape (RA4)[a]*
1. Length of the post-partum sex taboo (Inf 10)	NS
2. Attitude toward pre-marital sex (Psex)	NS
3. Age of marriage for males (Agem)	NS
4. No. of taboos reflecting male avoidance of female sexuality (All)	NS
Variables Related to Intergroup and Interpersonal Violence	
5. Raiding other groups for wives (Wie)	$r = -.29$ (N = 83, p = .004)
6. Degree of Interpersonal violence (Viol)	$r = .47$ (N = 90, p = .000)
7. Ideology of Male Toughness (Macho)	$r = -.42$ (N = 73, p = .000)
8. War	$r = .21$ (N = 86, p = .03)

Variables Related to Child Rearing

9. Character of father-daughter relationships (Fada)	r = −.20 (N = 65, p = .06)
10. Proximity of father in care of infants (Inf 23)	r = −.16 (N = 83, p = .08)
11. Character of mother-son relationships (Moso)	NS

Variables Related to Ideology of Male Dominance

12. Female power and authority (Stat)	r = −.22 (N = 83, p = .03)
13. Female political decision making (HO5)	r = −.33 (N = 88, p = .001)
14. Attitude toward women as citizens (HO8)	r = −.28 (N = 84, p = .005)
15. Presence of special places for men (Mho)	r = −.26 (N = 71, p = .01)
16. Presence of special places for women (Fho)	r = −.17 (N = 70, p = .08)

ᵃCode presented in Table 1. Correlation coefficient is Pearson r.

The correlations presented in Table 2 support the hypothesis that intergroup and interpersonal violence is enacted in sexual violence against females. Raiding other groups for wives is significantly associated with the incidence of rape. The intensity of interpersonal violence in a society is also positively correlated with the incidence of rape, as is the presence of an ideology which encourages men to be tough and aggressive. Finally, when warfare is reported as being frequent or endemic (as opposed to absent or occasional) rape is more likely to be present.

The character of relations between parents and children is not strongly associated with the incidence of rape. When the character of the father-daughter relationship is primarily indifferent, aloof, cold, and stern, rape is more likely to be present. The same is true when fathers are distant from the care of infants. However, there is no relationship between the nature of the mother-son tie (as measured in this study) and the incidence of rape.

There is considerable evidence supporting the notion that rape is an expression of a social ideology of male dominance. Female power and authority is lower in rape-prone societies. Women do not participate in public decision making in these societies and males express contempt for women as decision makers. In addition, there is greater sexual separation in rape-prone societies as indicated by the presence of structures or places where the sexes congregate in single-sex groups.

The correlates of rape presented in Table 2 strongly suggest that rape is the playing out of a socio-cultural script in which the expression of personhood for males is directed by, among other things, interpersonal violence and an ideology of toughness. If we see the sexual act as the ultimate emotional expression of the self, then it comes as no surprise that male sexuality is phrased in physically aggressive terms when other expressions of self are phrased in these terms. This explanation does not rule out the importance of the relationship between parents and children, husbands and wives. Raising a violent son requires certain behavior patterns in parents, behaviors that husbands may subsequently act out as adult males. Sexual repression does not explain the correlations presented in Table 2. Rape is not an instinct triggered by celibacy, enforced for whatever reason. Contrary to what some social scientists assume, men are not animals whose sexual behavior is programmed by instinct. Men are human beings whose sexuality is biologically based and culturally encoded.

Conclusion

Rape in tribal societies is part of a cultural configuration that includes interpersonal violence, male dominance, and sexual separation. In such societies, as the Murphys (1974, p. 197) say about the Mundurucu: "men . . . use the penis to dominate their women." The question remains as to what motivates the rape-prone cultural configuration. Considerable evidence (see Sanday, 1981) suggests that this configuration evolves in societies faced with depleting food resources, migration, or other factors contributing to a dependence on male destructive capacities as opposed to female fertility.

In tribal societies women are often equated with fertility and growth, men with aggression and destruction. More often than not, the characteristics associated with maleness and femaleness are equally valued. When people perceive an imbalance between the food supply and population needs, or when populations are in competition for diminishing resources, the male role is accorded greater prestige. Females are perceived as objects to be controlled as men struggle to retain or to gain control of their environment. Behaviors and attitudes prevail that separate the sexes and force men into a posture of proving their manhood. Sexual violence is one of the ways in which men remind themselves that they are superior. As such, rape is part of a broader struggle for control in the face of difficult circumstances. Where men are in harmony with their environment, rape is usually absent.

The insights garnered from the cross-cultural study of rape in tribal societies bear on the understanding and treatment of rape in our own. Ours is a heterogeneous society in which more men than we like to think feel that they do not have mastery over their destiny and who learn from the script provided by nightly television that violence is a way of achieving the material rewards that all Americans expect. It is important to understand that violence is socially and not biologically programmed. Rape is not an integral part of male nature, but the means by which men programmed for violence express their sexual selves.

Men who are conditioned to respect the female virtues of growth and the sacredness of life do not violate women. It is significant that in societies where nature is held sacred, rape occurs only rarely. The incidence of rape in our society will be reduced to the extent that boys grow to respect women and the qualities so often associated with femaleness in other societies—namely, nurturance, growth, and nature. Women can contribute to the socialization of boys by making these respected qualities in their struggle for equal rights.

References

Abrahamsen, D. *The psychology of crime.* New York: Columbia University Press, 1960.

Amir, M. *Patterns in forcible rape.* Chicago, IL: University of Chicago Press, 1971.

Ardrey, R. *The territorial imperative.* New York: Dell, 1966.

Blanguernon, C. *Le hogger (The hogger).* Paris: B. Arthaud, 1955 (Translated from the French for the Human Relations Files by Thomas Turner).

Broude, G. J. & Greene, S. J. Cross-cultural codes on twenty sexual attitudes and practices. *Ethnology,* 1976, *15*(4), 409–430.

Brownmiller, S. *Against our will.* New York: Simon & Schuster, 1975.

Dorsey, J. O. *Omaha sociology.* Smithsonian Institution, Bureau of Ethnology, Third Annual Report, 1881–82, pp. 205–370. Washington, D.C.: U.S. Government Printing Office, 1884.

Elwin, V. *The muria and their ghotul.* Bombay: Geoffrey Cumberlege, Oxford University Press, 1947.

Erdland, P. A. *Die Marshall-insulaner (The Marshall islanders).* Munster: Anthropos Bibliothek Ethnologica Monographs 1914, 2(1) (Translated by Richard Neuse for Human Relations Area Files).

Evans-Pritchard, E. E. *The Azande.* London: Oxford University Press, 1971.

Hallowell, A. I. *Culture and experience.* Philadelphia, PA: University of Pennsylvania Press, 1955.

Harris, M. *Cannibals and kings.* New York: Vintage/Random House, 1977.

Hoebel, E. A. *The Cheyennes.* New York: Holt, Rinehart & Winston, 1960.

Lagae, C. R. Les Azande ou Niam-Niam. *Bibliothèque—Congo* (Vol. 18). Brussels: Vromant & Cie., 1926 (Translated for Human Relations Area Files), New Haven, CT: HRAF.

Lambert, H. E. *Kikuyu social and political institutions.* London: Oxford University Press, 1956.

LeVine, R. A. Gusii sex offenses: A study in social control. *American Anthropologist*, 1959, *61*, 965–990.

Lorenz, K. *On aggression*. London: Methuen, 1966.

Maiskii, I. *Sovremennaia Mongolia (Contemporary Mongolia)*. Irkutsk: Gosudarstvennoe Izdatel'stvo, Irkutskoe Otedelenie, 1921 (Translated from the Russian for *Human Relations Area Files* by Mrs. Dayton and J. Kunitz).

Malinowski, B. *The sexual life of savages in north-western Melanesia*. London: G. Routledge & Sons, 1929.

Maybury-Lewis, D. *Akwe-Shavante society*. Oxford: Clarendon Press, 1967.

Mead, M. *The changing culture of an indian tribe*. New York: Columbia University Press, 1932.

Murdock, G. P. & White, D. R. Standard cross-cultural sample. *Ethnology*, 1969, *8*, 329–369.

Murphy Y. & Murphy, R. *Women of the forest*. New York: Columbia University Press, 1974.

Rattray, R. S. *Ashanti*. Oxford: Clarendon Press, 1923.

———. *Religion and art in Ashanti*. Oxford: Clarendon Press, 1927.

Sanday, P. R. *Female power and male dominance: On the origins of sexual inequality*. New York: Cambridge University Press, 1981.

Spencer, Baldwin & Gillen, F. J. *The Arunta* (2 Vols.). London: Macmillan & Co., 1927.

Stoller, R. J. *Sexual excitement*. New York: Pantheon Books, 1979.

Stout, D. B. *San Blas Cura acculturation*. New York: Viking Fund Publications in Anthropology, 1947, *9*.

Tiger, L. *Men in groups*. New York: Random House, 1969.

Turnball, C. *Wayward servants*. New York: Natural History Press, 1965.

Wolfgang, M. E. & Ferracuti, F. *The subculture of violence*. London: Tavistock, 1967.

10

"Riding the Bull at Gilley's": Convicted Rapists Describe the Rewards of Rape

~

Diana Scully
Joseph Marolla

O VER THE PAST SEVERAL DECADES, rape has become a "medicalized" social problem. That is to say, the theories used to explain rape are predicated on psychopathological models. They have been generated from clinical experiences with small samples of rapists, often the therapists' own clients. Although these psychiatric explanations are most appropriately applied to the atypical rapist, they have been generalized to all men who rape and have come to inform the public's view on the topic.

Two assumptions are at the core of the psychopathological model; that rape is the result of idiosyncratic mental disease and that it often includes an uncontrollable sexual impulse (Scully and Marolla, 1985). For example, the presumption of psychopathology is evident in the often cited work of Nicholas Groth (1979). While Groth emphasizes the nonsexual nature of rape (power, anger, sadism), he also concludes, "Rape is always a symptom of some psychological dysfunction, either temporary and transient or chronic and repetitive" (Groth, 1979:5). Thus, in the psychopathological view, rapists lack the ability to control their behavior; they are "sick" individuals from the "lunatic fringe" of society.

In contradiction to this model, empirical research has repeatedly failed to find a consistent pattern of personality type or character

From Diana Scully and Joseph Marolla, " 'Riding the Bull at Gilley's': Convicted Rapists Describe the Rewards of Rape," *Social Problems* 32, no. 3 (February 1985): 251–63. © 1985 by the Society for the Study of Social Problems. Reprinted by permission of the University of California Press and Diana Scully.

disorder that reliably discriminates rapists from other groups of men (Fisher and Rivlin, 1971; Hammer and Jacks, 1955; Rada, 1978). Indeed, other research has found that fewer than 5 percent of men were psychotic when they raped (Abel et al., 1980).

Evidence indicates that rape is not a behavior confined to a few "sick" men but many men have the attitudes and beliefs necessary to commit a sexually aggressive act. In research conducted at a midwestern university, Koss and her coworkers reported that 85 percent of men defined as highly sexually aggressive had victimized women with whom they were romantically involved (Koss and Leonard, 1984). A recent survey quoted in *The Chronicle of Higher Education* estimates that more than 20 percent of college women are the victims of rape and attempted rape (Meyer, 1984). These findings mirror research published several decades earlier which also concluded that sexual aggression was commonplace in dating relationships (Kanin, 1957, 1965, 1967, 1969; Kirkpatrick and Kanin, 1957).[1] In their study of 53 college males, Malamuth, Haber and Feshback (1980) found that 51 percent indicated a likelihood that they, themselves, would rape if assured of not being punished.

In addition, the frequency of rape in the United States makes it unlikely that responsibility rests solely with a small lunatic fringe of psychopathic men. Johnson (1980), calculating the lifetime risk of rape to girls and women aged twelve and over, makes a similar observation. Using Law Enforcement Assistance Association and Bureau of Census Crime Victimization Studies, he calculated that, excluding sexual abuse in marriage and assuming equal risk to all women, 20 to 30 percent of girls now 12 years old will suffer a violent sexual attack during the remainder of their lives. Interestingly, the lack of empirical support for the psychopathological model has not resulted in the demedicalization of rape, nor does it appear to have diminished the belief that rapists are "sick" aberrations in their own culture. This is significant because of the implications and consequences of the model.

A central assumption in the psychopathological model is that male sexual aggression is unusual or strange. This assumption removes rape from the realm of the everyday or "normal" world and places it in the category of "special" or "sick" behavior. As a consequence, men who rape are cast in the role of outsider and a connection with normative male behavior is avoided. Since, in this view, the source of the behavior is thought to be within the psychology of the individual, attention is diverted away from culture or social structure as contributing factors. Thus, the psychopathological model ignores evidence which links sexual aggression to environmental variables and which suggests that rape, like all behavior, is learned.

Cultural Factors in Rape

Culture is a factor in rape, but the precise nature of the relationship between culture and sexual violence remains a topic of discussion. Ethnographic data from preindustrial societies show the existence of rape-free cultures (Broude and Green, 1976; Sanday, 1979), though explanations for the phenomena differ.[2] Sanday (1979) relates sexual violence to contempt for female qualities and suggests that rape is part of a culture of violence and an expression of male dominance. In contrast, Blumberg (1979) argues that in preindustrial societies women are more likely to lack important life options and to be physically and politically oppressed where they lack economic power relative to men. That is, in preindustrial societies relative economic power enables women to win some immunity from men's use of force against them.

Among modern societies, the frequency of rape varies dramatically, and the United States is among the most rape-prone of all. In 1980, for example the rate of reported rape and attempted rape for the United States was eighteen times higher than the corresponding rate for England and Wales (West, 1983). Spurred by the Women's Movement, feminists have generated an impressive body of theory regarding the cultural etiology of rape in the United States. Representative of the feminist view, Griffin (1971) called rape "The All-American Crime."

The feminist perspective views rape as an act of violence and social control which functions to "keep women in their place" (Brownmiller, 1975; Kasinsky, 1975; Russell, 1975). Feminists see rape as an extension of normative male behavior, the result of conformity or overconformity to the values and prerogatives which define the traditional male sex role. That is, traditional socialization encourages males to associate power, dominance, strength, virility, and superiority with masculinity, and submissiveness, passivity, weakness, and inferiority with femininity. Furthermore, males are taught to have expectations about their level of sexual needs and expectations for corresponding female accessibility which function to justify forcing sexual access. The justification for forced sexual access is buttressed by legal, social, and religious definitions of women as male property and sex as an exchange of goods (Bart, 1979). Socialization prepares women to be "legitimate" victims and men to be potential offenders (Weis and Borges, 1973). Herman (1984) concludes that the United States is a rape culture because both genders are socialized to regard male aggression as a natural and normal part of sexual intercourse.

Feminists view pornography as an important element in a larger system of sexual violence; they see pornography as an expression of a rape-prone culture where women are seen as objects available for use by men (Morgan, 1980; Wheeler, 1985). Based on his content analysis of 428 "adults only" books, Smith (1976) makes a similar observation. He notes that, not only is rape presented as part of normal male/ female sexual relations, but the woman, despite her terror, is always depicted as sexually aroused to the point of cooperation. In the end, she is ashamed but physically gratified. The message—women desire and enjoy rape—has more potential for damage than the image of the violence per se.³

The fusion of these themes—sex as an impersonal act, the victim's uncontrollable orgasm, and the violent infliction of pain—is commonplace in the actual account of rapists. Scully and Marolla (1984) demonstrated that many convicted rapists denied their crime and attempted to justify their rapes by arguing that their victim had enjoyed herself despite the use of a weapon and the infliction of serious injuries, or even death. In fact, many argued, they had been instrumental in making *her* fantasy come true.

The images projected in pornography contribute to a vocabulary of motive which trivializes and neutralizes rape and which might lessen the internal controls that otherwise would prevent sexually aggressive behavior. Men who rape use this culturally acquired vocabulary to justify their sexual violence.

Another consequence of the application of psychopathology to rape is it leads one to view sexual violence as a special type of crime in which the motivations are subconscious and uncontrollable rather than overt and deliberate as with other criminal behavior. Black (1983) offers an approach to the analysis of criminal and/or violent behavior which, when applied to rape, avoids this bias.

Black (1983) suggests that it is theoretically useful to ignore that crime is criminal in order to discover what such behavior has in common with other kinds of conduct. From his perspective, much of the crime in modern societies, as in preindustrial societies, can be interpreted as a form of "self help" in which the actor is expressing a grievance through aggression and violence. From the actor's perspective, the victim is deviant and his own behavior is a form of social control in which the objective may be conflict management, punishment, or revenge. For example, in societies where women are considered the property of men, rape is sometimes used as a means of avenging the victim's husband or father (Black, 1983). In some cultures rape is used as a form of punishment. Such was the tradition among the puritanical, patriarchal Cheyenne where men were valued for their ability as warriors. It was Cheyenne custom that a wife suspected of being unfaithful could be "put on the prairie" by her husband. Military confreres then were invited to "feast" on the prairie (Hoebel, 1954; Llewellyn and Hoebel, 1941). The ensuing mass rape was a husband's method of punishing his wife.

Black's (1983) approach is helpful in understanding rape because it forces one to examine the goals that some men have learned to achieve through sexually violent means. Thus one approach to understanding why some men rape is to shift attention from individual psychopathology to the important question of what rapists gain from sexual aggression and violence in a culture seemingly prone to rape.

In this paper, we address this question using data from interviews conducted with 114 convicted, incarcerated rapists. Elsewhere, we discussed the vocabulary of motive, consisting of excuses and justifications, that these convicted rapists used to explain themselves and their crime (Scully and Marolla, 1984).[4] The use of these culturally derived excuses and justifications allowed them to view their behavior as either idiosyncratic or situationally appropriate and thus it reduced their sense of moral responsibility for their actions. Having disavowed deviance, these men revealed how they had used rape to achieve a number of objectives. We find that some men used rape for revenge or punishment while, for others, it was an "added bonus"—a last-minute decision made while committing another crime. In still other cases, rape was used to gain sexual access to women who were unwilling or unavailable, and for some it was a source of power and sex without any personal feelings. Rape was also a form of recreation, a diversion or an adventure and, finally, it was something that made these men "feel good."

Methods[5]

Sample

During 1980 and 1981 we interviewed 114 convicted rapists. All of the men had been convicted of the rape or attempted rape (n = 8) of an adult woman and subsequently incarcerated in a Virginia prison. Men convicted of other types of sexual offense were omitted from the sample.

In addition to their convictions for rape, 39 percent of the men also had convictions for burglary or robbery, 29 percent for abduction, 25 percent for sodomy, 11 percent for first or second degree murder, and 12 percent had been convicted of more than one rape. The majority of the men had previous criminal histories but only 23 percent had a record of past sex offenses and only 26 percent had a history of emotional problems. Their sentences for rape and accompanying crimes ranged from ten years to seven life sentences plus 380 years for one man. Twenty-two percent of the rapists were serving at least one life sentence. Forty-six percent of the rapists were white, 54 percent black. In age, they ranged from 18 to 60 years but the majority were between 18 and 35 years. Based on a statistical profile of felons in all Virginia prisons prepared by the Virginia Department of Corrections, it appears that this sample of rapists was disproportionately white and, at the time of the research, somewhat better educated and younger than the average inmate.

All participants in this research were volunteers. In constructing the sample, age, education, race, severity of current offense and past criminal record were balanced within the limitations imposed by the characteristics of the volunteer pool. Obviously the sample was not random and thus may not be typical of all rapists, imprisoned or otherwise.

All interviews were hand recorded using an 89-page instrument which included a general background, psychological, criminal, and sexual history, attitude scales and 30 pages of open-ended questions intended to explore rapists' own perceptions of their crime and themselves. Each author interviewed half of the sample in sessions that ranged from three to seven hours depending on the desire or willingness of the participant to talk.

Validity

In all prison research, validity is a special methodological concern because of the reputation inmates have for "conning." Although one goal of this research was to understand rape from the perspective of men who have raped, it was also necessary to establish the extent to which rapists' perceptions deviated from other descriptions of their crime. The technique we used was the same others have used in prison research; comparing factual information obtained in the interviews, including details of the crime, with reports on file at the prison (Athens, 1977; Luckenbill, 1977; Queen's Bench Foundation, 1976). In general, we found that rapists' accounts of their crime had changed very little since their trials. However, there was a tendency to understate the amount of violence they had used and, especially among certain rapists, to place blame on their victims.

How Offenders View the Rewards of Rape

Revenge and Punishment

As noted earlier, Black's (1983) perspective suggests that a rapist might see his act as a legitimized form of revenge or punishment. Additionally, he asserts that the idea of "collective liability" suggests that all people in a particular category are held accountable for the conduct of each of their counterparts. Thus, the victim of a violent act may merely represent the category of individual being punished.

These factors—revenge, punishment, and the collective liability of women—can be used to explain a number of rapes in our research. Several cases will illustrate the ways in which these factors combined in various types of rape. Revenge-rapes were among the most brutal and often included beatings, serious injuries, and even murder.

Typically, revenge-rapes included the element of collective liability. That is, from the rapist's perspective, the victim was a substitute for the woman he wanted to avenge. As explained elsewhere (Scully and Marolla, 1984), an upsetting event, involving a woman, preceded a significant number of rapes. When they raped, these men were angry because of a perceived indiscretion, typically related to a rigid, moralistic standard of sexual conduct, which they required from "their woman" but, in most cases, did not abide by themselves. Over and over these rapists talked about using rape "to get even" with their wives or other significant woman.[6] Typical is a young man who, prior to the rape, had a violent argument with his wife over what eventually proved to be her misdiagnosed case of venereal disease. She assumed the disease had been contracted through him, an accusation that infuriated him. After fighting with his wife, he explained that he drove around "thinking about hurting someone." He encountered his victim, a stranger, on the road where her car had broken down. It appears she accepted his offered ride because her car was out of commission. When she realized that rape was pending, she called him "a son of a bitch," and attempted to resist. He reported flying into a rage and beating her, and he confided,

> I have never felt that much anger before. If she had resisted, I would have killed her . . . The rape was for revenge. I didn't have an orgasm. She was there to get my hostile feelings off on.

Although not the most common form of revenge-rape, sexual assault continues to be used in retaliation against the victim's male partner. In one such case, the offender, angry because the victim's husband owed him money, went to the victim's home to collect. He confided, "I was going to get it one way or another." Finding the victim alone, he explained, they started to argue about the money and,

> I grabbed her and started beating the hell out of her. Then I committed the act,[7] I knew what I was doing. I was mad. I could have stopped but I didn't. I did it to get even with her and her husband.

Griffin (1971:33) points out that when women are viewed as commodities, "In raping another man's woman, a man may aggrandize his own manhood and concurrently reduce that of another man."

Revenge-rapes often contained an element of punishment. In some cases, while the victim was not the initial object of the revenge, the intent was to punish her because of something that transpired after the decision to rape had been made or during the course of the rape itself. This was the case with a young man whose wife had recently left him. Although they were in the process of reconciliation, he remained angry and upset over the separation. The night of the rape, he met the victim and her friend in a bar where he had gone to watch a fight on TV. The two women apparently accepted a ride from him but, after taking her friend home, he drove the victim to his apartment. At his apartment, he found a note from his wife indicating she had stopped by to watch the fight with him. This increased his anger because he preferred his wife's company. Inside his apartment, the victim allegedly remarked that she was sexually interested in his dog, which, he reported, put him in a rage. In the ensuing attack, he raped and pistol-whipped the victim. Then he forced a vacuum cleaner hose, switched on suction, into her vagina and bit her breast, severing the nipple. He stated:

> I hated at the time, but I don't know if it was her (the victim). (Who could it have been?) My wife? Even though we were getting back together, I still didn't trust her.

During his interview, it became clear that this offender, like many of the men, believed men have the right to discipline and punish women. In fact, he argued that most of the men he knew would also have beaten the victim because "that kind of thing (referring to the dog) is not acceptable among my friends."

Finally, in some rapes, both revenge and punishment were directed at victims because they represented women whom these offenders perceived as collectively responsible and liable for their problems. Rape was used "to put women in their place" and as a method of proving their "manhood" by displaying dominance over a female. For example, one multiple rapist believed his actions were related to the feeling that women thought they were better than he was.

> Rape was a feeling of total dominance. Before the rapes, I would always get a feeling of power and anger. I would degrade women so I could feel there was a person of less worth than me.

Another, especially brutal, case involved a young man from an upper-middle-class background, who spilled out his story in a seven-hour interview conducted in his solitary confinement cell. He described himself as tremendously angry, at the time, with his girlfriend whom he believed was involved with him in a "storybook romance," and from whom he expected complete fidelity. When she went away to college and became involved with another man, his revenge lasted eighteen months and involved the rape and murder of five women, all strangers who lived in his community. Explaining his rape-murders, he stated:

> I wanted to take my anger and frustration out on a stranger, to be in control, to do what I wanted to do. I wanted to use and abuse someone as I felt used and abused. I was killing my girlfriend. During the rapes and murders, I would think about my girlfriend. I hated the victims because they probably messed men over. I hated women because they were deceitful and I was getting revenge for what happened to me.

An Added Bonus

Burglary and robbery commonly accompany rape. Among our sample, 39 percent of rapists had also been convicted of one or the other of these crimes committed in connection with rape. In some cases, the original intent was rape, and robbery was an afterthought. However, a number of the men indicated that the reverse was true in their situation. That is, the decision to rape was made subsequent to their original intent which was burglary or robbery.

This was the case with a young offender who stated that he originally intended only to rob the store in which the victim happened to be working. He explained that when he found the victim alone,

> I decided to rape her to prove I had guts. She was just there. It could have been anybody.

Similarly, another offender indicated that he initially broke into his victim's home to burglarize it. When he discovered the victim asleep, he decided to seize the opportunity "to satisfy an urge to go to bed with a white woman, to see if it was different." Indeed, a number of men indicated that the decision to rape had been made after they realized they were in control of the situation. This was also true of an unemployed offender who confided that his practice was to steal whenever he needed money. On the day of the rape, he drove to a local supermarket and paced the parking lot, "staking out the situation." His pregnant victim was the first person to come along alone and "she was an easy target." Threatening her with a knife, he reported the victim as saying she would do anything if he didn't harm her. At that point, he decided to force her to drive to a deserted area where he raped her. He explained:

> I wasn't thinking about sex. But when she said she would do any-thing not to get hurt, probably because she was pregnant, I thought, "why not."

The attitude of these men toward rape was similar to their attitude toward burglary and robbery. Quite simply, if the situation is right, "why not." From the perspective of these rapists, rape was just another part of the crime—an added bonus.

Sexual Access

In an effort to change public attitudes that are damaging to the victims of rape and to reform laws seemingly premised on the assumption that women both ask for and enjoy rape, many writers emphasize the violent and aggressive character of rape. Often such arguments appear to discount the part that sex plays in the crime. The data clearly indicate that from the rapists' point of view rape is in part sexually motivated. Indeed, it is the sexual aspect of rape that distinguishes it from other forms of assault.

Groth (1979) emphasizes the psychodynamic function of sex in rape arguing that rapists' aggressive needs are expressed through sexuality. In other words, rape is a means to an end. We argue, however, that rapists view the act as an end in itself and that sexual access most obviously demonstrates the link between sex and rape. Rape as a means of sexual access also shows the deliberate nature of this crime. When a woman is unwilling or seems unavailable for sex, the rapist can seize what isn't volunteered. In discussing his decision to rape, one man made this clear.

> All the guys wanted to fuck her . . . a real fox, beautiful shape. She was a beautiful woman and I wanted to see what she had.

The attitude that sex is a male entitlement suggests that when a woman says "no," rape is a suitable method of conquering the "offending" object. If, for example, a woman is picked up at a party or in a bar or while hitchhiking (behavior which a number of the rapists saw as a signal of sexual availability), and the woman later resists sexual advances, rape is presumed to be justified. The same justification operates in what is popularly called "date rape." The belief that sex was their just compensation compelled a number of rapists to insist they had not raped. Such was the case of an offender who raped and seriously beat his victim when, on their second date, she refused his sexual advances.

> I think I was really pissed off at her because it didn't go as planned. I could have been with someone else. She led me on but wouldn't deliver . . . I have a male ego that must be fed.

The purpose of such rapes was conquest, to seize what was not offered.

Despite the cultural belief that young women are the most sexually desirable, several rapes involved the deliberate choice of a victim relatively older than the assailant.[8] Since the rapists were themselves rather young (26 to 30 years of age on the average), they were expressing a preference for sexually experienced, rather than elderly, women. Men who chose victims older than themselves often said they did so because they believed that sexually experienced women were more desirable partners. They raped because they also believed these women would not be sexually attracted to them.

Finally, sexual access emerged as a factor in the accounts of black men who consciously chose to rape white women.[9] The majority of rapes in the United States today are intraracial. However, for the past 20 years, according to national data based on reported rapes as well as victimization studies, which include unreported rapes, the rate of black on white (B/W) rape has significantly exceeded the rate of white on black (W/B) rape (LaFree, 1982).[10] Indeed, we may be experiencing a historical anomaly, since, as Brownmiller (1975) has documented, white men have freely raped women of color in the past. The current structure of interracial rape, however, reflects contemporary racism and race relations in several ways.

First, the status of black women in the United States today is relatively lower than the status of white women. Further, prejudice, segregation, and other factors continue to militate against interracial coupling. Thus, the desire for sexual access to higher status, unavailable women, an important function in B/W rape, does not motivate white men to rape black women. Equally important, demographic and geographic barriers interact to lower the incidence of W/B rape. Segregation as well as the poverty expected in black neighborhoods undoubtedly discourages many whites from choosing such areas as a target for housebreaking or robbery. Thus, the number of rapes that would occur in conjunction with these crimes is reduced.

Reflecting in part the standards of sexual desirability set by the dominant white society, a number of black rapists indicated they had been curious about white women. Blocked by racial barriers from legitimate sexual relations with white women, they raped to gain access to them. They described raping white women as "the ultimate experience" and "high status among friends. It gave me a feeling of status, power, macho." For another man, raping a white woman had a special appeal because it violated a "known taboo," making it more dangerous, and thus more exciting, to him than raping a black woman.

Impersonal Sex and Power

The idea that rape is an impersonal rather than an intimate or mutual experience appealed to a number of rapists, some of whom suggested it was their preferred form of sex. The fact that rape allowed them to control rather than care encouraged some to act on this preference. For example, one man explained,

> Rape gave me the power to do what I wanted to do without feeling I had to please a partner or respond to a partner. I felt in control, dominant. Rape was the ability to have sex without caring about the woman's response. I was totally dominant.

Another rapist commented:

> Seeing them laying there helpless gave me the confidence that I could do it . . . With rape, I felt totally in charge. I'm bashful, timid. When a woman wanted to give in normal sex, I was intimidated. In the rapes, I was totally in command, she totally submissive.

During his interview, another rapist confided that he had been fantasizing about rape for several weeks before committing his offense. His belief was that it would be "an exciting experience—a new high." Most appealing to him was the idea that he could make his victim "do it all for him" and that he would be in control. He fantasized that she "would submit totally and that I could have anything I wanted." Eventually, he decided to act because his older brother told him, "forced sex is great, I wouldn't get caught and, besides, women love it." Though now he admits to his crime, he continues to believe his victim "enjoyed it." Perhaps we should note here that the appeal of impersonal sex is not limited to convicted rapists. The amount of male sexual activity that occurs in homosexual meeting places as well as the widespread use of prostitutes suggests that avoidance of intimacy appeals to a large segment of the male population. Through rape men can experience power and avoid the emotions related to intimacy and tenderness. Further, the popularity of violent pornography suggests that a wide variety of men in this culture have learned to be aroused by sex fused with violence (Smith, 1976). Consistent with this observation, recent experimental research conducted by Malamuth et al. (1980) demonstrates that men are aroused by images that depict women as orgasmic under conditions of violence and pain. They found that for female students, arousal was high when the victim experienced an orgasm and *no* pain, whereas male students were highly aroused when the victim experienced an orgasm and pain. On the basis of their results, Malamuth et al. (1980) suggest that forcing a woman to climax despite her pain and abhorrence of the assailant makes the rapist feel powerful; he has gained control over the only source of power historically associated with women, their bodies. In the final analysis, dominance was the objective of most rapists.

Recreation and Adventure

Among gang rapists, most of whom were in their late teens or early twenties when convicted, rape represented recreation and adventure, another form of delinquent activity. Part of rape's appeal was the sense of male camaraderie engendered by participating collectively in a dangerous activity. To prove one's self capable of "performing" under these circumstances was a substantial challenge and also a source of reward. One gang rapist articulated this feeling very clearly:

> We felt powerful, we were in control. I wanted sex and there was peer pressure. She wasn't like a person, no personality, just domination on my part. Just to show I could do it—you know, macho.

Our research revealed several forms of gang rape. A common pattern was hitchhike-abduction rape. In these cases, the gang, cruising an area, "looking for girls," picked up a female hitchhiker for the purpose of having sex. Though the intent was rape, a number of men did not view it as such because they were convinced that women hitchhiked primarily to signal sexual availability and only secondarily as a form of transportation. In these cases, the unsuspecting victim was driven to a deserted area, raped, and in the majority of cases physically injured. Sometimes, the victim was not hitchhiking; she was abducted at knife- or gunpoint from the street usually at night. Some of these men did not view this type of attack as rape either because they believed a woman walking alone at night to be a prostitute. In addition, they were often convinced "she enjoyed it."

"Gang date" rape was another popular variation. In this pattern, one member of the gang would make a date with the victim. Then, without her knowledge or consent, she would be driven to a predetermined location and forcibly raped by each member of the group. One young man revealed this practice was so much a part of his group's recreational routine, they had rented a house for the purpose. From his perspective, the rape was justified because "usually the girl had a bad reputation, or we knew it was what she liked."

During his interview, another offender confessed to participating in twenty or thirty such "gang date" rapes because his driver's license had been revoked making it difficult for him to "get girls." Sixty percent of the time, he claimed, "they were girls known to do this kind of thing," but "frequently, the girls didn't want to have sex with all of us." In such cases, he said, "It might start out as rape but, then, they (the women) would quiet down and none ever reported it to the police." He was convicted for gang rape, which he described as "the ultimate thing I ever did," because unlike his other rapes, the victim, in this case, was a stranger whom the group abducted as she walked home from the library. He felt the group's past experience with "gang date" rape had prepared them for this crime in which the victim was blindfolded and driven to the mountains where, though it was winter, she was forced to remove her clothing. Lying on the snow, she was raped by each of the four men several times before being abandoned near a farmhouse. This young man continued to believe that if he had spent the night with her, rather than abandoning her, she would not have reported to the police.[11]

Solitary rapists also used terms like "exciting," "a challenge," "an adventure," to describe their feelings about rape. Like the gang rapists, these men found the element of danger made rape all the more exciting. Typifying this attitude was one man who described his rape as intentional. He reported:

> It was exciting to get away with it (rape), just being able to beat the system, not women. It was like doing something illegal and getting away with it.

Another rapist confided that for him "rape was just more exciting and compelling" than a normal sexual encounter because it involved forcing a stranger. A multiple rapist asserted, "It was the excitement and fear and the drama that made rape a big kick."

Feeling Good

At the time of their interviews, many of the rapists expressed regret for their crime and had empirically low self-esteem ratings. The experience of being convicted, sentenced, and incarcerated for rape undoubtedly produced many, if not most, of these feelings. What is clear is that, in contrast to the well-documented severity of the immediate impact and, in some cases, the long-term trauma experienced by the victims of sexual violence, the immediate emotional impact on the rapists is slight.

When the men were asked to recall their feelings immediately following the rape, only eight percent indicated that guilt or feeling bad was part of their emotional response. The majority said they felt good, relieved, or simply nothing at all. Some indicated they had been afraid of being caught or felt sorry for themselves. Only two men out of 114 expressed any concern or feeling for the victim. Feeling good or nothing at all about raping women is not an aberration limited to men in prison. Smithyman (1978), in his study of "undetected rapists"—rapists outside of prison—found that raping women had no impact on their lives nor did it have a negative effect on their self-image.

Significantly a number of men volunteered the information that raping had a positive impact on their feelings. For some the satisfaction was in revenge. For example, the man who had raped and murdered five women:

> It seems like so much bitterness and tension had built up and this released it. I felt like I had just climbed a mountain and now I could look back.

Another offender characterized rape as habit forming: "Rape is like smoking. You can't stop once you start." Finally one man expressed the sentiments of many rapists when he stated,

> After rape, I always felt like I had just conquered something, like I had just ridden the bull at Gilley's.

Conclusions

This paper has explored rape from the perspective of a group of convicted, incarcerated rapists. The purpose was to discover how these men viewed sexual violence and what they gained from their behavior.

We found that rape was frequently a means of revenge and punishment. Implicit in revenge-rapes was the notion that women were collectively liable for the rapists' problems. In some cases, victims were substitutes for significant women on whom the men desired to take revenge. In other cases, victims were thought to represent all women, and rape was used to punish, humiliate, and "put them in their place." In both cases women were seen as a class, a category, not as individuals. For some men, rape was almost an afterthought, a bonus added to burglary or robbery. Other men gained access to sexually unavailable or unwilling women through rape. For this group of men, rape was a fantasy come true, a particularly exciting form of impersonal sex that enabled them to dominate and control women by exercising a singularly male form of power. These rapists talked of the pleasures of raping—how for them it was a challenge, an adventure, a dangerous and "ultimate" experience. Rape made them feel good and, in some cases, even elevated their self-image.

The pleasure these men derived from raping reveals the extreme to which they objectified women. Women were seen as sexual commodities to be used or conquered rather than as human beings with rights and feelings. One young man expressed the extreme of the contemptful view of women when he confided to the female researcher:

> Rape is a man's right. If a woman doesn't want to give it, the man should take it. Women have no right to say no. Women are made to have sex. It's all they are good for. Some women would rather take a beating, but they always give in; it's what they are for.

This man murdered his victim because she wouldn't "give in."

Undoubtedly, some rapes, like some of all crimes, are idiopathic. However, it is not necessary to resort to pathological motives to account for all rape or other acts of sexual violence. Indeed, we find that men who rape have something to teach us about the cultural roots of sexual aggression. They force us to acknowledge that rape is more than an idiosyncratic act committed by a few "sick" men. Rather, rape can be viewed as the end point in a continuum of sexually aggressive behaviors that reward men and victimize women.[12] In the way that the motives for committing any criminal act can be rationally determined, reasons for rape can also be determined. Our data demonstrate that some men rape because they have learned that in this culture sexual violence is rewarding. Significantly, the overwhelming majority of these rapists indicated they never thought they would go to prison for what they did. Some did not fear imprisonment because they did not define their behavior as rape. Others knew that women frequently do not report rape; and, of those cases that are reported, conviction rates are low, and therefore they felt secure. These men perceived rape as a rewarding, low-risk act. Understanding that otherwise normal men can and do rape is critical to the development of strategies for prevention.

We are left with the fact that all men do not rape. In view of the apparent rewards and cultural supports for rape, it is important to ask why some men do not rape. Hirschi (1969) makes a similar observation about delinquency. He argues that the key question is not "Why do they do it?" but rather "Why don't we do it?" (Hirschi, 1969:34). Likewise, we may be seeking an answer to the wrong question about sexual assault of women. Instead of asking men who rape, "Why?", perhaps we should be asking men who don't, "Why not?".

Notes

1. Despite the fact that these data have been in circulation for some time, prevention strategies continue to reflect the "lunatic fringe" image of rape. For example, security on college campuses, such as bright lighting and escort service, is designed to protect women against stranger rape while little or no attention is paid to the more frequent crime—acquaintance or date rape.

2. Broude and Green (1976) list a number of factors which limit the quantity and quality of cross-cultural data on rape. They point out that it was not customary in traditional ethnography to collect data on sexual attitudes and behavior. Further, where data do exist, they are often sketchy and vague. Despite this, the existence of rape-free societies has been established.

3. This factor distinguishes rape from other fictional depictions of violence. That is, in fictional murder, bombings, robberies, etc., victims are never portrayed as enjoying themselves. Such exhibits are reserved for pornographic displays of rape.

4. We also introduced a typology consisting of "admitters" (men who defined their behavior as rape) and "deniers" (men who admitted to sexual contact with the victim but did not define it as rape). In this paper we drop the distinction between admitters and deniers because it is not relevant to most of the discussion.

5. For a full discussion of the research methodology, sample, and validity, see Scully and Marolla (1984).

6. It should be noted that significant women, like rape victims, were also sometimes the targets of abuse and violence and possibly rape as well, although spousal rape is not recognized in Virginia law. In fact, these men were abusers. Fifty-five percent of rapists acknowledged that they hit their significant woman "at least once," and 20 percent admitted to inflicting physical injury. Given the tendency of these men to underreport the amount of violence in their crime, it is probably accurate to say they underreported their abuse of their significant women as well.

7. This man, as well as a number of others, either would not or could not bring himself to say the word "rape." Similarly, we also attempted to avoid using the word, a technique which seemed to facilitate communication.

8. When asked toward whom their sexual interests were primarily directed, 43 percent of the rapists indicated a preference for women "significantly older than themselves." When those who responded, "women of any age" are added, 65 percent of rapists expressed sexual interest in women older than themselves.

9. Feminists as well as sociologists have tended to avoid the topic of interracial rape. Contributing to the avoidance is an awareness of historical and contemporary social injustice. For example, Davis (1981) points out that fictional rape of white women was used in the South as a post-slavery justification to lynch black men. And LaFree (1980) has demonstrated that black men who assault white women continue to receive more serious sanctions within the criminal justice system when compared to other racial combinations of victim and assailant. While the silence has been defensible in light of historical racism, continued avoidance of the topic discriminates against victims by eliminating the opportunity to investigate the impact of social factors on rape.

10. In our sample, 66 percent of black rapists reported their victim(s) were white, compared to two white rapists who reported raping black women. It is important to emphasize that because of the biases inherent in rape reporting and processing, and because of the limitations of our sample, these figures do not

accurately reflect the actual racial composition of rapes committed in Virginia or elsewhere. Furthermore, since black men who assault white women receive more serious sanctions within the criminal justice system when compared to other racial combinations of victim and assailant (LaFree, 1980), B/W rapists will be overrepresented within prison populations as well as overrepresented in any sample drawn from the population.

11. It is important to note that the gang rapes in this study were especially violent, resulting in physical injury, even death. One can only guess at the amount of hitchhike-abduction and "gang-date" rapes that are never reported or, if reported, are not processed because of the tendency to disbelieve the victims of such rapes unless extensive physical injury accompanies the crime.

12. It is interesting that men who verbally harass women on the street say they do so to alleviate boredom, to gain a sense of youthful camaraderie, and because it's fun (Benard and Schlaffer, 1884)—the same reason men who rape give for their behavior.

References

Abel, Gene, Judith Becker, and Linda Skinner. 1980. "Aggressive behavior and sex." *Psychiatric Clinics of North America* 3:133–51.

Athens, Lonnie. 1977. "Violent crime: a symbolic interactionist study." *Symbolic Interaction* 1:56–71.

Bart, Pauline. 1979. "Rape as a paradigm of sexism in society—victimization and its discontents." *Women's Studies International Quarterly* 2:347–57.

Benard, Cheryl, and Edith Schlaffer. 1984. "The man in the street: why he harasses." Pp. 70–73 in Alison M. Jaggar and Paula S. Rothenberg (eds.), *Feminist Frameworks*. New York: McGraw-Hill.

Black, Donald. 1983. "Crime as social control." *American Sociological Review* 48:34–45.

Blumberg, Rae Lesser. 1979. "A paradigm for predicting the position of women: policy implications and problem." Pp. 113–42 in Jean Lipman-Blumen and Jessie Bernard (eds.), *Sex Roles and Social Policy*. London: Sage Studies in International Sociology.

Broude, Gwen, and Sarah Greene. 1976. "Cross-cultural codes on twenty sexual attitudes and practices." *Ethnology* 15:409–28.

Brownmiller, Susan. 1975. *Against Our Will*. New York: Simon and Schuster.

Davis, Angela. 1981. *Women, Race and Class*. New York: Random House.

Fisher, Gary, and E. Rivlin. 1971. "Psychological needs of rapists." *British Journal of Criminology* 11:182–85.

Griffin, Susan. 1971. "Rape: the all-American crime," *Ramparts*, September 10:26–35.

Groth, Nicholas. 1971. *Men Who Rape*. New York: Plenum Press.

Hammer, Emanuel, and Irving Jacks. 1955. "A study of Rorschack flexnor and extensor human movements." *Journal of Clinical Psychology* 11:63–67.

Herman, Dianne. 1984. "The rape culture." Pp. 10–39 in Jo Freeman (ed.), *Women: A Feminist Perspective*. Palo Alto: Mayfield.

Hirschi, Travis. 1969. *Causes of Delinquency*. Berkeley: University of California Press.

Hoebel, E. Adamson. 1954. *The Law of Primitive Man*. Boston: Harvard University Press.

Johnson, Allan Griswold. 1980. "On the prevalence of rape in the United States." *Signs* 6:136–46.

Kanin, Eugene. 1957. "Male aggression in dating-courtship relations." *American Journal of Sociology* 63:197–204.

———. 1965 ."Male sex aggression and three psychiatric hypotheses." *Journal of Sex Research* 1:227–29.

———. 1967. "Reference groups and sex conduct norm violation." *Sociological Quarterly* 8:495–504.

———. 1969. "Selected dyadic aspects of male sex aggression." *Journal of Sex Research* 5:12–28.

Kasinsky, Renee. 1975. "Rape: a normal act?" *Canadian Forum*, September: 18–22.

Kirkpatrick, Clifford, and Eugene Kanin. 1957. "Male sex aggression on a university campus." *American Sociological Review* 22:52–58.

Koss, Mary P., and Kenneth E. Leonard. 1984. "Sexually aggressive men: empirical findings and theoretical implications." Pp. 213–32 in Neil M. Malamuth and Edward Donnerstein (eds.), *Pornography and Sexual Aggression*. New York: Academic Press.

LaFree, Gary. 1980. "The effect of sexual stratification by race on official reactions to rape." *American Sociological Review* 45:824–54.

———. 1982. "Male power and female victimization: towards a theory of interracial rape." *American Journal of Sociology* 88:311–28.

Llewellyn, Karl N., and E. Adamson Hoebel. 1941. *The Cheyenne Way: Conflict and Case Law in Primitive Jurisprudence*. Norman: University of Oklahoma Press.

Luckenbill, David. 1977. "Criminal homicide as a situated transaction." *Social Problems* 25:176–87.

Malamuth, Neil, Scott Haber, and Seymour Feshback. 1980. "Testing hypotheses regarding rape: exposure to sexual violence, sex difference, and the "normality' of rapists." *Journal of Research in Personality* 14:121–37.

Malamuth, Neil, Maggie Heim, and Seymour Feshback. 1980. "Sexual responsiveness of college students to rape depictions: inhibitory and disinhibitory effects." *Social Psychology* 38:399–408.

Meyer, Thomas J. 1984. " 'Date rape': a serious problem that few talk about." *Chronicle of Higher Education*, December 5.

Morgan, Robin. 1980. "Theory and practice: pornography and rape." Pp. 134–40 in Laura Lederer (ed.), *Take Back the Night: Women on Pornography*. New York: William Morrow.

Queen's Bench Foundation. 1976. *Rape: Prevention and Resistance*. San Francisco: Queen's Bench Foundation.

Rada, Richard. 1978. *Clinical Aspects of Rape*. New York: Grune and Stratton.

Russell, Diana. 1975. *The Politics of Rape*. New York: Stein and Day.

Sanday, Peggy Reeves. 1979. *The Socio-Cultural Context of Rape*. Washington, D.C.: United States Department of Commerce, National Technical Information Service.

Scully, Diana, and Joseph Marolla. 1984. "Convicted rapists' vocabulary of motive: excuses and justifications." *Social Problems* 31:530–44.

———. 1985 "Rape and psychiatric vocabulary of motive: alternative perspectives." Pp. 294–312 in Ann Wolbert Burgess (ed.), *Rape and Sexual Assault: A Research Handbook*. New York: Garland Publishing.

Smith, Don. 1976. "The social context of pornography." *Journal of Communications* 26:16–24.

Smithyman, Samuel. 1978. "The undetected rapist." Unpublished dissertation: Claremont Graduate School.

Weis, Kurt, and Sandra Borges. 1973. "Victimology and rape: the case of the legitimate victim." *Issues in Criminology* 8:71–115.

West, Donald J. 1983. "Sex offenses and offending." Pp. 1–30 in Michael Tonry and Norval Morris (eds.), *Crime and Justice: An Annual Review of Research*. Chicago: University of Chicago Press.

Wheeler, Hollis. 1985. "Pornography and rape: a feminist perspective." Pp. 374–91 in Ann Wolbert Burgess (ed.), *Rape and Sexual Assault: A Research Handbook*. New York: Garland Publishing.

11

Rape Myths

~

Martha R. Burt

RAPE MYTHS ARE PREJUDICIAL, STEREOTYPED, or false beliefs about rape, rape victims, or rapists. Rape myths have the effect of denying that many instances involving coercive sex are actually rapes. To understand how a rape myth works, one must understand the legal definition of rape and then ask why, when faced with a sexual assault that fits this legal definition, many people are still not willing to call this assault a rape.

As used in this chapter, rape is defined as: penetration, however slight, of any bodily orifice, obtained against the victim's will by using force, or threat of force, of any part of the assailant's body or any object used by the assailant in the course of the assault.

This definition does not require resistance on the part of the victim. Its critical elements are that the sexual acts have occurred against the victim's will, by the assailant's use of force or the threat of force.

In a world without rape myths, the general public would understand that every act of coerced sex involving penetration is a rape. Unfortunately, the common perception does not match the legal definition, because rape myths influence the common perception. What is a rape to the general public? Much depends on how people answer this question and what specific acts their definitions include.

The rape definitions held by individuals in this culture may be broad and inclusive or narrow and restrictive. People whose definitions are at the inclusive extreme believe that all coerced sex is rape, whether the coercion used is physical, psychological, or economic.

From Martha Burt, "Rape Myths," in *Acquaintance Rape: The Hidden Crime*, ed. Andrea Parrot and Laurie Bechhofer (New York: John Wiley and Sons, 1991), 26–40. © 1991 by John Wiley and Sons. Reprinted by permission of John Wiley and Sons.

Those whose definitions lie at the restrictive extreme believe that there is no such thing as rape—no matter what occurred, these people will find a way, using rape myths, to conclude that no rape happened.

Most people's definition of rape falls somewhere between these two extremes, including some acts of coerced sex but also excluding many on the basis of belief in rape myths. People have in their heads an idea of a "real" rape. Usually their idea is a good deal narrower than the legal definition given above and excludes many types of rape that happen more frequently than the classic "real" rape. When they hear of a specific incident in which a woman says she was raped, they look at the incident, compare it to their idea of a "real" rape, and, all too often, decide that the woman was not "really" raped.

The classic "real" rape, for many people, is a rape by a stranger who uses a weapon—an assault done at night, outside (in a dark alley), with a lot of violence, resistance by the victim, and hence severe wounds and signs of struggle. In fact, except for "at night," every element of this "classic" rape scenario is absent for a majority of rape victims in this country. More than half of all rapes are committed by someone known to the victim; most do not involve a weapon, or injury beyond minor bruises or scratches; most occur indoors, in either the victim's or the assailant's home (Ageton, 1983; Amir, 1971; Burgess & Holmstrom, 1979; Koss, 1985; Macdonald, 1979; Russell, 1984; Warshaw, 1988).

Note how thoroughly the classic rape scenario excludes acquaintance and date rape from the category of "real" rape. A rape by a date or an acquaintance is not a rape by a stranger. Further, it is relatively rare for date or acquaintance rapes to involve a weapon or serious injury to the victim, and they are most likely to take place indoors. In addition, the victim often has engaged in some type of voluntary interaction with the assailant, which may be as slight as giving the time of day to a neighbor's brother-in-law or as extensive as being married to the assailant. The problem in determining whether a "real" rape occurred then becomes perceiving that voluntary interaction ended and coercion began.

Rape myths are the mechanism that people use to justify dismissing an incident of sexual assault from the category of "real" rape. Accepting or believing rape myths leads to a more restrictive definition of rape and is thus rape-supportive, because such beliefs deny the reality of many actual rapes. Rejecting these assaults as not being "real" rapes makes rape prosecution harder, the victim's recovery more difficult, and the assailant's actions safer. Rejecting or disbelieving rape myths has the opposite effect. It leads to including more concrete instances within the definition of what is a real rape (Burt & Albin, 1981).

There are, of course, important consequences for the victims of "unreal" rape—people blame them, belittle them, treat them badly, do not take their situation seriously, and do not offer needed support (Burt & Estep, 1981a). Since rapes by acquaintances are very likely to be considered "unreal" rapes, their victims may have a particularly hard time with certain aspects of recovery (Katz, 1986; Russell, 1984; Warshaw, 1988).

Analysis of Rape Myths

Rape myths are part of the general culture. People learn them in the same way they acquire other attitudes and beliefs—from their families, their friends, newspapers, movies, books, dirty jokes, and, lately, rock videos. I group rape myths into four main classifications of myths focused on the victim/woman (other myths, discussed below, focus on the assailant/man): nothing happened; no harm was done; she wanted or liked it; and she asked for or deserved it.

Nothing Happened

The first group of myths remove an incident from the category of a "real" rape by denying that any incident, either sex or rape, occurred at all. A number of myths promote the idea that women falsely accuse men of rape. For years, judges in rape trials cautioned juries to be wary of women's claims of rape by reading them the warning of Lord Hale, a British judge during the 18th century: "A rape accusation is easily made, and, once made, is difficult to defend against, even if the accused person is innocent." Juries were instructed to weigh the woman's claim with special care. Many people believe that women lie, "crying rape" to cover up an out-of-wedlock pregnancy or to get back at men who have jilted them or refused their advances. Yet according to police records, false reports are no more likely for rape than they are for other serious crimes (Lear, 1972). Many myths in this group have the effect of negating a claim of rape against someone known to the victim—an acquaintance, neighbor, family member, co-worker, ex-husband, or ex-lover—especially if the prerape relationship involved conflict.

Also in this category of "nothing happened" are myths that women's rape claims are sheer fantasy or wishful thinking. The elderly spinster calling the police to find the "rapist under the bed" is a common theme of dirty jokes, implying that the woman is sex-starved and making up her accusations to convince herself that she is desirable. And, women's "rape" fantasies usually involve very handsome and attractive men who find them so irresistible that masculine self-control is momentarily overwhelmed, and the men sweep them off their feet. These fantasies do not resemble real rapes: they lack the degradation, the ignoring of one's personhood, the threat of death, the fear of physical injury, and the forced necessity to have intimate contact with someone against one's will.

No Harm Was Done

The second group of myths remove an incident from the category of a "real" rape by denying that any harm was done. Sexual intercourse is admitted, but its coerced and harmful nature is denied. Beliefs that rape is "just sex" belong in this group. Remarks such as "If you're not a virgin, what difference does it make?" and "Relax and enjoy it" reflect this belief, implying that the rape is no different from other acts of sex the victim has experienced. They deny the violent, life-threatening nature of rape. Acquaintance rape involves the humiliation of realizing that the assailant does not care what the victim wants and that part of the payoff for the assailant is his ability to control the victim, ignore her wishes, and force her to do anything he says. Although it often involves less outright fear of death than stranger rape, acquaintance rape still involves force and fear of bodily injury.

Other rape myths in this category of "no harm done" are based on the assumption that a woman's value lies in her sexual exclusiveness. If she is not a virgin, or she is not the exclusive sexual property of her lawful husband, there is no more harm that can be done. Indeed, until very recently rape statutes in this country, as in England, were based on property rights incorporating this assumption. The person harmed by a rape was presumed to be the man who owned the woman—either her father, who had lost the marriage value of a virgin daughter, or her husband, who had lost the ability to enjoy her as exclusive sexual property. As of 1990, seven states still do not include marital rape as a prosecutable offense and an additional 26 states allowed prosecutions only under restricted circumstances. Laws allowing prosecution of marital rape are very recent; they have resulted from political pressure from women's groups. The earlier laws were based on the husband's property right to use his wife sexually and her presumed forfeiture of a right to refuse. (See Chapter 7 in this volume.)

Many "no harm done" myths refer to women of societally devalued status or women who are stereotyped as sexually available. The most extreme implication of these myths is that once a woman has "said yes" and had sex with one man, she is never again in a position where she can legitimately say "no." So, if a woman can be shown to have had sex with someone other than her husband, she is no longer worthy of the law's protection—she is fair game, or an "open territory victim" as Clark and Lewis (1977) phrased it. Prostitutes are a special case of the open territory victim, so devalued that many people believe that prostitutes cannot be raped (Silbert, 1988).

This is the type of myth that traps many minority women, whose experiences of sexual violation are not taken seriously because they are stereotyped as sleeping with many men and therefore already devalued. Any group of women stereotyped as being sexually active outside of marriage, such as divorcées or prostitutes, or any women who frequent places associated with being sexually available, such as bars, run the risk of being dismissed as unworthy of the law's protection or of sympathetic concern when they press a charge of rape.

Even if a woman is raped by a complete stranger under circumstances fitting the "classic" rape and in which her normal sexual behavior is completely irrelevant, once it becomes known that she belongs to a stereotyped group the general public is less likely to believe that she was the victim of a "real" rape. If her rape occurred in connection with dating, frequenting a bar, or other circumstances connected in the public mind with impropriety or promiscuity, her report of a rape will be received with even greater skepticism.

The myth that "only bad girls get raped" works to cast suspicion on any woman who has been raped. The reasoning goes, "If she was raped, she must have done something to bring it on, she must be a 'bad girl.' " Common defense attorney tactics follow directly from this premise; in their efforts to obtain a not-guilty verdict, defense attorneys will try to convince juries that victims are sexually promiscuous. Too often, this defense tactic works, even in states with laws rewritten specifically to exclude this type of testimony as prejudicial to the victim (Berger, 1977; Borgida, 1981; New York Task Force on Women in the Courts, 1986-87; Wood, 1973).

She Wanted It

The third group of myths remove an incident from the category of a "real" rape by maintaining that the woman wanted it, invited it, or liked it. The issue of consent lies at the crux of this type of myth. In one sense, these myths simply pose the question: Did she want to or did she have to? Did her observed behavior stem from personal motivation, in which case it was consensual sex, or from environmental coercion by an assailant, in which case it was rape?

Complications arise in answering this seemingly simple question because the culture's many myths concerning women and sex are distilled to a belief that "women never mean no." At some level, women are always presumed always to "want it," no matter what they say. Think of the meaning of some common phrases: "Your lips say 'no, no, no' but your eyes say 'yes, yes, yes,' " or "Come on, baby, you know you really want it." As a result of these assumptions about women and sex, the practical requirements of proof of environmental coercion ("real" rape) are often extreme, precisely because the situations activate rape myths and sexual stereotypes.

To differentiate a rape from "just sex," one must be convinced that the victim did not consent to the sexual acts performed. To people who have experience with victims and with rape trials, it is quite clear that in the public mind a victim's reputation or identity enters this judgment; women with certain reputations or identities (e.g., divorcées, minority women, women out alone at night) are stereotypically assumed to consent more readily, to more men, in more situations. Having assumed a generalized propensity to consent and attached it to whole classes of women, this line of reasoning then particularizes this argument to this woman (victim) in this situation (alleged rape) and infers consent to this man (alleged assailant). Therefore, following this line of reasoning, this situation is not a rape.

One can also see why women who are raped by acquaintances or dates have a very hard time getting their listeners to credit their claim that what happened was actually a rape. The closer the prerape situation is to a context in which sex is a possibility (e.g., a party, a date, consensual necking or petting), the more difficult it is to convince the world that a rape occurred. The difficulties are further compounded by some people's perception that any interaction between a man and a woman is potentially sexual, and therefore anything that occurs should be considered to be sex, not rape. . . .

Among this group of myths is the idea that any healthy woman can resist a rapist if she really wants to, particularly if the rapist is someone she knows. The corollary is that if she got raped, she must not have resisted enough and therefore she wanted it or consented to it. Frighteningly, some people also still believe that women like to be treated violently and that force is sexually stimulating to women. This line of reasoning ultimately comes down to: "There's no such thing as rape."

She Deserved It

The fourth group of myths remove an incident from the category of "real" rape by claiming that the woman deserved it or did something to bring it on. These myths admit that there was sex and that the sex was forced, but they hold the woman responsible—therefore the act was not a rape. If she was flirting; if she was attractively dressed; if she was, in the man's perception, a tease; if she went out with a man, necked with him, and invited him to her apartment for coffee; even if she only said "hello" to him at the office—it was her fault. She "got into the game" of sexuality, this reasoning goes, and once in the game, society loads her with the full responsibility for whatever happens. The myths do not differentiate between her "asking for" companionship, friendship, and a date and her "asking for" rape. . . .

Women are also blamed or seen as deserving the rape if they put themselves in risky circumstances, even when they have no choice but to do so. If a woman hitchhikes, or is out late at night, even if she works late-night shifts, a rape is still her fault. There is no parallel for this in other crimes. If someone walking in a bad neighborhood is robbed, or if someone does not lock an apartment door and is burglarized, no one denies that the *crime* happened, even when it is clear that the victim used poor judgment. The robber or burglar is perceived as intending to commit a crime and actually carrying it out; the victim simply made it a little easier. Not so with rape, where the rape myths operate to blame the victim even when the facts show that a majority of rapists plan their rapes in advance, thus showing an intent to commit a crime independent of the behavior of any potential victim (Amir, 1971; Groth, 1979; Macdonald, 1979).

Myths Regarding Men

All of the myths discussed so far focus on woman—as does most of the cultural ideology. To have everyone judging the victim is a good smokescreen; the attacker usually gets away with hardly a glance. However, there are complementary myths about male sexuality and about rapists which also serve to reduce perceptions of the assailant's culpability. One is that only crazy men rape. Therefore, faced with a sane accused assailant, the average person finds it hard to imagine that he is a rapist. In fact, rapists are no more "insane" than the average man (Groth, 1979), and significant numbers of normal college men admit that they have raped (Koss, Leonard, Oros, & Beezley, 1985) or would rape if they could get away with it (Malamuth, 1981).

Second, the myths promote the idea that men cannot control their sexuality. The idea that wearing revealing clothing is provocation to rape implies that rape results from a spontaneous, unplanned response to a sexually attractive woman. This myth once again presumes that rape is simply forceful sex ("assault with a friendly weapon," as the joke has it) and that only sexually attractive women will be the targets of this male response ("Who would want to rape her?" said of a very unattractive woman). To be somewhat facetious, this myth implies that if a scantily clad woman walks down the street and a man sees her, he will go out of control, the situation can end only in rape, and the man is not responsible for it because he saw her knees and they drove him over the edge. Put this way, it should be obvious that this myth excuses men's assaultive behavior and helps remove such incidents from the category of "real" rapes. . . .

The Context of Rape Myths

Rape myths do not exist in a vacuum, however powerful they are in themselves. One of the things my research has documented (Burt, 1980; Burt & Albin, 1981) is the surrounding set of attitudes that support the myths. This research showed strong positive associations between acceptance of rape myths and higher levels of sex role stereotyping, adversarial sexual beliefs, sexual conservatism, and acceptance of interpersonal violence.

People's sense of themselves as male and female is tied into whether they believe rape myths or see males and females as relating to each others as adversaries. Contemplating this set of attitudes can be quite discouraging for the prospects of making serious changes in the cultural ideology of rape, because these attitudes represent an aspect of people's core identity and cannot readily be changed through public education programs that deal with facts. Anyone who has ever tried knows how hard it is to change core identities of what maleness means, what femaleness means, and what the underlying assumptions I have just described mean for sexual violence.

Check (1984) has further generalized my work by expanding my adversarial sexual beliefs scale beyond the sexual into the concept of general hostility toward women—an attitude that is also very strongly associated with rape myth acceptance and sex role stereotyping. Further, the culture reinforces these feelings by representing women as sly, manipulative, vindictive, and untrustworthy. If one has hostile feelings toward women, the culture will provide ample support for the "truth" of these feelings. Those who have hostile feelings will not therefore have to confront them as feelings, but will be able to sustain a (false) belief that women "really are" untrustworthy. However, if a woman feels hostile toward men, she will experience a lot of baiting and rejection. The culture does *not* support women's hostility toward men, however justified. Rather, women who express these feelings are called "manhaters," "ball breakers," and similar epithets.

Researchers have measured some important consequences of beliefs in rape myths and their supporting attitudes. The more one believes rape myths, the narrower is one's definition of a "real" rape, the less likely is one to convict someone of a rape, and the lighter the sentence is one to recommend in a mock jury situation (Borgida, 1981; Burt & Albin, 1981). There is an association between believing rape myths and admitting that one has had intercourse with a woman by force (Koss et al., 1985). High myth acceptors are also more likely to say that they would rape if they thought they could get away with it (Malamuth, 1981). Finally, high myth acceptors are more aroused by violent pornography (Malamuth & Donnerstein, 1984).

All of these beliefs and attitudes form an interlocking web of victim blame. The culture reinforces the behavior, and the behavior reinforms the culture and becomes the reality. A continuing cycle of beliefs denies real victim status to women and makes it very hard to be a woman who has been raped. . . .

Other cultural elements such as dirty jokes and movies reinforce rape myths. With dirty jokes, the questions to ask are: Who is the target of aggression, who is "it" in the jokes, and who is the audience for the jokes? Who squirms, who is put down? Another question is: What image of male and female sexuality is portrayed by dirty jokes? By and large, women are the targets of aggression in dirty jokes, both as characters in the jokes and as the audience to whom they are told. Dirty jokes generally portray women as sexually insatiable (and therefore too demanding of the male), always ready to go, never saying no, and seductive. Women's bodies and genitals are portrayed as foul and their bodily fluids as harmful. They are depicted as unfaithful, untrustworthy, and untruthful, as whores who have no real affection for their faithful men. Jokes about rape incorporate all of the myths described above but concentrate mostly on the idea that women like rape, or really cooperate, and therefore there is no such thing as rape.

Movies likewise reinforce rape myths. Pornographic films do this outright, by portraying rape incidents in which the woman ultimately responds with enjoyment, and by frequent and repeated association of sex and violence. But movies for the general public are culpable in their own way, from the famous scene in *Gone with the Wind* to more modern versions such as *Swept Away* and *Blume in Love*.

Teenagers and young women are the most likely victims of rape, and most will be raped by people they know. These victims are very likely to believe an extensive array of rape myths that lead them to accept responsibility for their own rapes in dating, party, and acquaintance situations (Goodchilds, Zellman, Johnson, & Giarusso, 1988).

Films aimed at the teenage audience reinforce these myths and teach young women that sex is likely to be violent and violence is frequently the price one pays for being sexual. Slasher films, now very popular with teenagers, implicitly reinforce violence against women. The victims are almost invariably young, attractive women alone (with no male protector); these films associate emotional climax and release with stalking and ultimately committing violence on women, repeatedly (sometimes as many as ten times in a single movie). Finally, rock videos commonly portray strong associations between sex and violence. Adolescents who spend a lot of time watching rock videos are highly likely to believe rape myths and to hold other beliefs that foster women's sexual victimization (Deiter & Heeter, 1989). The next generation is being taught to acquiesce to its own victimization.

The Function of Rape Myths

The analysis that has guided my research was developed by women in the antirape movement in the early 1970s. The evolution of this analysis and explanations of the causes and consequences of sexual assault occurred hand-in-hand. The analysis assisted attempts to understand sexual assault: the daily experience of trying to help sexual assault victims provided both a great push for theory to guide counseling practice and data for theory development. This analysis, developed by feminists, offers a radical critique of women's victimization through sexual assault and other sex- and sex-role-related phenomena such as battering, incest, prostitution, and pornography. Feminist analysis approaches women's sexual victimization in a way that shifts the focus away from victim reactions and immediate contributing factors, both of which often fail to address the question of why victimization occurs in the first place. Feminists started to ask who benefits from women's sexual victimization and focused their attention on the structural conditions that promote certain forms of victimization as mechanisms for maintaining the current distribution of power between the sexes. That distribution of power is embodied in patriarchy.

Most present societies, including our own, are patriarchies. Patriarchy is a system designed to maintain societal power, control, and privilege in male hands. Many writers have examined the mechanisms used to maintain male advantage, including economic and familial structures, and child-rearing and socialization practices (see Chafetz, 1984; Eagly, 1987; and Epstein, 1988 for the social science perspective; and Benjamin, 1988; and Westkott, 1986 for the psychoanalytic perspective). Far less analysis illuminates the support provided for patriarchy by culture and ideology and, ultimately, by overt physical and sexual violence; that which exists has been produced by feminists (Benjamin, 1988; Brownmiller, 1975; Burt, 1980, 1983a, b; 1988; Burt & Albin, 1981; Burt & Estep, 1981a, b; Clark and Lewis, 1977; Deiter & Heeter, 1989; Dinnerstein, 1976; Farley, 1978; Griffin, 1981; Holliday, 1978; MacKinnon, 1982; Miller, 1976; Rowbotham, 1973; Webster, 1978; Westkott, 1986).

To retain themselves in control, groups in power may use many means, including overt violence and coercion, training or socialization, and cultural beliefs about what is "right," "good," "true," and "natural." The part of patriarchal ideology relevant to this chapter is our culture's set of beliefs about what is right, good, true, and natural about men, women, and their relationship to each other. Rape myths are part of this ideology.

Ideologies are most easily seen when they are not our own. Under those circumstances it is also easy to see that the ideology supports one group's interests and suppresses those of other groups. This may be why the word *ideology* has a slightly pejorative connotation in the United States. It is relatively easy to see that beliefs about the cultural inferiority and mental incapacities of colonized or enslaved peoples, which were prevalent among western powers during periods of empire building, were both false and supportive of the exploitive interests of the colonizers. Believing a people to be childlike, lazy, and incapable of looking out for its own best interests is a strong justification for taking it over, whether as a colony or by making slaves of its members. It is less easy to see or to admit that one's own beliefs are not necessary or natural. The purposes of an ideology, if it is functioning well, are to make a particular world view appear natural and normal, to make alternative belief structures impossible, and to make rebellion against the powerful group supported by the ideology unlikely.

The ideology that supports a patriarchal power structure contains several important elements. First is the belief that men are "better" than women—smarter, more active, more capable, stronger, and so forth (Vogel, Broverman, Broverman, Clarkson, & Rosenkrantz, 1972; Broverman, Broverman, Clarkson, Rosenkrantz, & Vogel, 1970; Chafetz, 1984; Eagly, 1987; Epstein, 1988). Second, patriarchy's ideology appropriates certain behaviors to the male role as its exclusive prerogative. For our purposes, physical violence and sexuality are the two most important behaviors so appropriated (Benjamin, 1988; Brownmiller, 1975; MacKinnon, 1982). Patriarchy's ideology of sex roles encourages average expressions of violence and sexual behavior for males and tolerates extreme expressions. It also encourages suitable passive, complementary behavior for females. Conversely,

inappropriate cross-sex behavior is punished, and the strongest con-
demnations are reserved for women who "unnaturally" indulge in behavior that forms the core of male privilege—violence and sexuality
(New York Task Force on Women in the Courts, 1986-87; Schneider,
Jordan, & Arguedas, 1978). Finally, patriarchy's ideology contains
beliefs that deny, excuse, exonerate, or justify extreme forms of male
behavior that epitomize men's power position vis-à-vis women, such
as rape, wife-beating, and incest, or that blame the victims of these
acts for their own victimization.

Ideology usually operates to make the powerless (the potential
victims of violence) at least as likely to acquiesce in it as the powerful
(Fanon, 1966). Thus the powerless may believe in their own inferiority; rape victims often express a sense of self-blame for their rapes
(Katz & Burt, 1988). In essence, ideology works to reduce the need
for much overt violence to maintain power, because the powerless,
believing the ideology, will not act in their own behalf. Rape victims
often will not report a rape because they are humiliated and they fear
they will not be believed.

Research has begun to document instances of how a justifying
ideology accomplishes this end of stifling the powerless. Rape myths
justify and excuse rape (Burt, 1980, 1983a, 1988; Burt & Albin, 1981;
Schwendinger & Schwendinger, 1974; Weis & Borges, 1973) and deny
victims appropriate support (Burt & Estep, 1981a; Warshaw, 1988),
while an ideological commitment to the sanctity of the home with-
holds protection for women and children against violence in the
family (Calvert, 1974; Finkelhor, 1979; Gil, 1973; Greenblat, 1985;
Steinmetz & Straus, 1974; Walker, 1979).

Conclusion

Rape myths allow rapists to rape with near impunity. They teach women
to blame themselves for their own victimization. They transform rape
by acquaintances, friends, and intimates into no rape at all. They support the use of violence, coupled with sexuality, as a mechanism for
keeping women powerless. At base, every woman lives with the fear
of rape and modifies her behavior in large and small ways to reduce
the likelihood of becoming a rape victim (Burt & Estep, 1981b; Burt
& Katz, 1985; Riger & Gordon, 1988). The myths make clear to her
that avoiding rape is her responsibility and that she will find little
sympathy for her situation should she be so careless as to allow herself to be raped. They make especially clear the disbelief and blame
she will encounter should she be so foolish as to be raped by someone
she knows. Rape myths keep her quiet and keep her controlled. Rape

and the threat of male violence are one of patriarchy's mechanisms for maintaining male control.

References

Ageton, S. S. (1983). *Sexual assault among adolescents*. Lexington, MA: Lexington Books.

Amir, M. (1971). *Patterns in forcible rape*. Chicago, IL: University of Chicago Press.

Benjamin, J. (1988). *The bonds of love: Psychoanalysis, feminism and the problem of domination*. New York: Pantheon Books.

Berger, V. (1977). Man's trial, woman's tribulation: Rape cases in the courtroom. *Columbia Law Review, 77*, 1–103.

Borgida, E. (1981). Legal reform and rape laws: Social psychological and constitutional considerations. In L. Bickman (Ed.). *Applied social psychology annual* (Vol. 2). Beverly Hills, CA: Sage.

Broverman, I. K., Vogel, S. R., Broverman, D. M., Clarkson, F. E., & Rosenkrantz, P. S. (1972). Sex-role stereotypes: A current appraisal. *Journal of Social Issues, 28*, 59–72.

Broverman, I. K., Broverman, D. M., Clarkson, F. E., Rosenkrantz, P. S., & Vogel, S. R. (1970). Sex-role stereotypes and clinical judgments of mental health. *Journal of Consulting Psychology, 34*, 1–7.

Brownmiller, S. (1975). *Against our will: Men, women, and rape*. New York: Simon & Schuster.

Burgess, A. W., & Holmstrom, L. L. (1979). *Rape: Crisis and recovery*. Bowie, MD: Brady.

Burt, M. R. (1980). Cultural myths and supports for rape. *Journal of Personality and Social Psychology, 38*, 217–230.

Burt, M. R. (1983a). Justifying personal violence: A comparison of rapists and the general public. *Victimology: An International Journal, 8*, 131–150.

Burt, M. R. (1983b). A conceptual framework for victimological research. *Victimology: An International Journal, 8*, 261–268.

Burt, M. R. (1988). Cultural myth, violence against women, and the law. *Drew Gateway, 58*, 25–37.

Burt, M. R., & Albin, R. S. (1981). Rape myths, rape definitions, and probability of conviction. *Journal of Applied Social Psychology, 11*, 212–230.

Burt, M. R., & Estep, R. E. (1981a). Who is a victim: Definitional problems in sexual victimization. *Victimology: An International Journal, 6*, 15–28.

Burt, M. R., & Estep, R. E. (1981b). Apprehension and fear: Learning a sense of sexual vulnerability. *Sex Roles, 7*, 511–522.

Burt, M. R., & Katz, B. L. (1985). Rape, robbery, and burglary: Responses to actual and feared criminal victimization, with special focus on women and the elderly. *Victimology: An International Journal, 10,* 325–358.

Calvert, R. (1974). Criminal and civil liability in husband-wife assaults. In S. Steinmetz & M. Straus (Eds.), *Violence in the family* (pp. 88–90). New York: Dodd, Mead.

Chafetz, J. S. (1984). *Sex and advantage: A comparative macro-structural theory of sex stratification.* Totowa, NJ: Rowman & Allanheld.

Check, J. V. P. (1984). *The hostility toward women scale.* Unpublished doctoral dissertation, University of Manitoba.

Clark, L. M. G., & Lewis, D. J. (1977). *Rape: the price of coercive sexuality.* Toronto: The Women's Press.

Deiter, P., & Heeter, C. (1989, March). *"Shooting her with video, drugs, bullets and promises. . .": MTV videos and adolescent viewers' beliefs about sex, violence and sexual violence.* Paper presented at the annual meeting of the Association for Women in Psychology, Newport, RI.

Dinnerstein, D. (1976). *The mermaid and the minotaur: Sexual arrangements and human malaise.* New York: Harper & Row.

Eagly, A. (1987). *Sex differences in social behavior: A social role interpretation.* Hillsdale, NJ: Erlbaum.

Epstein, C. F. (1988). *Deceptive distinctions: Theory and research on sex, gender and the social order.* New Haven, CT: Yale University Press.

Fanon, F. (1966). *The wretched of the earth.* New York: Grove Press/ Evergreen.

Farley, J. (1978). *Sexual shakedown: The sexual harassment of women on the job.* New York: McGraw-Hill.

Finkelhor, D. (1979). *Sexually victimized children.* New York: Free Press.

Gil, D. G. (1973). *Violence against children* (2nd ed.). Cambridge, MA: Harvard University Press.

Goodchilds, J. D., Zellman, G. L., Johnson, P. B., & Giarruso, R. (1988). Adolescents and their perceptions of sexual interactions. In A. W. Burgess (Ed.), *Rape and sexual assault* (Vol. II, pp. 245–270). New York: Garland.

Greenblat, C. S. (1985). Don't hit your wife . . . unless . . .: Preliminary findings on normative support for the use of force by husbands. *Victimology: An International Journal, 10,* 221–241.

Griffin, S. (1981). *Pornography and silence.* New York: Harper & Row.

Groth, A. N. (1979). *Men who rape: The psychology of the offender.* New York: Plenum Press.

Holliday, L. (1978). *The violent sex: Male psychobiology and the evolution of consciousness.* Guerneville, CA: Bluestocking Books.

Katz, B. L. (1986, August). *Effects of familiarity with the rapist on post-rape recovery.* Paper presented at the annual meeting of the American Psychological Association, Washington, DC.

Katz, B. L., & Burt, M. R. (1988). Self-blame in recovery from rape: Help or hindrance? In A. W. Burgess (Ed.), *Rape and sexual assault* (Vol. II, pp. 191–212). New York: Garland.

Koss, M. P. (1985). The hidden rape victim: Personality, attitudinal, and situational characteristics. *Psychology of Women Quarterly, 9,* 193–212.

Koss, M. P., Leonard, K. E., Oros, C. J., & Beezley, D. A. (1985). Nonstranger sexual aggression: A discriminant analysis of the psychological characteristics of undetected offenders. *Sex Roles, 12,* 981–992.

Lear, M. W. (1972). Q: If you rape a woman and steal her TV, what can they get you for in New York? A: Stealing her TV. *New York Times Magazine,* January 30, 1972, 10–11.

Macdonald, J. M. (1979). *Rape: offenders and their victims.* Springfield, IL: Thomas.

MacKinnon, C. (1982). Feminism, marxism, method and the state: An agenda for theory. *Signs, Journal of Women in Culture and Society, 7,* 515–544.

Malamuth, N. M. (1981). Rape proclivity among males. *Journal of Social Issues, 37,* 138–157.

Malamuth, N. M., & Donnerstein, E. (Eds.). (1984). *Pornography and sexual aggression.* New York: Academic Press.

Miller, J. B. (1976). *Toward a new psychology of women.* Boston: Beacon Press.

New York Commission on Judicial Conduct. (1984). Matter of Fromer. *1985 Annual Report, 135,* October 25, 1984.

New York Task Force on Women in the Courts. (1986–87). Report of the New York Task Force on Women in the Courts. *Fordham Urban Law Journal, 15,* 1–198.

Riger, S., & Gordon, M. T. (1988). The impact of crime on urban women. In A. W. Burgess (Ed.), *Rape and sexual assault* (Vol. II, pp. 293–316). New York: Garland.

Rowbotham, S. (1973). *Woman's consciousness, man's world.* Hammondsworth, England: Penguin.

Russell, D. E. H. (1984). *Sexual exploitation.* Beverly Hills, CA: Sage.

Schneider, E. M., Jordan, S. B., & Arguedas, C. C. (1978). Representation of women who defend themselves in response to physical or sexual assault. *Heresies, 6,* 100.

Schwendinger, J., & Schwendinger, H. (1974). Rape myths: In legal, theoretical, and everyday practice. *Crime and Social Issues, 1,* 18–26.

Silbert, M. (1988). Compounding factors in the rape of street prostitutes. In A. W.. Burgess (Ed.), *Rape and sexual assault* (Vol. II, pp. 75–90). New York: Garland.

Steinmetz, S. K., & Straus, M. A. (Eds.). (1974). *Violence in the family.* New York: Dodd, Mead.

Walker, L. (1979). *Battered women.* New York: Harper & Row.

Warshaw, R. (1988). *I never called it rape: The* Ms. *report on recognizing, fighting, and surviving date and acquaintance rape.* New York: Harper & Row.

Webster, P. (1978). Politics of rape in primitive society. *Heresies, 6,* 16.

Weis, K., & Borges, S. (1973). Victimology and rape: The case of the legitimate victim. *Issues in Criminology, 8,* 71–115.

Westkott, M. (1986). *The feminist legacy of Karen Horney.* New Haven, CT: Yale University Press.

Wood, P. L. (1973). The victim in a forcible rape case: A feminist view. *American Criminal Law Review, 11,* 335–354.

12

Sexual Aggression, Masculinity, and Fathers

~

David Lisak

THE FEMINIST CRITIQUE OF RAPE has broadened the scope of social scientists' efforts to understand why men rape.[1] The critique has contextualized what had been a narrowly focused view by demonstrating the critical importance of sociological and cultural forces in producing sexual aggression. This transformation in understanding why rape occurs has progressed dialectically, fostered by a vigorous reaction to the original, individual-focused and psychopathology-oriented theories. As a result, the new perspectives often have been expounded in opposition to the old ones. Since they are conceptualized as opposing one another, the old perspective is rejected in favor of the new. Thus, over two decades, sociocultural and psychological perspectives on why men rape have emerged as antagonistic and often mutually exclusive approaches.

These two levels of analysis can be combined, however, to help explain the origins of some of the motivations which lead men to rape. I argue that cultural forces, by shaping both the proximal and distal environment in which male children are raised, contribute to the creation of psychological dynamics which in turn become the wellspring of attitudes, dispositions, and behaviors that lead to sexual aggression.

From David Lisak, "Sexual Aggression, Masculinity, and Fathers," *Signs: Journal of Women in Culture and Society* 16, no. 2 (1991): 238–43, 246–62. © 1991 by the University of Chicago Press. Reprinted by permission of the University of Chicago Press and David Lisak.

Since the history of psychological explanations of rapists' motivations is replete with references to pathogenic mothering, I want to emphasize that this essay is not about "smothering" mothers, "castrating" mothers, or mother-headed households. However, it is about women, who are the victims of rapists, whose lives are constrained and restricted in myriad ways by the fear of rape and by their efforts to avoid it, and whose parenting roles are constrained by a pervasive gender system that may encourage it.

The study of rape remains one of the most politically and psychologically sensitive areas within the social sciences. Researchers have only recently begun to document and understand its impact on the lives of women, often against virulent prejudices. Yet, even as comprehension has increased, there remains a tendency among many to deny the reality of this impact—the pain, often long term, with which the survivor lives, as well as the effects on the survivor's friends and family and on all women's ability to live their lives without fear. Then, if denial gives way at all, there is often a tendency to reject complex explanations for why men rape, and to look for a simple, powerful explanation that might yield an effective solution to the problem. This chapter does not provide a unitary or simple theory of why men rape. Rather, I argue that the combination of several contributing factors produces a constellation of motivations that are conducive to sexual aggression.

A decade of epidemiological and psychological research amply documents that at least one in four women are victims of rape or attempted rape during their lifetime.[2] The psychological repercussions have also been thoroughly documented. Survivors of rape often experience acute posttraumatic reactions and may suffer severe bouts of depression, anxiety, and fear as well as impaired social functioning. These repercussions often wane after several months, but serious psychological disturbance has been documented in survivors years after their assaults.[3]

Apart from challenging the widespread denial of the impact of rape, these research findings also have had a dramatic impact on the study of rapists. One of the first questions that emerged from the prevalence studies was, Who is doing this raping? Certainly it cannot be the men incarcerated for rape, for only a tiny handful of the rape survivors identified in these prevalence studies acknowledged that they had reported the rape to the authorities.[4] This presented a serious challenge to the existing knowledge base on rapists, which was founded on the study of men incarcerated in prisons or special treatment facilities for sex offenders. If these men represent only a tiny fraction of rapists, can the data gleaned from studying them be generalized to the vast population of rapists at large? . . .

Feminist-informed Study of Sexually Aggressive Men

In stark contrast to the old perspective on rape and rapists, the feminist analysis located the cause of rape in the culture in which it is embedded. As the myriad manifestations of a misogynist and patriarchal culture were articulated, it became increasingly clear that rape could be reasonably defined as a concrete acting out of culturally normative beliefs and images. The objectification of women in culture-wide images, such as in advertising, the denigration of women in pornography, and the institutional oppression of women as it is encoded in the legal system were all documented as examples of cultural norms that directly and inexorably lead to rape. In this new context, rapists were seen not as pathological deviants from societal norms but, rather, as normal men who act out in individual dramas what their surrounding culture perpetrates institutionally.[5]

Following these trends, research on why men rape shifted toward examining the ways in which culturally supported attitudes and norms foster sexually aggressive behavior, among imprisoned rapists, but with increasing emphasis on college men. This research demonstrated an association between rape myths, stereotyped sex role beliefs, and attitudes—the culture's misogynist messages—and both the propensity for, and actual perpetration of, sexual aggression.[6]

The successful demonstration of an association between culturally embedded attitudes and sexually aggressive behavior has strengthened the sociocultural perspective and perhaps encouraged a concurrent rejection of individual, psychologically based perspectives. Researchers adopting the sociocultural perspective have tended to equate the old psychopathology model—rapists as sexually maladjusted or psychotic—with any model taking a psychological view. For example, in a review of the etiology of rape, Ilsa Lottes saw little evidence that rapists could be differentiated from other criminals along dimensions of adjustment or pathology, and much evidence to support a sociocultural explanation of rape. Lottes concludes, "Adherents of the sociocultural etiology do not consider most rapists as sick and psychologically distinct from other groups of men."[7] This conclusion, which was originally based on the evidence for differential psychopathology among rapists, was explicitly broadened to reject the possibility that rapists may be psychologically distinct from nonrapists. Thus, psychopathology has been equated with psychology, and in the process the possibility of discovering meaningful psychological differences between rapists and nonrapists has been discarded.

Yet recent studies of sexually aggressive college men provide evidence that there are indeed consistent differences between rapists and nonrapists in certain psychological dimensions. Several different measures of hostility toward women and dominance motives, as well as factors that may underlie these characteristics, have successfully differentiated sexually aggressive from nonaggressive men in college student samples.[8] While these findings can be interpreted as the affective sequelae of rape-supportive attitudes, they may equally be seen as the emotional and psychodynamic precursors to those attitudes. Some men may be psychologically predisposed to so thoroughly adopt the ambient culture's misogyny that they are capable of using force to overcome a woman's resistance. If so, we need to explore the ingredients, cultural and individual, which synergistically produce this predisposition to rape.

There are actually few data available on which to base an analysis of these ingredients' interactions. For, despite the ubiquity of rape, there is relatively little research that attempts to unravel the complex network of factors that leads to sexually aggressive acts. One approach is to study unreported rapists, men who raped but who were never reported to authorities—a sample of men perhaps more representative of rapists than samples taken from prisons and treatment facilities.[9] These data can be augmented with information from other sources and by theoretical work that helps provide a framework for understanding the etiology of sexual aggression. . . .[10]

Motivations to Rape: Data from Unreported Rapists

The main body of the David Lisak and Susan Roth study consisted of the evaluation of fifteen unreported rapists and fifteen control subjects.[11] All of the subjects were junior- and senior-class males in full-time attendance at a major Southeastern university. They were recruited to the study via their responses on a questionnaire that, among other things, assessed the types of sexual interactions they had experienced. All subjects first went through a screening interview. In the case of rapists, this was to verify that they had committed acts that conform to most legal definitions of rape or attempted rape. In the case of the control subjects, it was to verify that they had not committed such acts. None of the rapists defined themselves as such, nor their behaviors as rape, and they were typically very open about describing the levels of force they had used in the course of sexual interactions. They provided highly detailed accounts of these episodes, leaving little room for suspicion that they were not describing, from memory, actual events.

Demographically, the majority of the subjects were from upper-middle-class backgrounds, and they came from virtually all regions of the United States. Of the fifteen rapists, thirteen were European-American and two were African-American. Among the control subjects, the ratio was fourteen to one. The occupations of the subjects' fathers were typically white collar and mostly high paying. Among the fathers of the rapists there were two high-ranking career military men, several business executives, a banker, a professor, and a surgeon. Three of the fathers held blue-collar jobs. Among the fathers of the control subjects, there were again several business executives, two medical doctors, a lawyer, a professor, and a high-level government bureaucrat. One of the fathers held a blue-collar job.[12]

While there were no apparent differences between the two groups in the fathers' occupations, there were some differences in the occupational status of the subjects' mothers. Among the rapists, nine of the twelve mothers did not work outside the home. Of the remaining three, one began working when the subject was ten years old, and two held full-time jobs throughout the subjects' childhood (a teacher and a food service worker). In contrast, among the control subjects, only four mothers did not work outside the home, and one of these was president of a community organization, heavily committed to volunteer activities. Of the remaining eight, six held full-time jobs throughout their children's childhood (three teachers, a social worker, a nurse, and a caterer), one began working when the subject turned ten, and one worked part time in the family business. In sum, the families of the rapists appeared to conform more closely to the stereotypical American nuclear family, in which the husband is the breadwinner and the wife attends to children and home.

The fifteen rapists were responsible for twenty-two rapes and five attempted rapes, almost all in nonstranger situations. All used force or threats of force to overcome a woman's resistance to either sexual intercourse or oral sex. In most cases the force consisted of the use of overwhelming body weight while pinning the woman's arms. In at least four cases, the victim was also struck or pushed around. In many cases, force was augmented by threats of further violence.[13]

The rapists scored significantly higher than control subjects on standardized measures of hostility toward women, underlying anger motivations, dominance as a motive for sexual interactions, underlying power motivations, and on two indices of hypermasculinity. The interviews were analyzed to assess the subjects' relationships with both parents. Each statement about either parent was coded either negative, positive, or neutral. Rapists made significantly more negative statements and significantly fewer positive statements about their fathers than did control subjects. They made significantly more negative statements about their mothers, but not fewer positive statements. Correlations between these parental variables and the standardized measures noted above indicated that, the worse the subject's relationship with his father, the more did he express hostility toward women, dominance over women, underlying power motivations, and hypermasculine attitudes. In contrast, subjects' relationships with their mothers did not correlate with any of these measures.[14]

While these quantitative data highlight marked differences between the rapists and control subjects, a deeper understanding of the nature and implications of these differences requires a qualitative analysis, in particular of the rapists' more negative relationships with their fathers and mothers. What follows are examples of the statements made by rapists and control subjects about each of their parents, the types of statements that contributed to each of three statistically significant findings, more negative statements about fathers and mothers by the rapists, and more positive statements about fathers by the controls.

First, let us look at the data on fathers. Three of the rapists' fathers were physically abusive toward their sons. Their violence ranged from infrequent, closed-fist striking to routine striking and beating, resulting in physical injury.[15] One of these rapists described such an incident when he was fifteen years old: "Once I got into a real argument with him. He started egging me on, so I called him a dick. He slugged me in the face, then dragged my face across the carpet. I was bleeding from my forehead to my chin. I wimped out and screamed, 'I'm sorry, I'm sorry.' "

Much more commonly, rapists described their fathers as both physically and emotionally distant. Most fathers were successful professionals whose work kept them away from home for long stretches. Once home, they were frequently described as tired and unavailable to their sons. One rapist described his father this way:

> He's so tied into his business that it takes him away from family life. His business trips come first. He's always traveling to markets and overseas. And the work pressures get to him. When he's home he goes downstairs and watches TV or works in the yard. . . . Our family doesn't go on many vacations. He doesn't like to take time away from the office. He's really dedicated. He gets one month vacation, but he only takes two weeks, and even then he spends most of that with his colleagues hunting and fishing.

Other rapists focused more on their fathers' emotional absence and unavailability. One described his father as "so unemotional he's almost numb." Another described meal times this way: "He'd come home and go to his room. Then we'd eat. He'd be silent and often really angry at the table. Everything I did was wrong. If we were alone together in a room I'd feel really uncomfortable."

Many of the rapists complained of never spending any time with their fathers alone and said they felt they had little or nothing in common with them. Five of the rapists also expressed clear disappointment in their fathers, ranging from mild expressions, such as "I always wanted my Dad to [back me up] but he never did," to more overt disappointment: "He's a frustrated person in a lot of ways. He always wanted to be famous and powerful in the world and he chose a dull life as a banker. . . . He got fired as the vice president of one bank. . . . He would go to work where he was just a cog and he'd often come home cranky. He had a tendency to yell. He would be pent up inside and then explode," to outright contempt: "I blamed her but I also blamed him for having no backbone and never standing up to her. . . . My stepmother made all the decisions. All the money, everything's in her name or jointly owned. I lost respect for him for that."

While several of the control subjects described mildly ambivalent relationships with their fathers, the vast majority described relationships characterized by greater warmth, closeness, and interaction than those of the rapists. Some of the control subjects were effusive in their listing of their father's qualities and in their admiration for their father: "My hero was my Dad. He had this big beard. He was always free and liberal and fun. He was always relaxed, laid back. He can deal with things well. I've always tried to emulate that and his manners and his expressions. I'd always try to copy his manners." This subject did voice some negative feelings about not spending as much time with his father as he would have liked, but the disappointment was embedded in positive characterizations. For example, he said, "We'd play basketball, but not enough," and went on to say that he and his father did things together "every day after work." In contrast to many of the rapists, he also described his father as "openly affectionate." Explicit descriptions of their father's warmth were present in the protocols of four of the control subjects, who used terms such as "loving," "caring," "warm," and "affectionate."

One of the starkest differences between the control subjects and rapists was in the frequency with which the controls described themselves as "like" their father in some way. Six of the control subjects made such references. They described having similar interests as their fathers, and having similar personality traits—some they viewed as positive and others as less so. Examples included:

> He has a lot of excuses when he doesn't come through with something. Then he'll come through. I tend to be like that, too.
>
> I'm majoring in biology. My father's a biologist actually, a professor.
>
> I see myself being a lot more like my father now.
>
> I'm a lot like him. He partied hard in college also. He could have done better. . . . In childhood you're closer to your mother but later I found out my Dad and I had more and more in common and we are more similar than with my mother.
>
> I'm the spitting image of him.
>
> He was a lot like me, laid back, but when he believed in something he was very stubborn. . . . All my life I wanted to be a doctor like my Dad, but I think the amount of work is extremely hard on family life.

This last statement reflects another difference between the control subjects and the rapists. As noted earlier, some of the controls talked about not seeing enough of their fathers but did so without the bitterness that was present in some of the rapists' statements. The controls described their fathers as wanting to spend more time with them than circumstances allowed or voicing regrets about the lack of time. For example, the control subject quoted above decided not to pursue a career in medicine because of the workload and its consequences. "When I go home I can see Dad in his chair. We used to talk a lot, and he'd tell me that he regretted devoting so much to work and career that he missed out on family life. He didn't want me to make the same mistake." Other subjects described how their fathers spent time with them even in the midst of busy schedules: "He's pretty busy, but he always has time Sunday for a couple of beers with me and a football game"; "even when he was working so much we'd go out into the backyard and play ball together."

The differences between rapists and control subjects in the number of negative statements about mothers were less consistent than the differences in the father variables. Only one rapist made as many positive as negative comments about his father; the rest made more negative comments and often many more. In contrast, every control subject made more positive than negative comments about his father: this ratio also applied to the control subjects' descriptions of their mothers. In contrast, among the rapists, six had positive ratios—they made more positive than negative comments about their mothers—and four had negative ratios.

The negative statements about mothers made by the rapists were of three main types: descriptions of negative personality traits; descriptions of behaviors; and descriptions of conflicts. Negative personality traits included "depressed," "flighty," "irresponsible," "weak," "incredibly aggressive," "dependent," and "anxious." Negative behaviors included "nagging," "yelling," "overbearing," "intrusive," "inquisitive," and behaviors which the rapists experienced as controlling and restrictive. Many of these characterizations were made in the context of describing conflicts with their mothers, and these almost invariably centered around issues of autonomy. For instance: "She was always yelling and screaming at us. . . . I'd always try to do exactly the opposite of what she wanted"; "Mom thought dances were evil and wouldn't let us go"; "I'd come home in a bad mood and Mom would be real inquisitive. Sometimes I wouldn't want to talk but she'd keep asking."

Two rapists in particular described protracted conflicts with their mothers that centered on their efforts to get involved in activities and relationships outside the home. One rapist described his mother's reaction to his first dating foray, and his departure for college: "She didn't like the idea of her only son having a girlfriend, leaving the nest. She was really upset. I think I went out with [my first girlfriend] out of rebellion. . . . She would always tease me about this girl in front of my friends. . . . She didn't want me to leave, or have a girlfriend, or go to college. She drove me here and cried on my bed she was so upset."

Another rapist, whose father died when he was six years old, described a long history of intense conflicts with his mother over very similar issues. He said she treated him and his sister "almost like we were an extension of her own life," forcing them to stay home and study and dramatically restricting their social activities. He described one incident this way: "In ninth grade I told my Mom I wanted to go to Homecoming dance. There was a girl I wanted to ask. But my Mom wanted me to go with this other girl from the church. So my Mom called the girl's Mom and arranged it. I didn't like that girl at all. My Mom picked her up and gave us a ride there. I had wanted my friend to drive us but my Mom wouldn't allow it. It wasn't fun. It was very embarrassing. . . . She wanted total control of my life."

Sexual Aggression and Male Gender Development

The widespread gender-based division of parental responsibilities in this culture has allocated certain roles to the feminine gender and others to the masculine. As a result, mothers are the primary caretakers of children, especially during the early, formative years of childhood. This mother-centered child-rearing practice has important implications for both the gender identification and psychological development of children, implications that have been articulated by scholars such as Nancy Chodorow and Dorothy Dinnerstein.[16] When early child care is exclusively the responsibility of women, a child will experience basic, developmental processes in relation not only to a particular person but also to that person's gender.

One of these basic developmental processes is what psychologists from many different perspectives have termed the formation of the self, or ego. Although the language used to describe this process varies across perspectives, a common thread is that the self arises out of the infant's interaction with its environment, the world of things and people around it. The particulars of that environment are heavily determined by culture and subculture. Chodorow and Dinnerstein argue that the practice of mother-centered child rearing becomes a fundamental aspect of the infant's environment, one with important implications for the child's development. Dinnerstein writes:

> The earliest roots of antagonism to women lie in the period before the infant has any clear idea of where the self ends and the outside world begins, or any way of knowing that the mother is a separately sentient being. At this stage a woman is the helpless child's main contact with the natural surround, the center of everything the infant wants and feels drawn to, fears losing and feels threatened by. She is the center also of the non-self, an unbounded, still unarticulated region within which the child labors to define itself and to discover the outlines of durable objects, creatures, themes. She is this global, inchoate, all-embracing presence before she is a person, a discrete finite human individual with a subjectivity of her own.
>
> When she does become a person, her person-ness is shot through for the child with these earlier qualities. And when it begins to be clear that this person is a female in a world of males and females, femaleness comes to be the name for, the embodiment of, these global and inchoate and all-embracing qualities, qualities very hard indeed to reconcile with person-ness as one has begun to feel it inside oneself.[17]

Jungian psychologists have contributed another dimension to this process of self-development. They argue for the importance of an intrapsychic aspect—the consolidation of ego consciousness in relation to states of unconsciousness. According to this perspective, unconsciousness is the source from which ego consciousness—the capacity for conscious awareness and self-reflection—emerges. Infants are initially wholly unconscious beings, with only a flickering of consciousness and with no sense of either self or other. While the ego gradually emerges out of the infant's growing repertoire of capacities and accumulating experiences, consciousness also emerges and expands. The infant gradually learns to differentiate between inner and outer world, between inner images, dreams, impulses, and fantasies and the world of external stimuli.[18]

Thus, these two processes of early development, integrally intertwined, run parallel. In both, there is the implication that a new entity—the self, ego consciousness—emerges from something that preceded it. In the case of the self, it is the infant's immediate environment, particularly its principal caretakers, that preceded it. In the case of ego consciousness, it is states of unconsciousness (sleep, twilight fantasy states) that preceded it. Further, at both levels, the emerging entity is destined to experience that which preceded it ambivalently—as both a life-giving source and a restraining, regressive pull. This ambivalence is built into the relationship, since the new entity that is developing can only experience and define itself in relation to that from which it is emerging. Thus, the embracing arms that protected are simultaneously and increasingly experienced also as enveloping, perhaps even engulfing. The comforting solace of sleep becomes the enemy of an ego consciousness straining to stretch its contact with, and awareness of, an increasingly captivating external world.

Given this context, and as a consequence of the gender-based division of early child care, the developing infant's sense of self and its emerging ego consciousness become intertwined with "female" and with all of the profound, and profoundly ambivalent, experiences of this early and foundational stage of development. To the child, it is in relation to a female that it experiences vulnerability and protection, dependency and being cared for, the reciprocation of emotional intimacy, and the intense pleasures of sensual contact. It is also in relation to a female that the child experiences the beginnings of agency, will, and boundaries and the threats and restraints to these newly discovered capacities. Thus, the female is inevitably cast as the omnipotent Goddess who is both the bottomless source of nurturance and comfort and also a restraining and a potentially devouring threat. Simultaneously, the female becomes associated with the threat of ego dissolution—the loss of ego consciousness. . . .[19]

The interview material on rapists in the Lisak and Roth study is consistent with these theoretical approaches. The basic conflict with mothers centered on their involvement with their sons, while the conflict with fathers centered on their noninvolvement. Thus, the complaints made by several rapists that their mothers constrained their autonomy must be viewed in the context of the psychodynamics of mother-child relations in gender-based child-rearing practices. The rapists' responses to many of the questionnaire items suggest that these child-rearing practices may lead to an association of the "fear of reengulfment" with all women. On the questionnaires, the rapists endorsed many items that expressed a view of women as potentially hostile, powerful adversaries whom they must control and dominate lest they be controlled and dominated. Many of their stories dealt with the threat of being "trapped," "devoured," or in some way ambushed by a female. Women are described as "cold," "heartless," "deceitful," and "callous." A very common story line involved a woman who entices men with the promise of sexual access but who then heartlessly reneges and rejects them.[20]

This association between women and the force that threatens to suppress both self and ego consciousness—an association perpetuated by traditional parenting arrangements—is a crucial backdrop for the male child's gender identification process. He carries this powerful psychological legacy into what has been dubbed the "oedipal" stage, the phase of childhood during which the gender identification process takes a major step. Through a combination of pressures both from within and beyond his family, the male child begins to learn, consciously and unconsciously, the meaning of gender and his particular place in a gender-divided world. He learns that he must suppress a part of himself—the part labeled "feminine" by his culture—the part that he discovered and experienced in the context of that primary relationship with his mother.[21] In effect, the culture first puts him in the arms of someone whom it labels "woman," so that he associates the vulnerability, dependency, and emotional intimacy he discovered in that relationship with "female," and then, a few years later, the culture demands that he deny those very aspects of himself because they are "feminine" and he must now be "masculine." This demand is the basis of what Chodorow terms the male's "negative identification." He must first define what he is not—a female—and then he must find a new self-definition as a male.

The role of the father in this transformation depends on more than his mere presence, for he must provide his son with an opportunity to internalize "masculinity," not merely imitate it. Internalization of the masculine gender, a process that is greatly facilitated by the internalization of aspects of the father, is necessary if the male child is to comply successfully with cultural expectations of masculinity. Thus, if some aspect of the father's personality or behavior seriously interferes with this internalization process, then the son's ability to execute the self-mutilation—that is, embrace a "masculine identification"—may be jeopardized.[22]

There is a sizable research literature on the effects of inadequate fathering on various aspects of male development, including "masculine identification." It provides some data and considerable theoretical argument to suggest that inadequate fathering, in the context of the traditional nuclear family, may impair "masculine identification" and can result in an array of adverse consequences, from various forms of psychopathology to low self-esteem, poor cognitive development, antisocial behavior, and hypermasculine behavior.[23]

The research literature on male juvenile delinquency is replete with references to the etiological significance of father absence and inadequate fathering. One study comparing delinquents and nondelinquents on the quality of their relationships with their parents yielded findings very similar to those from the Lisak and Roth study of unreported rapists. Compared to nondelinquents, delinquents had more negative perceptions of their mothers in three of ten categories (including more "rejecting" and more "demanding"). However, the data on fathers were even more striking. In seven of the ten categories delinquents had significantly more negative perceptions. These categories included more "rejecting," "demanding," and "neglecting" and less "loving."[24]

Walter Miller argued that delinquents are molded by the values of a subculture that places an inordinate value on "toughness," characterized by a hypermasculine array of behaviors and attitudes, including an absence of sentimentality and a view of women as objects to be conquered. The origins of this concern with toughness, he argued, are in the lack of a consistent male figure in the upbringing of many delinquents. This absence creates difficulty in identifying with and learning the male role, with a consequent "compulsive reaction formation" of hypermasculine behavior. These youths then congregate, forming juvenile gangs that become the paternally deprived male's first real opportunity to learn the male role. Thus, the gang becomes a preeminent source for the youth's masculine identification—a gang made up of other, equally insecure youths. Together, they form a subculture exalting the hypermasculine values which protect them from their underlying insecurities, values that often lead to antisocial behavior. A similar dynamic has been argued by several other delinquency researchers.[25]

These theories on the links between paternal deprivation, insecure masculine identification, and gang subculture may offer some explanation for the data provided by Eugene Kanin.[26] He argued that the college date rapists he interviewed were influenced by peer groups that exalted sexual conquest as a primary measure of self-esteem. Kanin viewed the peer group as the originator of the individual male's pre-occupation with conquest. The delinquency data suggest a more complex relationship, in which insecure males are drawn to such peer groups out of a common need to bolster their insecure masculine identification: the culture and activities of the peer group—misogynist beliefs and aggressive behavior directed at women—are designed to answer this common need.

Father-distant Child Rearing and the Culture of Violence

Support for this theory is also to be found in cross-cultural research on the societal correlates of child-rearing practices. Robert Munroe, Ruth Munroe, and John Whiting show that there is considerable evidence from cross-cultural research that indicates that in societies characterized by mother-centered child rearing and relative father absence, male children typically experience "sex identity conflicts" in the course of development.[27] This pervasive conflict has "covert"' manifestations, such as the couvade, wherein males may express their underlying feminine identifications by mimicking female pregnancy symptoms. It may also have "overt" manifestations, such as various forms of hypermasculine behavior that serve as a defense against the underlying and antecedent feminine identification.

Beatrice Whiting argued that interpersonal violence perpetrated by males results, in part, from "protest masculinity," which is in turn a consequence of particular child-rearing practices. In a detailed study of six societies, Whiting gave evidence that protest masculinity is more prevalent in societies where men and women are more segregated (meals, social activities, and work), and where children sleep with their mothers and have little contact with their fathers until they are six to fourteen years old. Whiting argues that males who are raised in these conditions—the equivalent of "father absence" in the delinquency literature—face a "sex-identity conflict" when they are thrust into the male world. Significantly, Whiting clearly attributes the conflict not to any innate need for the male to achieve a masculine identification but to the conflicting demands of his culture. She writes, "It will be a problem for those boys who have formed a strong identification with women only if the people in the world make it clear that being a man is very different from being a woman and that men are more important and more powerful. For these boys there is a dramatic change in their evaluation of who controls resources. . . ."[28]

Finding a cross-cultural association between father-distant child rearing and the prevalence of "macho" behavior, denigration of females and violence, Scott Coltrane concludes that women are accorded more respect in societies in which they share some control over resources and in which mothers and fathers are both engaged in child care. "When fathers help take care of children, boys grow up with fewer needs to define themselves in opposition to women and men are less inclined to hypermasculine displays of male superiority."[29]

These cross-cultural studies suggest that, at the level of individual development, within any given society, there will exist intracultural differences that will parallel those demonstrated in the cross-cultural research cited above. Thus, differences in child-rearing practices between societal subcultures or even families may be comparable to differences between cultures, producing parallel differences in male gender development. Thus, the rapists, who largely were raised in father-distant, traditional, European-American nuclear families, showed many similarities to the male behavior described in societies characterized by father-distant child-rearing practices. They showed evidence of hypermasculine behavior and dispositions, hostility toward women, dominance, and a propensity to perpetrate violence against women.

This accumulation of evidence from cross-cultural research and delinquency studies provides a coherent framework within which to understand the demonstrated differences in the Lisak and Roth study between the unreported rapists and the control subjects: their anger and power motivations, their hypermasculine attitudes, their more ambivalent relationships with their mothers, and their more starkly negative relationships with their fathers.

Perhaps the major implication of this theoretical framework is that the ultimate solution to the problem of rape will be a fundamental alteration in our concept of gender—in its dethronement from its stature as an indelible part of the natural order. Exposing the nefarious and tragic collusion between a gender-divided society and male sexual aggression must be part of the process of eroding its status.

However, while this erosion takes place, a critical examination of the consequences of father-distant child rearing may help to mitigate some of the adverse effects of gendering on personality development. If we must dichotomize ourselves along gender lines, let us at least not dichotomize certain fundamental roles, such as the parenting of children, which have such far-reaching effects on how the children conceptualize themselves and their relations with other people.

Notes

1. See Susan Brownmiller, *Against Our Will* (New York: Simon & Schuster, 1975); Andra Medea and Kathleen Thompson, *Against Rape* (New York: Farrar,

Straus & Giroux, 1974); and Diana Russell, *The Politics of Rape* (New York: Stein & Day, 1975) for examples of the feminist critique of rape.

2. Two of the most widely cited and methodologically sound epidemiological studies are Diana Russell, "The Prevalence and Incidence of Forcible Rape and Attempted Rape of Females," *Victimology* 7, no. 1 (1982): 81–93; and Mary Koss, Christine Gidycz, and Nadine Wisniewski, "The Scope of Rape: Incidence and Prevalence of Sexual Aggression and Victimization in a National Sample of Higher Education Students," *Journal of Consulting and Clinical Psychology* 55, no. 2 (1987): 162–70.

3. For data on the repercussions of rape, see Susan Roth, Kathy Wayland, and Mary Woolsey, "Victimization History and Victim-Assailant Relationships as Factors in Recovery from Sexual Assault," *Journal of Traumatic Stress* 3, no. 1 (1990): 169–80; and Dean Kilpatrick et al., "Mental Health Correlates of Criminal Victimization: A Random Community Sample," *Journal of Consulting and Clinical Psychology* 53, no. 6 (1985): 866–73. For a phenomenological description of the aftermath of sexual trauma, see Susan Roth and Leslie Lebowitz, "The Experience of Sexual Trauma," *Journal of Traumatic Stress* 1, no. 1 (1988): 79–107.

4. Koss, Gidycz, and Wisniewski reported that 5 percent of victims reported their assaults to the authorities. In Russell, the figure was 9.5 percent. Furthermore, only a small proportion of men reported for rape are actually convicted and sent to prison.

5. See n. 1 above for examples of the cultural analysis of rape.

6. See Diana Scully and Joseph Marolla, "Convicted Rapists' Vocabulary of Motive: Excuses and Justification," *Social Problems* 31, no. 5 (1984): 530–44, for data on the attitudes of convicted rapists; and Neil Malamuth, "Predictors of Naturalistic Sexual Aggression," *Journal of Personality and Social Psychology* 50, no. 2 (1986): 953–62, for data on the attitudes of self-reported sexually aggressive college men.

7. Ilsa Lottes, "Sexual Socialization and Attitudes toward Rape," in *Rape and Sexual Assault*, vol. 2, ed. Ann Wolbert Burgess (New York: Garland, 1988), 195.

8. See, e.g., Malamuth; and David Lisak and Susan Roth, "Motivational Factors in Nonincarcerated Sexually Aggressive Men," *Journal of Personality and Social Psychology* 55, no. 5 (1988): 795–802.

9. Lisak and Roth, "Motivational Factors," and David Lisak and Susan Roth, "Motives and Psychodynamics of Self-reported, Unincarcerated Rapists," *American Journal of Orthopsychiatry* 60, no. 2 (1990): 268–80.

10. The psychological perspective that will be articulated in this article is typically characterized as "psychodynamic," reflecting its emphasis on unconscious and dynamic motivational factors. It is only one among several psychological perspectives that have been applied to the understanding of rapists. Thus, it should be viewed as one part of an aggregate explanation and not as an attempt to provide a unitary theory of why men rape.

11. For further details of this study, see Lisak and Roth, "Motives and Psychodynamics" (n. 9 above).

12. Demographic information and data on family relationships are given for twelve subjects from each group, since three rapists dropped out of the study before their evaluation was completed.

13. It should be noted that while the level of overt threat and violence associated with acquaintance rapes is often less than that associated with stranger

rapes—e.g., there were no reports of weapons used—the experience for the victim is still one of extreme helplessness and terror. Further, there is evidence that the long-term repercussions for victims of acquaintance rapes are often as serious as those for victims of stranger rapes. See Leslie Lebowitz, "The Phenomenology of the Survivor of Rape" (Ph.D. diss., Duke University, 1990), for a detailed analysis of survivors' experiences of both stranger and acquaintance rapes. See Roth, Wayland, and Woolsey (n. 3 above); and Thomas McCahill, Linda Meyer, and Arthur Fischman, *The Aftermath of Rape* (Lexington, Mass.: Lexington, 1979), for data on the psychological repercussions of acquaintance rape.

14. See Lisak and Roth, "Motives and Psychodynamics," for details of the quantitative results.

15. Not surprisingly, these three rapists were among the four who reported using the highest levels of force during the rapes they committed, including choking, striking, and severe forms of intimidation and threat.

16. See Dorothy Dinnerstein, *The Mermaid and the Minotaur* (New York: Harper Colophon, 1976); and Nancy Chodorow, *The Reproduction of Mothering* (Berkeley: University of California Press, 1978).

17. Dinnerstein, 93.

18. See Erich Neumann, *The Origins and History of Consciousness* (Princeton, N.J.: Princeton University Press, 1954), for a comprehensive analysis of the development of consciousness from the Jungian perspective.

19. Dinnerstein's description of the relationship between the infant and the mother and Neumann's descriptions of the relationship between consciousness and unconsciousness are remarkably parallel. While Neumann casts the association between the mother and the unconscious in universal, archetypal terms, Dinnerstein sees similar associations but casts them within the framework of mother-centered child-rearing practices.

20. Many of the rapists produced projective stories that dealt with the themes of initiation, fear of women's power, and a need to control women. Initiation themes were often expressed in stories of men who go off to war or on solo adventures; in many cases these stories ended in failure rather than heroic deeds. The most prevalent examples of the fear of women's power were stories which implicitly or explicitly compared women to spiders who entrap and then kill their prey—men. The rapists' need to control and dominate women was expressed in myriad forms, from fantasies of having sex with dead or unconscious women, to stories about men manipulating women into having sex or tricking them into intimacy only to leave them once their "conquest" is complete.

21. It should be noted that intracultural variations will have an impact on how threatening "feminine" aspects of personality are for the developing male. For example, a male raised in a father-distant or father-absent home, but one in which gender norms are mitigated by countercultural influences, may not perceive these aspects of himself as "feminine," although he will still have to confront the wider culture, its gender biases, and its pressures to conform with "appropriate" gender behavior. See Sandra Bem, "Gender Schema Theory and Its Implications for Child Development: Raising Gender-aschematic Children in a Gender-schematic Society," *Signs: Journal of Women in Culture and Society* 8, no. 4 (Summer 1983): 598–616. "Gender Schema Theory," articulated by Bem, also predicts that certain individuals, because of differences in socialization histories, will be more attuned to gender as a category and will be more likely to sustain rigid schemas about their own gender-appropriate behavior and that of other people around them.

22. See Nancy Chodorow, *The Reproduction of Mothering* (Berkeley: University of California Press, 1978), for a thorough analysis of the connection between mother-centered child rearing and the male's need to reject parts of himself identified with the mother and for a comprehensive description of the process of identification; and Eleanor Maccoby and Carol Jacklin, *The Psychology of Sex Differences* (Stanford, Calif.: Stanford University Press, 1974), 328–362, for a review of studies that suggest a particularly salient role for the father in the gendering of the son through socialization.

23. See Henry Biller, *Paternal Deprivation* (Lexington, Mass: Lexington, 1974), for a review of the literature on the effects of paternal absence and deficiency. It should be noted that in citing this research I am not trying to argue that insecure or incomplete masculine identification leads to mental health problems of an objective nature. Rather, the evidence suggests that it can lead to problems in adapting to a gender-divided environment.

24. Gene Medinnus, "Delinquents' Perceptions of Their Parents," *Journal of Consulting Psychology* 29, no. 6 (1965): 592–93.

25. See Joan McCord, William McCord, and Emily Thurber, "Some Effects of Paternal Absence on Male Children," *Journal of Abnormal and Social Psychology* 64, no. 5 (1962): 361–69; Walter Miller, "Lower Class Culture as a Generating Milieu of Gang Delinquency," *Journal of Social Issues* 14, no. 3 (1958): 5–19; David Lynn and William Sawrey, "The Effects of Father-Absence on Norwegian Boys and Girls," *Journal of Abnormal and Social Psychology* 59, no. 2 (1959): 258–62; and John Nash, "The Father in Contemporary Culture and Current Psychological Literature," *Child Development* 36, no. 1 (1965): 261–95.

26. Eugene Kanin, "Date Rape: Unofficial Criminals and Victims," *Victimology* 9, no. 1 (1984): 95–108, and "Date Rapists: Differential Sexual Socialization and Relative Deprivation," *Archives of Sexual Behavior* 14, no. 3 (1985): 219–31.

27. Robert Munroe, Ruth Munroe, and John Whiting, "Male Sex-Role Resolutions," In *Handbook of Cross-cultural Human Development*, ed. Ruth Munroe, Robert Munroe, and Beatrice Whiting (New York: STM Press, 1981), 611–32.

28. Beatrice Whiting, "Sex Identity Conflict and Physical Violence: A Comparative Study," *American Anthropologist* 67, pt. 2, no. 6 (1965): 123–40.

29. Scott Coltrane, "Hypermasculinity and Gender Difference in Cross-cultural Perspective" (University of California, Riverside, typescript), 22, and "Father-Child Relationships and the Status of Women: A Cross-cultural Study," *American Journal of Sociology* 93, no. 5 (1988): 1060–95.

IV   Institutional and
Cultural Context

Various institutional and cultural factors have an impact on the likelihood of rape and the social responses to rape. The first two articles address forces within our society that encourage sexual assault. In "Fraternities and Rape on Campus," Florida State University sociologists Patricia Yancey Martin and Robert Hummer argue that all-male fraternities create a socio-cultural context that fosters sexual coercion in relations with women. The authors identify specific norms and organizational practices of fraternities that contribute to coercive, often violent, sex: a narrow, stereotyped definition of masculinity that emphasizes competition, dominance, and sexual prowess; the treatment of women as commodities and sexual prey; excessive use of alcohol; preoccupation with group loyalty and secrecy; and the pervasiveness of physical force and aggression. Martin and Hummer conclude that until fraternities change these norms and practices, they will remain unsafe places for women.

The role of pornography in producing sexual aggression has been a subject of great discussion among social scientists. Two respected participants in this debate, Edward Donnerstein and Daniel Linz, professors at the University of California, Santa Barbara, address this issue in "Mass Media, Sexual Violence, and Male Viewers." Published in 1986, their article remains one of the best analyses of the scholarly literature on this subject. They investigate the impact of sexual violence in the media and provide an accessible overview of the literature on the relationship between pornography and rape. According to the authors, current research demonstrates that exposure to sexually violent images facilitates men's sexual aggression against women, lessens sensitivity to rape, and increases acceptance of rape myths. These images are found not only in some forms of pornography but also in the mainstream media, including prime-time television and popular films. Donnerstein and Linz emphasize that what is harmful is sexual violence in the media, not sexual explicitness.

Perceptions of and responses to rape in this country have been profoundly shaped by racism, a theme explored in the next chapter. Taking a broad historical view, Jennifer Wriggins, a law professor at the University of Maine, analyzes the racially biased treatment of rape within the legal system from slavery to the present in "Rape, Racism, and the Law." She contends that throughout this period, the criminal justice system has treated most seriously the rape of white women by black men, has punished African-American men disproportionately for the crime of rape, and has ignored the sexual victimization of African-American women.

Finally, "Gender, Ethnicity, and Sexual Assault" examines the influence of ethnicity and gender on the likelihood of experiencing sexual assault, the circumstances surrounding the assault, and its consequences. Based on a study of over three thousand adult residents of Los Angeles, Susan Sorenson and Judith Siegel, psychologists in the School of Public Health at the University of California, Los Angeles, found a lower rate of sexual assault among Hispanics than among non-Hispanic whites, which they attribute in part to the stronger community and familial bonds among the former group. Unlike most studies of sexual assault, Sorenson and Siegel included men as well as women in their sample. They found that men reported lower rates of sexual assault than did women, but that, once assaulted, men and women were equally likely to be victimized again.

13

Fraternities and Rape on Campus

~

Patricia Yancey Martin
Robert A. Hummer

R APES ARE PERPETRATED ON DATES, at parties, in chance encounters, and in specially planned circumstances. That group structure and processes, rather than individual values or characteristics, are the impetus for many rape episodes was documented by Blanchard (1959) 30 years ago (also see Geis 1971), yet sociologists have failed to pursue this theme (for an exception, see Chancer 1987). A recent review of research (Muehlenhard and Linton 1987) on sexual violence or rape devotes only a few pages to the situational contexts of rape events, and these are conceptualized as potential risk factors for individuals rather than qualities of rape-prone social contexts.

Many rapes, far more than come to the public's attention, occur in fraternity houses on college and university campuses, yet little research has analyzed fraternities at American colleges and universities as rape-prone contexts (cf. Ehrhart and Sandler 1985). Most of the research on fraternities reports on samples of individual fraternity men. . . . With minor exceptions, little research addresses the group and organizational context of fraternities or the social construction of fraternity life (for exceptions, see Letchworth 1969; Longino and Kart 1973; Smith 1964).

Gary Tash, writing as an alumnus and trial attorney in his fraternity's magazine, claims that over 90 percent of all gang rapes on college campuses involve fraternity men (1988, p. 2). Tash provides

From Patricia Yancey Martin and Robert A. Hummer, "Fraternities and Rape on Campus," *Gender and Society* 3, no. 4 (December 1989): 457–73. © 1989 by Sociologists for Women in Society. Reprinted by permission of Sage Publications.

no evidence to substantiate this claim, but students of violence against women have been concerned with fraternity men's frequently reported involvement in rape episodes (Adams and Abarbanel 1988). Ehrhart and Sandler (1985) identify over 50 cases of gang rapes on campus perpetrated by fraternity men, and their analysis points to many of the conditions that we discuss here. Their analysis is unique in focusing on conditions in fraternities that make gang rapes of women by fraternity men both feasible and probable. They identify excessive alcohol use, isolation from external monitoring, treatment of women as prey, use of pornography, approval of violence, and excessive concern with competition as precipitating conditions to gang rape (also see Merton 1985; Roark 1987).

The study reported here confirmed and complemented these findings by focusing on both conditions and processes. We examined dynamics associated with the social construction of fraternity life with a focus on processes that foster the use of coercion, including rape, in fraternity men's relations with women. Our examination of men's social fraternities on college and university campuses as groups and organizations led us to conclude that fraternities are a physical and sociocultural context that encourages the sexual coercion of women. We make no claims that all fraternities are "bad" or that all fraternity men are rapists. Our observations indicated, however, that rape is especially probable in fraternities because of the kinds of organizations they are, the kinds of members they have, the practices their members engage in, and a virtual absence of university or community oversight. Analyses that lay blame for rapes by fraternity men on "peer pressure" are, we feel, overly simplistic (cf. Burkhart 1989; Walsh 1989). We suggest, rather, that fraternities create a sociocultural context in which the use of coercion in sexual relations with women is normative and in which the mechanisms to keep this pattern of behavior in check are minimal at best and absent at worst. We conclude that unless fraternities change in fundamental ways, little improvement can be expected.

Methodology

Our goal was to analyze the group and organizational practices and conditions that create in fraternities an abusive social context for women. We developed a conceptual framework from an initial case study of an alleged gang rape at Florida State University that involved four fraternity men and an 18-year-old coed. The group rape took place on the third floor of a fraternity house and ended with the "dumping" of the woman in the hallway of a neighboring fraternity house. According to newspaper accounts, the victim's blood-alcohol concentration, when she was discovered, was .349 percent, more than three times the legal limit for automobile driving and an almost lethal amount. One law enforcement officer reported that sexual intercourse occurred during the time the victim was unconscious: "She was in a life-threatening situation" (*Tallahassee Democrat*, 1988b). When the victim was found, she was comatose and had suffered multiple scratches and abrasions. Crude words and a fraternity symbol had been written on her thighs (*Tampa Tribune*, 1988). When law enforcement officials tried to investigate the case, fraternity members refused to cooperate. This led, eventually, to a five-year ban of the fraternity from campus by the university and by the fraternity's national organization.

In trying to understand how such an event could have occurred, and how a group of over 150 members (exact figures are unknown because the fraternity refused to provide a membership roster) could hold rank, deny knowledge of the event, and allegedly lie to a grand jury, we analyzed newspaper articles about the case and conducted open-ended interviews with a variety of respondents about the case and about fraternities, rapes, alcohol use, gender relations, and sexual activities on campus. Our data included over 100 newspaper articles on the initial gang rape case; open-ended interviews with Greek (social fraternity and sorority) and non-Greek (independent) students (N = 20); university administrators (N = 8, five men, three women); and alumni advisers to Greek organizations (N = 6). Open-ended interviews were held also with judges, public and private defense attorneys, victim advocates, and state prosecutors regarding the processing of sexual assault cases. Data were analyzed using the grounded theory method (Glaser 1978; Martin and Turner 1986). In the following analysis, concepts generated from the data analysis are integrated with the literature on men's social fraternities, sexual coercion, and related issues.

Fraternities and the Social Construction of Men and Masculinity

Our research indicated that fraternities are vitally concerned—more than with anything else—with masculinity (cf. Kanin 1967). They work hard to create a macho image and context and try to avoid any suggestion of "wimpishness," effeminacy, and homosexuality. Valued members display, or are willing to go along with, a narrow conception of masculinity that stresses competition, athleticism, dominance, winning, conflict, wealth, material possessions, willingness to drink alcohol, and sexual prowess vis-à-vis women.

Valued Qualities of Members

When fraternity members talked about the kind of pledges they prefer, a litany of stereotypical and narrowly masculine attributes and behaviors was recited and feminine or woman-associated qualities and behaviors were expressly denounced (cf. Merton 1985). Fraternities seek men who are "athletic," "big guys," good in intramural competition, "who can talk college sports." Males "who are willing to drink alcohol," "who drink socially," or "who can hold their liquor" are sought. Alcohol and activities associated with the recreational use of alcohol are cornerstones of fraternity social life. Nondrinkers are viewed with skepticism and rarely selected for membership.*

Fraternities try to avoid "geeks," nerds, and men said to give the fraternity a "wimpy" or "gay" reputation. Art, music, and humanities majors, majors in traditional women's fields (nursing, home economics, social work, education), men with long hair, and those whose appearance or dress violate current norms are rejected. Clean-cut, handsome men who dress well (are clean, neat, conforming, fashionable) are preferred. One sorority woman commented that "the top ranking fraternities have the best looking guys." . . . Thus, a fraternity's reputation and status depend on members' possessions of stereotypically masculine qualities. Good grades, campus leadership, and community service are "nice" but masculinity and dominance—for example, in athletic events, physical size of members, athleticism of members—counts most.

Certain social skills are valued. Men are sought who "have good personalities," are friendly, and "have the ability to relate to girls" (cf. Longino and Kart 1973). One fraternity man, a junior, said: "We watch a guy [a potential pledge] talk to women . . . we want guys who can relate to girls." Assessing a pledge's ability to talk to women is, in part, a preoccupation with homosexuality and a conscious avoidance of men who seem to have effeminate manners or qualities. If a member is suspected of being gay, he is ostracized and informally drummed out of the fraternity. A fraternity with a reputation as wimpy or tolerant of gays is ridiculed and shunned by other fraternities. Militant heterosexuality is frequently used by men as a strategy to keep each other in line (Kimmel 1987).

Financial affluence or wealth, a male-associated value in American culture, is highly valued by fraternities. In accounting for why the

---

*Recent bans by some universities on open-keg parties at fraternity houses have resulted in heavy drinking before coming to a party and an increase in drunkenness among those who attend. This may aggravate, rather than improve, the treatment of women by fraternity men at parties.

fraternity involved in the gang rape that precipitated our research project had been recognized recently as "the best fraternity chapter in the United States," a university official said: "They were good-looking, a big fraternity, had lots of BMWs." After the rape, newspaper stories described the fraternity members' affluence, noting the high number of members who owned expensive cars (*St. Petersburg Times*, 1988).

The Status and Norms of Pledges

A pledge (sometimes called an associate member) is a new recruit who occupies a trial membership status for a specific period of time. The pledge period (typically ranging from 10 to 15 weeks) gives fraternity brothers an opportunity to assess and socialize new recruits. Pledges evaluate the fraternity also and decide if they want to become brothers. The socialization experience is structured partly through assignment of a Big Brother to each pledge. Big Brothers are expected to teach pledges how to become a brother and to support them as they progress through the trial membership period. Some pledges are repelled by the pledging experience, which can entail physical abuse; harsh discipline; and demands to be subordinate, follow orders, and engage in demeaning routines and activities, similar to those used by the military to "make men out of boys" during boot camp.

Characteristics of the pledge experience are rationalized by fraternity members as necessary to help pledges unite into a group, rely on each other, and join together against outsiders. The process is highly masculinist in execution as well as conception. A willingness to submit to authority, follow orders, and do as one is told is viewed as a sign of loyalty, togetherness, and unity. Fraternity pledges who find the pledge process offensive often drop out. Some do this by openly quitting, which can subject them to ridicule by brothers and other pledges, or they may deliberately fail to make the grades necessary for initiation or transfer schools and decline to reaffiliate with the fraternity on the new campus. One fraternity pledge who quit the fraternity he had pledged described an experience during pledgeship as follows:

> This one guy was always picking on me. No matter what I did, I was wrong. One night after dinner, he and two other guys called me and two other pledges into the chapter room. He said, "Here, X, hold this 25 pound bag of ice at arms' length 'till I tell you to stop." I did it even though my arms and hands were killing me. When I asked if I could stop, he grabbed me around the throat and lifted me off the floor. I thought he would choke me to death. He cussed me and called me all kinds of names. He took one of my fingers and twisted it until

it nearly broke. . . . I stayed in the fraternity for a few more days, but then I decided to quit. I hated it. Those guys are sick. They like seeing you suffer.

Fraternities' emphasis on toughness, withstanding pain and humiliation, obedience to superiors, and using physical force to obtain compliance contributes to an interpersonal style that deemphasizes caring and sensitivity but fosters intragroup trust and loyalty. If the least macho or most critical pledges drop out, those who remain may be more receptive to, and influenced by, masculinist values and practices that encourage the use of force in sexual relations with women and the covering up of such behavior (cf. Kanin 1967). . . .

Practices of Brotherhood

Practices associated with fraternity brotherhood that contribute to the sexual coercion of women include a preoccupation with loyalty, group protection and secrecy, use of alcohol as a weapon, involvement in violence and physical force, and an emphasis on competition and superiority.

LOYALTY, GROUP PROTECTION, AND SECRECY. Loyalty is a fraternity preoccupation. Members are reminded constantly to be loyal to the fraternity and to their brothers. Among other ways, loyalty is played out in the practices of group protection and secrecy. The fraternity must be shielded from criticism. Members are admonished to avoid getting the fraternity in trouble and to bring all problems "to the chapter" (local branch of a national social fraternity) rather than to outsiders. Fraternities try to protect themselves from close scrutiny and criticism by the Interfraternity Council (a quasi-governing body composed of representatives from all social fraternities on campus), their fraternity's national office, university officials, law enforcement, the media, and the public. Protection of the fraternity often takes precedence over what is procedurally, ethically, or legally correct. Numerous examples were related to us of fraternity brothers' lying to outsiders to "protect the fraternity."

Group protection was observed in the alleged gang rape case with which we began our study. Except for one brother, a rapist who turned state's evidence, the entire remaining fraternity membership was accused by university and criminal justice officials of lying to protect the fraternity. Members consistently failed to cooperate even though the alleged crimes were felonies, involved only four men (two of whom were not even members of the local chapter), and the victim of the crime nearly died. According to a grand jury's findings, fraternity officers repeatedly broke appointments with law enforcement officials, refused to provide police with a list of members, and refused to cooperate with police and prosecutors investigating the case (*Florida Flambeau*, 1988).

Secrecy is a priority value and practice in fraternities, partly because full-fledged membership is premised on it (for confirmation, see Ehrhart and Sandler 1985; Longino and Kart 1973; Roark 1987). Secrecy is also a boundary-maintaining mechanism, demarcating in-group from out-group, us from them. Secret rituals, handshakes, and mottoes are revealed to pledge brothers as they are initiated into full brotherhood. Since only brothers are supposed to know a fraternity's secrets, such knowledge affirms membership in the fraternity and separates a brother from others. Extending secrecy tactics from protection of private knowledge to protection of the fraternity from criticism is a predictable development. Our interviews indicated that individual members knew the difference between right and wrong, but fraternity norms that emphasize loyalty, group protection, and secrecy often overrode standards of ethical correctness.

ALCOHOL AS WEAPON. Alcohol use by fraternity men is normative. They use it on weekdays to relax after class and on weekends to "get drunk," "get crazy," and "get laid." The use of alcohol to obtain sex from women is pervasive—in other words, it is used as a weapon against sexual reluctance. According to several fraternity men whom we interviewed, alcohol is the major tool used to gain sexual mastery over women (cf. Adams and Abarbanel 1988; Ehrhart and Sandler 19855). One fraternity man, a 21-year-old senior, described alcohol use to gain sex as follows: "There are girls that you know will fuck, then some you have to put some effort into it. . . . You have to buy them drinks or find out if she's drunk enough. . . ."

A similar strategy is used collectively. A fraternity man said that at parties with Little Sisters: "We provide them with 'hunch punch' and things get wild. We get them drunk and most of the guys end up with one." " 'Hunch punch,' " he said, "is a girls' drink made up of overproof alcohol and powdered Kool-Aid, no water or anything, just ice. It's very strong. Two cups will do a number on a female." He had plans in the next academic term to surreptitiously give hunch punch to women in a "prim and proper" sorority because "having sex with prim and proper sorority girls is definitely a goal." These women are a challenge because they "won't openly consume alcohol and won't get openly drunk as hell." Their sororities have "standards committees" that forbid heavy drinking and easy sex.

In the gang rape case, our sources said that many fraternity men on campus believed the victim had a drinking problem and was thus an "easy make." According to newspaper accounts, she had been drinking alcohol on the evening she was raped; the lead assailant is alleged to have given her a bottle of wine after she arrived at his fraternity house. Portions of the rape occurred in a shower, and the victim was reportedly so drunk that the assailants had difficulty holding her in a standing position (*Tallahassee Democrat*, 1988a). While raping her, her assailants repeatedly told her they were members of another fraternity under the apparent belief that she was too drunk to know the difference. Of course, if she was too drunk to know who they were, she was too drunk to consent to sex (cf. Allgeier 1986; Tash 1988). . . .

VIOLENCE AND PHYSICAL FORCE. Fraternity men have a history of violence (Ehrhart and Sandler 1985; Roark 1987). Their record of hazing, fighting, property destruction, and rape has caused them problems with insurance companies (Bradford 1986; Pressley 1987). Two university officials told us that fraternities "are the third riskiest property to insure behind toxic waste dumps and amusement parks." Fraternities are increasingly defendants in legal actions brought by pledges subjected to hazing (Meyer 1986; Pressley 1987) and by women who were raped by one or more members. In a recent alleged gang rape incident at another Florida university, prosecutors failed to file charges but the victim filed a civil suit against the fraternity nevertheless (*Tallahassee Democrat*, 1989).

COMPETITION AND SUPERIORITY. Interfraternity rivalry fosters in-group identification and out-group hostility. Fraternities stress pride of membership and superiority over other fraternities as major goals. Interfraternity rivalries take many forms, including competition for desirable pledges, size of pledge class, size of membership, size and appearance of fraternity house, superiority in intramural sports, highest grade-point averages, giving the best parties, gaining the best or most campus leadership roles, and, of great importance, attracting and displaying "good looking women." Rivalry is particularly intense over members, intramural sports, and women (cf . Messner 1989).

Fraternities' Commodification of Women

In claiming that women are treated by fraternities as commodities, we mean that fraternities knowingly, and intentionally, use women for their benefit. Fraternities use women as bait for new members, as servers of brothers' needs, and as sexual prey.

Women as Bait

Fashionably attractive women help a fraternity attract new members. As one fraternity man, a junior, said, "They are good bait." Beautiful, sociable women are believed to impress the right kind of pledges and give the impression that the fraternity can deliver this type of woman to its members. Photographs of shapely, attractive coeds are printed in fraternity brochures and videotapes that are distributed and shown to potential pledges. The women pictured are often dressed in bikinis, at the beach, and are pictured hugging the brothers of the fraternity. One university official says such recruitment materials give the message; "Hey, they're here for you, you can have whatever you want," and, "we have the best looking women. Join us and you can have them too." Another commented: "Something's wrong when males join an all-male organization as the best place to meet women. It's so illogical."

Fraternities compete in promising access to beautiful women. One fraternity man, a senior, commented that "the attraction of girls [i.e., a fraternity's success in attracting women] is a big status symbol for fraternities." One university official commented that the use of women as a recruiting tool is so well entrenched that fraternities that might be willing to forgo it say they cannot afford to unless other fraternities do so as well. One fraternity man said, "Look, if we don't have Little Sisters, the fraternities that do will get all the good pledges." Another said, "We won't have as good a rush [the period during which new members are assessed and selected] if we don't have these women around."

In displaying good-looking, attractive, skimpily dressed, nubile women to potential members, fraternities implicitly, and sometimes explicitly, promise sexual access to women. One fraternity man commented that "part of what being in a fraternity is all about is the sex" and explained how his fraternity uses Little Sisters to recruit new members:

> We'll tell the sweetheart [the fraternity's term for Little Sister], "You're gorgeous; you can get him." We'll tell her to fake a scam and she'll go hang all over him during a rush party, kiss him, and he thinks he's done wonderful and wants to join. The girls think it's great too. It's flattering for them.

Women as Servers

The use of women as servers is exemplified in the Little Sister program. Little Sisters are undergraduate women who are rushed and selected in a manner parallel to the recruitment of fraternity men. They are affiliated with the fraternity in a formal but unofficial way and are able, indeed required, to wear the fraternity's Greek letters. Little Sisters are not full-fledged fraternity members, however; and fraternity national offices and most universities do not register or regulate them.

Each fraternity has an officer called Little Sister Chairman who over-sees their organization and activities. The Little Sisters elect officers among themselves, pay monthly dues to the fraternity, and have well-defined roles. Their dues are used to pay for the fraternity's social events, and Little Sisters are expected to attend and hostess fraternity parties and hang around the house to make it a "nice place to be." One fraternity man, a senior, described Little Sisters this way: "They are very social girls, willing to join in, be affiliated with the group, de-voted to the fraternity." Another member, a sophomore, said: "Their sole purpose is social—attend parties, attract new members, and 'take care' of the guys."

Our observations and interviews suggested that women selected by fraternities as Little Sisters are physically attractive, possess good social skills, and are willing to devote time and energy to the frater-nity and its members. One undergraduate woman gave the following job description for Little Sisters to a campus newspaper:

> It's not just making appearances at all the parties but entails many more responsibilities. You're going to be expected to go to all the intramural games to cheer the brothers on, support and encourage the pledges, and just be around to bring some extra life to the house. [As a Little Sister] you have to agree to take on a new responsibility other than studying to maintain your grades and managing to keep your checkbook from bouncing. You have to make time to be a part of the fraternity and support the brothers in all they do. (*The Toma-hawk*, 1988)

The title of Little Sister reflects women's subordinate status; fra-ternity men in a parallel role are called Big Brothers. Big Brothers assist a sorority primarily with the physical work of sorority rushes, which, compared to fraternity rushes, are more formal, structured, and intensive. Sorority rushes take place in the daytime and fraternity rushes at night so fraternity men are free to help. According to one fraternity member, Little Sister status is a benefit to women because it gives them a social outlet and "the protection of the brothers." The gender-stereotypic conceptions and obligations of these Little Sister and Big Brother statuses indicate that fraternities and sororities promote a gen-der hierarchy on campus that fosters subordination and dependence in women, thus encouraging sexual exploitation and the belief that it is acceptable.

Women as Sexual Prey

Little Sisters are a sexual utility. Many Little Sisters do not belong to sororities and lack peer support for refraining from unwanted sexual relations. One fraternity man (whose fraternity has 65 members and 85 Little Sisters) told us they had recruited "wholesale" in the prior year to "get lots of new women." The structural access to women that the Little Sister program provides and the absence of normative supports for refusing fraternity members' sexual advances may make women in this program particularly susceptible to coerced sexual encounters with fraternity men.

Access to women for sexual gratification is a presumed benefit of fraternity membership, promised in recruitment materials and strategies and through brothers' conversations with new recruits. One fraternity man said: "We always tell the guys that you get sex all the time, there's always new girls. . . . After I became a Greek, I found out I could be with females at will." A university official told us that, based on his observations, "no one [i.e., fraternity men] on this campus wants to have 'relationships.' They just want to have fun [i.e., sex]." Fraternity men plan and execute strategies aimed at obtaining sexual gratification, and this occurs at both individual and collective levels.

Individual strategies include getting a woman drunk and spending a great deal of money on her. As for collective strategies, most of our undergraduate interviewees agreed that fraternity parties often culminate in sex and that this outcome is planned. One fraternity man said fraternity parties often involve sex and nudity and can "turn into orgies." Orgies may be planned in advance, such as the Bowery Ball party held by one fraternity. A former fraternity member said of this party:

> The entire idea behind this is sex. Both men and women come to the party wearing little or nothing. There are pornographic pinups on the walls and usually porno movies playing on the TV. The music carries sexual overtones. . . . They just get schnockered [drunk] and, in most cases, they also get laid.

When asked about the women who come to such a party, he said: "Some Little Sisters just won't go. . . . The girls who do are looking for a good time, girls who don't know what it is, things like that."

Other respondents denied that fraternity parties are orgies but said that sex is always talked about among the brothers and they all know "who each other is doing it with." One member said that most of the time, guys have sex with their girlfriends "but with socials, girlfriends aren't allowed to come and it's their [members'] big chance [to have sex with other women]." The use of alcohol to help them get women into bed is a routine strategy at fraternity parties.

Conclusions

In general, our research indicated that the organization and member-ship of fraternities contribute heavily to coercive and often violent sex. Fraternity houses are occupied by same-sex (all men) and same-age (late teens, early twenties) peers whose maturity and judgment is often less than ideal. Yet fraternity houses are private dwellings that are mostly off-limits to, and away from scrutiny of, university and community representatives, with the result that fraternity house events seldom come to the attention of outsiders. Practices associated with the social construction of fraternity brotherhood emphasize a macho conception of men and masculinity, a narrow, stereotyped conception of women and femininity, and the treatment of women as commodi-ties. Other practices contributing to coercive sexual relations and the cover-up of rapes include excessive alcohol use, competitiveness, and normative support for deviance and secrecy (cf. Bogal-Allbritten and Allbritten 1985; Kanin 1967).

Some fraternity practices exacerbate others. Brotherhood norms require "sticking together" regardless of right or wrong; thus rape epi-sodes are unlikely to be stopped or reported to outsiders, even when witnesses disapprove. The ability to use alcohol without scrutiny by authorities and alcohol's frequent association with violence, includ-ing sexual coercion, facilitates rape in fraternity houses. Fraternity norms that emphasize the value of maleness and masculinity over fe-maleness and femininity and that elevate the status of men and lower the status of women in members' eyes undermine perceptions and treat-ment of women as persons who deserve consideration and care (cf. Ehrhart and Sandler 1985; Merton 1985).

Androgynous men and men with a broad range of interests and attributes are lost to fraternities through their recruitment practices. Masculinity of a narrow and stereotypical type helps create attitudes, norms, and practices that predispose fraternity men to coerce women sexually, both individually and collectively (Allgeier 1986; Hood 1989; Sanday 1981, 1986). Male athletes on campus may be similarly dis-posed for the same reasons (Kirshenbaum 1989; Telander and Sullivan 1989). . . .

Our research led us to conclude that fraternity norms and prac-tices influence members to view the sexual coercion of women, which is a felony crime, as sport, a contest, or a game (cf. Sato 1988). This sport is played not between men and women but between men and men. Women are the pawns or prey in the interfraternity rivalry game; they prove that a fraternity is successful or prestigious. The use of women in this way encourages fraternity men to see women as objects and sexual coercion as sport. Today's societal norms support young women's rights to engage in sex at their discretion, and coercion is unnecessary in a mutually desired encounter. However, nubile young women say they prefer to be "in a relationship" to have sex while young men say they prefer to "get laid" without a commitment (Muehlenhard and Linton 1987). These differences may reflect, in part, American puritanism and men's fears of sexual intimacy or perhaps intimacy of any kind. In a fraternity context, getting sex without giving emotionally demonstrates "cool" masculinity. More important, it poses no threat to the bonding and loyalty of the fraternity brotherhood (cf. Farr 1988). Drinking large quantities of alcohol before having sex suggests that "scoring" rather than intrinsic sexual pleasure is a primary concern of fraternity men.

Unless fraternities' composition, goals, structures, and practices change in fundamental ways, women on campus will continue to be sexual prey for fraternity men. As all-male enclaves dedicated to opposing faculty and administration and to cementing in-group ties, fraternity members eschew any hint of homosexuality. Their version of masculinity transforms women, and men with womanly characteristics, into the out-group. "Womanly men" are ostracized; feminine women are used to demonstrate members' masculinity. Encouraging renewed emphasis on their founding values (Longino and Kart 1973), service orientation and activities (Lemire 1979), or members' moral development (Marlowe and Auvenshine 1982) will have little effect on fraternities' treatment of women. A case for or against fraternities cannot be made by studying individual members. The fraternity qua group and organization is at issue. Located on campus along with many vulnerable women, embedded in a sexist society, and caught up in masculinist goals, practices, and values, fraternities' violation of women—including forcible rape—should come as no surprise.

References

Allgeier, Elizabeth. 1986. "Coercive versus Consensual Sexual Interactions." G. Stanley Hall Lecture to American Psychological Association Annual Meeting, Washington, DC, August.

Adams, Aileen, and Gail Abarbanel. 1988. *Sexual Assault on Campus: What Colleges Can Do*. Santa Monica, CA: Rape Treatment Center.

Blanchard, W. H. 1959. "The Group Process in Gang Rape." *Journal of Social Psychology* 49:259–66.

Bogal-Allbritten, Rosemarie B., and William L. Allbritten. 1985. "The Hidden Victims: Courtship Violence Among College Students." *Journal of College Student Personnel* 43:201–4.

Bohrstedt, George W. 1969. "Conservatism, Authoritarianism and Religiosity of Fraternity Pledges." *Journal of College Student Personnel* 27:36–43.

Bradford, Michael. 1986. "Tight Market Dries Up Nightlife at University." *Business Insurance* (March 2): 2, 6.

Burkhart, Barry. 1989. Comments in Seminar on Acquaintance/Date Rape Prevention: A National Video Teleconference, February 2.

Burkhart, Barry R., and Annette L. Stanton. 1985. "Sexual Aggression in Acquaintance Relationships." Pp. 43–65 in *Violence in Intimate Relationships*, edited by G. Russell. Englewood Cliffs, NJ: Spectrum.

Byington, Diane B., and Karen W. Keeter. 1988. "Assessing Needs of Sexual Assault Victims on a University Campus." Pp. 23–31 in *Student Services: Responding to Issues and Challenges*. Chapel Hill: University of North Carolina Press.

Chancer, Lynn S. 1987. "New Bedford, Massachusetts, March 6, 1983–March 22, 1984: The 'Before and After' of a Group Rape." *Gender & Society* 1:239–60.

Ehrhart, Julie K., and Bernice R. Sandler. 1985. *Campus Gang Rape: Party Games?* Washington, DC: Association of American Colleges.

Farr, K. A. 1988. "Dominance Bonding Through the Good Old Boys Sociability Network." *Sex Roles* 18:259–77.

Florida Flambeau. 1988. "Pike Members Indicted in Rape." (May 19): 1, 5.

Fox, Elaine, Charles Hodge, and Walter Ward. 1987. "A Comparison of Attitudes Held by Black and White Fraternity Members." *Journal of Negro Education* 56:521–34.

Geis, Gilbert. 1971. "Group Sexual Assaults." *Medical Aspects of Human Sexuality* 5:101–13.

Glaser, Barney G. 1978. *Theoretical Sensitivity: Advances in the Methodology of Grounded Theory.* Mill Valley, CA: Sociology Press.

Hood, Jane. 1989. "Why Our Society Is Rape-Prone." *New York Times*, May 16.

Hughes, Michael J., and Robert B. Winston, Jr. 1987. "Effects of Fraternity Membership on Interpersonal Values." *Journal of College Student Personnel* 45:405–11.

Kanin, Eugene J. 1967. "Reference Groups and Sex Conduct Norm Violations." *The Sociological Quarterly* 8:495–504.

Kimmel, Michael, ed. 1987. *Changing Men: New Directions in Research on Men and Masculinity.* Newbury Park, CA: Sage.

Kirshenbaum, Jerry. 1989. "Special Report, An American Disgrace: A Violent and Unprecedented Lawlessness Has Arisen Among College Athletes in All Parts of the Country." *Sports Illustrated* (February 27): 16–19.

Lemire, David. 1979. "One Investigation of the Stereotypes Associated with Fraternities and Sororities." *Journal of College Student Personnel* 37:54–57.

Letchworth, G. E. 1969. "Fraternities Now and in the Future." *Journal of College Student Personnel* 10:118–22.

Longino, Charles F., Jr., and Cary S. Kart. 1973. "The College Fraternity: An Assessment of Theory and Research." *Journal of College Student Personnel* 31:118–25.

Marlowe, Anne F., and Dwight C. Auvenshine. 1982. "Greek Membership: Its Impact on the Moral Development of College Freshmen." *Journal of College Student Personnel* 40:53–57.

Martin, Patricia Yancey, and Barry A. Turner. 1986. "Grounded Theory and Organizational Research." *Journal of Applied Behavioral Science* 22:141–57.

Merton, Andrew. 1985. "On Competition and Class: Return to Brotherhood." *Ms.* (September):60–65, 121–22.

Messner, Michael. 1989. "Masculinities and Athletic Careers." *Gender & Society* 3:71–88.

Meyer, T. J. 1986. "Fight Against Hazing Rituals Rages on Campuses." *Chronicle of Higher Education* (March 12):34–36.

Miller, Leonard D. 1973. "Distinctive Characteristics of Fraternity Members." *Journal of College Student Personnel* 31:126–28.

Muehlenhard, Charlene L., and Melaney A. Linton. 1987. "Date Rape and Sexual Aggression in Dating Situations: Incidence and Risk Factors." *Journal of Counseling Psychology* 34:186–96.

Pressley, Sue Anne. 1987. "Fraternity Hell Night Still Endures." *Washington Post* (August 11):B1.

Rapaport, Karen, and Barry R. Burkhart. 1984. "Personality and Attitudinal Characteristics of Sexually Coercive College Males." *Journal of Abnormal Psychology* 93:216–21.

Roark, Mary L. 1987. "Preventing Violence on College Campuses." *Journal of Counseling and Development* 65:367–70.

Sanday, Peggy Reeves. 1981. "The Socio-Cultural Context of Rape: A Cross-Cultural Study." *Journal of Social Issues* 37:5–27.

———. 1986. "Rape and the Silencing of the Feminine." Pp. 84–101 in *Rape*, edited by S. Tomaselli and R. Porter. Oxford: Basil Blackwell.

St. Petersburg Times. 1988. "A Greek Tragedy." (May 29):1F, 6F.

Sato, Ikuya. 1988. "Play Theory of Delinquency: Toward a General Theory of 'Action.' " *Symbolic Interaction* 11:191–212.

Smith, T. 1964. "Emergence and Maintenance of Fraternal Solidarity." *Pacific Sociological Review* 7:29–37.

Tallahassee Democrat. 1988a. "FSU Fraternity Brothers Charged." (April 27):1A, 12A.

———. 1988b. "FSU Interviewing Students About Alleged Rape." (April 24):1D.

———. 1989. "Woman Sues Stetson in Alleged Rape" (March 19):3B.

Tampa Tribune. 1988. "Fraternity Brothers Charged in Sexual Assault of FSU Coed." (April 27):6B.

Tash, Gary B. 1988. "Date Rape." *The Emerald of Sigma Pi Fraternity* 75(4):1–2.

Telander, Rick, and Robert Sullivan. 1989. "Special Report, You Reap What You Sow." *Sports Illustrated* (February 27):20–34.

The Tomahawk. 1988. "A Look Back at Rush, A Mixture of Hard Work and Fun." (April/May):3D.

Walsh, Claire. 1989. Comments in Seminar on Acquaintance/Date Rape Prevention: A National Video Teleconference, February 2.

Wilder, David H., Arlyne E. Hoyt, Dennis M. Doren, William E. Hauck, and Robert D. Zettle. 1978. "The Impact of Fraternity and Sorority Membership on Values and Attitudes." *Journal of College Student Personnel* 36:445–49.

Wilder, David H., Arlyne E. Hoyt, Beth Shuster Surbeck, Janet C. Wilder, and Patricia Imperatrice Carney. 1986. "Greek Affiliation and Attitude Change in College Students." *Journal of College Student Personnel* 44:510–19.

14

Mass Media, Sexual Violence, and Male Viewers

~

Edward Donnerstein
Daniel Linz

THE INFLUENCE OF PORNOGRAPHY on male viewers has been a topic of concern for behavioral scientists for many years, as well as a recent volatile political and legal question. Often research on pornography and its effects on behavior or attitudes is concerned with sexual explicitness. But it is not an issue of sexual explicitness; rather, it is an issue of violence against women and the role of women in "pornography" that is of concern to us here. Research over the last decade has demonstrated that sexual images per se do not facilitate aggressive behavior, change rape-related attitudes, or influence other forms of antisocial behaviors or perceptions. It is the violent images in pornography that account for the various research effects. This will become clearer as the research on the effects of sexual violence in the media is discussed. It is for these and other reasons that the term "aggressive pornography" or "sexually violent mass media images" is preferred. We will occasionally use the term "pornography" in this article for communication and convenience.

In this chapter we will examine the research on aggressive pornography and the research that examines nonpornographic media images of violence against women, the major focus of recent research and the material that provokes negative reactions. Our final section will examine the research on nonviolent pornography. We will also

From Edward Donnerstein and Daniel Linz, "Mass Media, Sexual Violence, and Male Viewers: Current Theory and Research," *American Behavioral Scientist* 29, no. 5 (May/June 1986): 601–18. © 1986 by Sage Publications. Reprinted by permission of Sage Publications.

refer to various ways in which this research has been applied to current political debate on pornography and offer suggestions to mitigate the negative effects from exposure to certain forms of pornography and sexually violent mass media.

Research on the Effects of Aggressive Pornography

By "aggressive pornography" we refer to X-rated images of sexual coercion in which force is used or implied against a woman in order to obtain certain sexual acts, as in scenes of rape and other forms of sexual assault. One unique feature of these images is their reliance upon "positive victim outcomes," in which rape and other sexual assaults are depicted as pleasurable, sexually arousing, and beneficial to the female victim. In contrast to other forms of media violence in which victims suffer, die, and do not enjoy their victimization, aggressive pornography paints a rosy picture of aggression. The myths regarding violence against women are central to the various influences this material has upon the viewer. This does not imply that there are not images of suffering, mutilation, and death; there are. The large majority of images, however, show violence against women as justified, positive, and sexually liberating. Even these more "realistic" images, however, can influence certain viewers under specific conditions. We will address this research later.

There is some evidence that these images increased through the 1970s (e.g., Malamuth and Spinner, 1980). However, more recent content analysis suggests that the increase has abated in the 1980s (Scott, 1985). The Presidential Commission on Obscenity and Pornography of 1970 did not examine the influence of aggressive pornography, mainly because of its low frequency. This is important to note, as it highlights differences between the commission and the position outlined in this article. The major difference is not in the findings but in the type of material being examined. (The Commission on Obscenity and Pornography was interested only in sexually explicit media images.)

In many aggressive pornographic depictions, as noted, the victim is portrayed as secretly desiring the assault and as eventually deriving sexual pleasure from it (e.g., Donnerstein and Berkowitz, 1982; Malamuth, Heim, and Feshbach, 1980). From a cognitive perspective, such information may suggest to the viewer that even if a woman seems repelled by a pursuer, she will eventually respond favorably to forceful advances, aggression, and overpowering by a male assailant (Brownmiller, 1975). The victim's pleasure could further heighten the aggressor's. Viewers might then come to think, at least for a short while, that their own sexual aggression would also be profitable, thus reducing restraints or inhibitions against aggression (Bandura, 1977). These views diminish the moral reprehensibility of any witnessed assault on a woman and, indeed, suggest that the sexual attack may have a highly desirable outcome for both victim and aggressor. Men having such beliefs might therefore be more likely to attack a woman after they see a supposedly "pleasurable" rape. Furthermore, as there is a substantial aggressive component in the sexual assault, it could be argued that the favorable outcome lowers the observers' restraints against aggression toward women. Empirical research in the last few years, which is examined below, as well as such cases as the New Bedford rape in which onlookers are reported to have cheered the rape of a woman by several men, suggests that the above concerns may be warranted.

Aggressive Pornography and Sexual Arousal

Although it was once believed that only rapists show sexual arousal to depictions of rape and other forms of aggression against women (e.g., Abel, Barlow, Blanchard, and Guild, 1977), research by Malamuth and his colleagues (e.g., Malamuth, 1981b, 1984; Malamuth and Check, 1983; Malamuth and Donnerstein, 1982; Malamuth, Haber, and Feshbach, 1980; Malamuth, Heim, and Feshbach, 1980) indicates that a nonrapist population will evidence increased sexual arousal to media-presented images of rape. This increased arousal occurs primarily when the female victim shows signs of pleasure and arousal, the theme most commonly presented in aggressive pornography. In addition, male subjects who indicate that there is some likelihood that they themselves would rape display increased sexual arousal to *all* forms of rape depictions, similar to the reactions of known rapists (e.g., Malamuth, 1981a, 1981b; Malamuth and Donnerstein, 1982). Researchers have suggested that this sexual arousal measure serves as an objective index of a proclivity to rape. Using this index, an individual whose sexual arousal to rape themes was found to be similar to or greater than his arousal to nonaggressive depictions would be considered to have an inclination to rape (Abel et al., 1977; Malamuth, 1981a; Malamuth and Donnerstein, 1982).

Aggressive Pornography and Attitudes Toward Rape

There are now considerable data indicating that exposure to aggressive pornography may alter the observer's perception of rape and the rape victim. For example, exposure to a sexually explicit rape scene in which the victim shows a "positive" reaction tends to produce a lessened sensitivity to rape (i.e., Malamuth and Check, 1983), increased acceptance of rape myths and interpersonal violence against women (e.g., Malamuth and Check, 1981), and increases in the self-reported possibility of raping (e.g., Malamuth, 1981a). This self-reported possibility of committing rape is highly correlated with (a) sexual arousal to rape stimuli, (b) aggressive behavior and a desire to hurt women, and (c) a belief that rape would be a sexually arousing experience for the rapist (see Malamuth, 1981a; Malamuth and Donnerstein, 1982). Exposure to aggressive pornography may also lead to self-generated rape fantasies (e.g., Malamuth, 1981b).

Aggressive Pornography and Aggression Against Women

Recent research (e.g., Donnerstein, 1980a, 1980b, 1983, 1984; Donnerstein and Berkowitz, 1982) has found that exposure to aggressive pornography increases aggression against women in a laboratory context. The same exposure does not seem to influence aggression against other men. This increased aggression is most pronounced when the aggression is seen as positive for victim and occurs for both angered and nonangered individuals.

Although this research suggests that aggressive pornography can influence the male viewer, the relative contribution of the sexual and the aggressive components of the material remains unclear. Is it the sexual nature of the material or the messages about violence that are crucial? This is an extremely important question. In many discussions of this research the fact that the material is aggressive is forgotten and it is assumed that the effects occur due to the sexual nature of the material. As we noted earlier, the sexual nature of the material is not the major issue. Recent empirical studies shed some light on this issue.

The Influence of Nonpornographic Depictions of Violence Against Women

It has been alleged that images of violence against women have increased not only in pornographic materials but also in more readily accessible mass media materials (*Newsweek*, 1985). Scenes of rape and violence have appeared in daytime TV soap operas and R-rated movies shown on cable television. These images are sometimes accompanied by the theme, common in aggressive pornography, that women enjoy or benefit from sexual violence. For example, several episodes of the daytime drama, "General Hospital," were devoted to a rape of one of the well-known female characters by an equally popular male character. At first the victim was humiliated; later the two characters married. A similar theme is expressed in the popular film, *The Getaway*. In this film described by Malamuth and Check (1981),

> Violence against women is carried out both by the hero and the antagonist. The hero, played by Steve McQueen, is portrayed in a very "macho" image. At one point, he slaps his wife several times causing her to cry from the pain. The wife, played by Ali McGraw, is portrayed as deserving this beating. As well, the antagonist in the movie kidnaps a woman (Sally Struthers) and her husband. He rapes the woman but the assault is portrayed in a manner such that the woman is depicted as a willing participant. She becomes the antagonist's girlfriend and they both taunt her husband until he commits suicide. The woman then willingly continues with the assailant and at one point frantically searches for him. (p. 439)

In a field experiment Malamuth and Check (1981a) attempted to determine whether or not the depiction of sexual violence contained in *The Getaway* and in another film with similar content influenced the viewer's perceptions and attitudes toward women. A total of 271 male and female students participated in a study they were led to believe focused on movie ratings. One group watched, on two different evenings, *The Getaway* and *Swept Away* (which also shows women as victims of aggression within erotic contexts). A group of control subjects watched neutral, feature-length movies. These movies were viewed in campus theaters as part of the Campus Film Program. The results of a "Sexual Attitudes Survey," conducted several days after the screenings, indicated that viewing the sexually aggressive films significantly increased male but not female acceptance of interpersonal violence and tended to increase rape myth acceptance. These effects occurred not with X-rated materials but with "prime-time" materials.

A recent study by Donnerstein and Berkowitz (1985) sought to examine more systematically the relative contributions of aggressive and sexual components of aggressive pornography. In a series of studies, male subjects were shown one of four different films: (1) the standard aggressive pornography used in studies discussed earlier; (2) an X-rated film that contained no forms of aggression or coercion and was rated by subjects to be as sexual as the first; (3) a film that contained scenes of aggression against a woman but without any sexual content and was considered less sexual and also less arousing (physiologically) than the previous two films; and (4) a neutral film. Although the aggressive pornographic film led to the highest aggression against women, the aggression-only film produced more aggressive behavior than the sex-only film. In fact, the sex-only film produced no different results than the neutral film. Subjects were also examined for their attitudes about rape and their willingness to say they might commit a rape. The most calloused attitudes and the highest percentage indicating some likelihood to rape were found in the aggression-only conditions; and the X-rated sex-only film was the lowest.

This research suggests that violence against women need not occur in a pornographic or sexually explicit context in order for the depictions to have an impact on both attitudes and behavior. Angered individuals became more aggressive toward a female target after exposure to films judged not to be sexually arousing but that depict a woman as a victim of aggression. This supports the claim by Malamuth and Check (1983) that sexual violence against women need not be portrayed in a pornographic fashion for greater acceptance of interpersonal violence and rape myths. . . .

An important element in the effects of exposure to aggressive pornography is violence against women. Because much commercially available media contain such images, researchers have begun to examine the impact of more popular film depictions of violence against women. Of particular interest have been R-rated "slasher" films, which combine graphic and brutal violence against women within a sexual context. These types of materials do not fit the general definition of pornography, but we believe their impact is stronger.

The Effects of Exposure to R-Rated Sexualized Violence

In a recent address before the International Conference on Film Classification and Regulation, Lord Harlech of the British Film Board noted the increase in R-rated sexually violent films and their "erotisizing" and "glorification" of rape and other forms of sexual violence. According to Harlech,

> Everyone knows that murder is wrong, but a strange myth has grown up, and been seized on by filmmakers, that rape is really not so bad, that it may even be a form of liberation for the victim, who may be acting out what she secretly desires—and perhaps needs—with no harm done. . . . Filmmakers in recent years have used rape as an exciting and titillating spectacle in pornographic films, which are always designed to appeal to men.

As depictons of sex and violence become increasingly graphic, especially in feature-length movies shown in theaters, officials at the National Institute of Mental Health are becoming concerned:

Films had to be made more and more powerful in their arousal effects. Initially, strong excitatory reactions [may grow] weak or vanish entirely with repeated exposure to stimuli of a certain kind. This is known as "habituation." The possibility of habituation to sex and violence has significant social consequences. For one, it makes pointless the search for stronger and stronger arousers. But more important is its potential impact on real life behavior. If people become inured to violence from seeing much of it, they may be less likely to respond to real violence.

This loss of sensitivity to real violence after repeated exposure to films with sex and violence, or "the dilemma of the detached bystander in the presence of violence," is currently a concern of our research program. Although initial exposure to a violent rape scene may act to create anxiety and inhibitions about such behavior, researchers have suggested that repeated exposure to such material could counter these effects. The effects of long-term exposure to R-rated sexually violent mass media portrayals is the major focus of our ongoing research program investigating how massive exposure to commercially released violent and sexually violent films influence (1) viewer perceptions of violence, (2) judgments about rape and rape victims, (3) general physiological desensitization to violence, and (4) aggressive behavior.

This research presents a new approach to the study of mass media violence. First, unlike many previous studies in which individuals may have seen only 10-30 minutes of material, the current studies examine 10 hours of exposure. Second, we are able to monitor the process of subject's desensitization over a longer period of time than previous experiments. Third, we examine perceptual and judgmental changes regarding violence, particularly violence against women.

In the program's first study, Linz, Donnerstein, and Penrod (1984) monitored desensitization of males to filmed violence against women to determine whether this desensitization "spilled over" into other decision making about victims. Male subjects watched nearly ten hours (five commercially released feature-length films, one a day for five days) of R-rated or X-rated fare—either R-rated sexually violent films such as *Tool Box Murders*, *Vice Squad*, *I Spit On Your Grave*, *Texas Chainsaw Massacre*; X-rated movies that depicted sexual assault; or X-rated movies that depicted only consensual sex (nonviolent). The R-rated films were much more explicit with regard to violence than they were with regard to sexual content. After each movie the men completed a mood questionnaire and evaluated the films on several dimensions. The films were counterbalanced so that comparisons could be made of the same films being shown on the first and last day of viewing. Before participation in the study, subjects were screened for levels of hostility, and only those with low hostility scores were in-cluded to help guard against the possibility of a overly hostile indi-vidual imitating the filmed violence during the week of the films. This is also theoretically important because it suggests that any effects we found would occur with a normal population. (It has been suggested by critics of media violence research that only those who are *already* predisposed toward violence are influenced by exposure to media violence. In this study, those individuals have been eliminated.) After the week of viewing the men watched yet another film. This time, however, they saw a videotaped reenactment of an actual rape trial. After the trial they were asked to render judgments about how respon-sible the victim was for her own rape and how much injury she had suffered.

Most interesting were the results from the men who had watched the R-rated films such as *Texas Chainsaw Massacre* or *Maniac*. Ini-tially, after the first day of viewing, the men rated themselves signifi-cantly above the norm for depression, anxiety, and annoyance on a mood adjective checklist. After each subsequent day of viewing, these scores dropped until, on the fourth day of viewing, the males' levels of anxiety, depression, and annoyance were indistinguishable from baseline norms. What happened to the viewers as they watched more and more violence?

We believe they were becoming desensitized to violence, particu-larly against women, which entailed more than a simple lowering of arousal to the movie violence. The men actually began to perceive the films differently as time went on. On day one for example, on the average, the men estimated that they had seen four "offensive scenes." By the fifth day, however, subjects reported only half as many offen-sive scenes (even though exactly the same movies, but in reverse or-der, were shown). Likewise, their ratings of the violence within the films receded from day one to day five. By the last day the men rated the movies less graphic and less gory and estimated fewer violent scenes than on the first day of viewing. Most startling, by the last day of viewing graphic violence against women the men were rating the material as significantly less debasing and degrading to women, more humorous, more enjoyable, and claimed a greater willingness to see this type of film again. This change in perception due to repeated ex-posure was particularly evident in comparisons of reactions to two specific films—*I Spit On Your Grave* and *Vice Squad*. Both films con-tain sexual assault; however, rape is portrayed more graphically in *I Spit On Your Grave* and more ambiguously in *Vice Squad*. Men who were exposed first to *Vice Squad* and then to *I Spit On Your Grave* gave nearly identical ratings of sexual violence. However, subjects who had seen the more graphic movie first saw much less sexual violence (rape) in the more ambiguous film.

The subject's evaluations of a rape victim after viewing a reenacted rape trial were also affected by the constant exposure to brutality against women. The victim of rape was rated as significantly more worthless and her injury as significantly less severe by those exposed to filmed violence when compared to a control group of men who saw only the rape trial and did not view films. Desensitization to filmed violence on the last day was also significantly correlated with assignment of greater blame to the victim for her own rape. (These types of effects were not observed for subjects who were exposed to sexually explicit but nonviolent films.)

Mitigating the Effects of Exposure to Sexual Violence

This research strongly suggests a potential harmful effect from exposure to certain forms of aggressive pornography and other forms of sexualized violence. There is now, however, some evidence that these negative changes in attitudes and perceptions regarding rape and violence against women can be not only eliminated but positively changed. Malamuth and Check (1983) found that if male subjects who had participated in such an experiment were later administered a carefully constructed debriefing, they would be actually less accepting of certain rape myths than control subjects exposed to depictions of intercourse (without a debriefing). Donnerstein and Berkowitz (1981) showed that not only are the negative effects of previous exposure eliminated, but even up to four months later, debriefed subjects have more "sensitive" attitudes toward rape than control subjects. These debriefings consisted of (1) cautioning subjects that the portrayal of the rape they have been exposed to is completely fictitious in nature, (2) educating subjects about the violent nature of rape, (3) pointing out to subjects that rape is illegal and punishable by imprisonment, and (4) dispelling the many rape myths that are perpetrated in the portrayal (e.g., in the majority of rapes, the victim is promiscuous or has a bad reputation, or that many women have an unconscious desire to be raped).

Surveys of the effectiveness of debriefings for male subjects with R-rated sexual violence has yielded similar positive results. Subjects who participated in the week-long film exposure study that was followed by certain type of debriefing changed their attitudes in a positive direction. The debriefings emphasized the fallacious nature of movie portrayals suggesting that women deserve to be physically violated and emphasized that processes of desensitization may have occurred due to long-term exposure to violence. The results indicated an immediate effect for debriefing with subjects scoring lower on rape myth acceptance after participation than they scored before participation in the film viewing sessions. These effects remained, for the most part, six weeks later. The effectiveness of the debriefing for the subjects who participated in two later experiments (one involving two weeks of exposure to R-rated violent films) indicated that even after seven months, subjects' attitudes about sexual violence showed significant positive change compared to the preparticipation levels.

This research suggests that if the calloused attitudes about rape and violence presented in aggressive pornography and other media representations of violence against women are learned, they can likewise be "unlearned." Furthermore, if effective debriefings eliminate these negative effects, it would seem possible to develop effective "prebriefings" that would also counter the impact of such materials. Such programs could become part of sex education curricula for young males. Given the easy access and availability of many forms of sexual violence to young males today, such programs would go a long way toward countering the impact of such images.

The Impact of Nonaggressive Pornography

An examination of early research and reports in the area of nonaggressive pornography would have suggested that effects of exposure to erotica were, if anything, nonharmful. For instance:

—It is concluded that pornography is an innocuous stimulus which leads quickly to satiation and that the public concern over it is misplaced. (Howard, Liptzin, and Reifler, 1973, p. 133)

—Results . . . fail to support the position that viewing erotic films produces harmful social consequences. (Mann, Sidman, and Starr, 1971, p. 113)

—If a case is to be made against "pornography" in 1970, it will have to be made on grounds other than demonstrated effects of damaging personal or social nature. (President's Commission on Obscenity and Pornography, 1970, p. 139)

A number of criticisms of these findings, however (e.g., Cline, 1974; Dienstbier, 1977; Wills, 1977), led to a reexamination of the issue of exposure to pornography and subsequent aggressive behavior. Some, such as Cline (1974), saw major methodological and interpretive problems with the Pornography Commission report; others (e.g., Liebert and Schwartzberg, 1977) believed that the observations were premature. Certainly the relationship between exposure to pornography and subsequent aggressive behavior was more complex than first believed. For the most part, recent research has shown that exposure to *nonaggressive* pornography can have one of two effects.

A number of studies in which individuals have been predisposed to aggress and later exposed to nonaggressive pornography have revealed increases in aggressive behavior (e.g., Baron and Bell, 1977; Donnerstein, Donnerstein and Evans, 1975; Malamuth, Feshback, and Jaffe, 1977; Meyer, 1972; Zillmann, 1971, 1979). Such findings have been interpreted in terms of a general arousal model, which states that under conditions in which aggression is a dominant response, any source of emotional arousal will tend to increase aggressive behavior in disinhibited subjects (c.g., Bandura, 1977; Donnerstein, 1983). A second group of studies (e.g., Baron, 1977; Baron and Bell, 1973; Frodi, 1977; Donnerstein et al., 1975; Zillmann and Sapolsky, 1977) reports the opposite—that exposure to pornography of a nonaggressive nature can actually reduce subsequent aggressive behavior.

These results appear contradictory, but recent research (e.g., Baron, 1977; Donnerstein, 1983; Donnerstein et al., 1975; Zillmann, 1979) has begun to reconcile seeming inconsistencies. It is now believed that as pornographic stimuli become more arousing, they give rise to increases in aggression. At a low level of arousal, however, the stimuli distract individuals, and attention is directed away from previous anger. Acting in an aggressive manner toward a target is incompatible with the pleasant feelings associated with low-level arousal (see Baron, 1977; Donnerstein, 1983). There is also evidence that individuals who find the materials "displeasing" or "pornographic" will also increase their aggression after exposure, whereas those who have more positive reactions to the material will not increase their aggression even to highly arousing materials (Zillmann, 1979).

The research noted above was concerned primarily with same-sex aggression. The influence of nonaggressive pornography on aggression against women tends to produce mixed effects. Donnerstein and Barret (1978) and Donnerstein and Hallam (1978) found that nonaggressive pornography had no effect on subsequent aggression unless constraints against aggressing were reduced. This was accomplished by both angering male subjects by women and giving subjects multiple chances to aggress. Donnerstein (1983) tried to reduce aggressive inhibitions through the use of an aggressive model but found no increase in aggression after exposure to an X-rated nonviolent film. It seems, therefore, that nonaggressive sexual material does not lead to aggression against women except under specific conditions (e.g., when inhibitions against aggression are deliberately lowered by the experimenter).

Almost without exception, studies reporting the effects on non-violent pornography have relied on short-term exposure; most subjects have been exposed to only a few minutes of pornographic material. More recently, Zillmann and Bryant (1982, 1984) demonstrated that *long-term* exposure (4 hours and 48 minutes over a six-week period) to pornography that does not contain overt aggressiveness may cause male and female subjects to (1) become more tolerant of bizarre and violent forms of pornography, (2) become less supportive of statements about sexual equality, and (3) become more lenient in assigning punishment to a rapist whose crime is described in a newspaper account. Furthermore, extensive exposure to the nonaggressive pornography significantly increased males' sexual callousness toward women. This latter finding was evidenced by increased acceptance of statements such as, "A man should find them, fool them, fuck them, and forget them," "A woman doesn't mean 'no' until she slaps you," and "If they are old enough to bleed, they are old enough to butcher." Zillmann and others (e.g., Berkowitz, 1984) have offered several possible explanations for this effect, suggesting that certain viewer attitudes are strengthened through long-term exposure to nonviolent pornographic material.

A common scenario of the material used in the Zillmann research is that women are sexually insatiable by nature. Even though the films shown do not feature the infliction of pain or suffering, women are portrayed as extremely permissive and promiscuous, willing to accommodate any male sexual urge. *Short-term* exposure to this view of women (characteristic of early studies of nonviolent pornography) may not be sufficient to engender changes in viewers' attitudes congruent with these portrayals. However, attitudinal changes might be expected under conditions of long-term exposure. Continued exposure to the idea that women will do practically anything sexually may *prime* or encourage other thoughts regarding female promiscuity (Berkowitz, 1984). This increase in the availability of thoughts about female promiscuity or the ease with which viewers can imagine instances in which a female has been sexually insatiable may lead viewers to inflate their estimates of how willingly and frequently women engage in sexual behavior. The availability of thoughts about female insatiability may also affect judgments about sexual behavior such as rape, bestiality, and sadomasochistic sex. Further, these ideas may endure. Zillmann and Bryant (1982), for example, found that male subjects still had a propensity to trivialize rape three weeks after exposure to nonviolent pornography. It is important to point out, however, that in these studies long-term exposure did not increase aggressive behavior but in fact decreased subsequent aggression.

Unfortunately, the role that images of female promiscuity and insatiability play in fostering callous perceptions of women can only be speculated upon at this point because no research has systematically manipulated film content in an experiment designed to facilitate or inhibit viewer cognitions. One cannot rule out the possibility, for example, that simple exposure to many sexually explicit depictions (regardless of their "insatiability" theme) accounts for the attitudinal changes found in their study. Sexual explicitness and themes of insatiability are experimentally confounded in this work.

Another emerging concern among political activists about pornography is its alleged tendency to degrade women (Dworkin, 1985; MacKinnon, 1985). This concern has been recently expressed in the form of municipal ordinances against pornography originally drafted by Catherine MacKinnon and Andrea Dworkin that have been introduced in a variety of communities, including Minneapolis and Indianapolis. One central feature of these ordinances is that pornography is the graphic "sexually explicit subordination of women" that also includes "women presented in scenarios of degradation, injury, abasement, torture, shown as filthy or inferior, bleeding, bruised, or hurt in a context that makes these conditions sexual" (City County general ordinance No. 35, City of Indianapolis, 1984). These ordinances have engendered a great deal of controversy, as some individuals have maintained that they are a broad form of censorship. A critique of these ordinances can be found in a number of publications (e.g., Burstyn, 1985; Russ, 1985).

The framers of the ordinance suggest that after viewing such material "a general pattern of discriminatory attitudes and behavior, both violent and non-violent, that has the capacity to stimulate various negative reactions against women will be found" (p. 8. Defendants' memorandum, United States District Court for the Southern District of Indiana, Indianapolis Division, 1984). Experimental evidence is clear with respect to the effects of pornography showing *injury, torture, bleeding, bruised*, or *hurt* women in sexual contexts. What has not been investigated is the effect of material showing *women in scenarios of degradation, as inferior and abased.*

No research has separated the effect of sexual explicitness from degradation, as was done with aggressive pornography, to determine whether the two interact to foster negative evaluations of women. Nearly all experiments conducted to date have confounded sexual explicitness with presentation of women as a subordinate, objectified class. Only one investigation (Donnerstein, 1984) has attempted to disentangle sexual explicitness and violence. The results of this short-term exposure investigation, discussed above, revealed that although the combination of sexual explicitness and violence against a woman (the violent pornographic condition) resulted in the highest levels of subsequent aggression against a female target, the nonexplicit depiction that depicted only violence resulted in aggression levels nearly as high and attitudes that were more calloused. The implication of this research is that long-term exposure to material that may not be explicitly sexual but that depicts women in scenes of degradation and subordination may have a negative impact on viewer attitudes. This is one area in which research is still needed.

Conclusions

Does pornography influence behaviors and attitudes toward women? The answer is difficult and centers on the definition of pornography. There is no evidence for any "harm"-related effects from sexually explicit materials. But research may support potential harm effects from aggressive materials. *Aggressive* images are the issue, not sexual images. The message about violence and the sexualized nature of violence is crucial. Although these messages may be part of some forms of pornography, they are also pervasive media messages in general, from prime-time TV to popular films. Males in our society have callous attitudes about rape. But where do these attitudes come from? Are the media, and in particular pornography, the cause? We should be reluctant to place the blame on the media. If anything, the media act to reinforce already existing attitudes and values regarding women and violence. They are a contributor, but only one of many.

As social scientists we have devoted a great deal of time to searching for causes of violence against women. Perhaps it is time to look for ways to reduce this violence. This article has noted several studies that report techniques to mitigate the influence of exposure to sexual violence in the media, which involves changing attitudes about violence. The issue of pornography and its relationship to violence will continue for years, perhaps without any definitive answers. We may never know if there is any real causal influence. We *do* know, however, that rape, and other forms of violence against women are pervasive. How we change this situation is of crucial importance, and our efforts need to be directed to this end.

References

Abel, G., Barlow, D., Blanchard, E., and Guild, D. (1977). The components of rapists' sexual arousal. *Archives of General Psychiatry*, 34, 395–403, 895–903.

Bandura, A. (1977). *Social learning theory.* Englewood Cliffs, NJ: Prentice-Hall.

Baron, R. A. (1977). *Human aggression.* New York: Plenum Press.

Baron, R. A. (1984). The control of human aggression: A strategy based on incompatible responses. In R. Green and E. Donnerstein (Eds.), *Aggression: Theoretical and empirical reviews* (vol. II). New York: Academic Press.

Baron, R. A., and Bell, P. A. (1977). Sexual arousal and aggression by males: Effects of type of erotic stimuli and prior provocation. *Journal of Personality and Social Psychology,* 35, 79–87.

Berkowitz, L. (1974). Some determinants of impulsive aggression: Role of mediated associations with reinforcements for aggression. *Psychological Review,* 81, 165–179.

Brownmiller, S. (1975). *Against our will: Men, women and rape.* New York: Simon & Schuster.

Burstyn, V. (1985). *Women against censorship.* Manchester, NH: Salem House.

Burt, M. R. (1980). Cultural myths and supports for rape. *Journal of Personality and Social Psychology,* 38, 217–230.

Check, J. V. P., and Malamuth, N. (1983). Violent pornography, feminism, and social learning theory. *Aggressive Behavior,* 9, 106–107.

Check, J. V. P., and Malamuth, N. (in press). Can participation in pornography experiments have positive effects? *Journal of Sex Research.*

Cline, V. B. (Ed.). (1974). *Where do you draw the line?* Salt Lake City, UT: Brigham Young University Press.

Dienstbier, R. A, (1977). Sex and violence: Can research have it both ways? *Journal of Communication,* 27, 176–188.

Donnerstein, E. (1980a). Pornography and violence against women. *Annals of the New York Academy of Sciences,* 347, 277–288.

Donnerstein, E. (1980b). Aggressive-erotica and violence against women. *Journal of Personality and Social Psychology,* 39, 269–277.

Donnerstein, E. (1983). Erotica and human aggression. In R. Green and E. Donnerstein (Eds.), *Aggression: Theoretical and empirical reviews.* New York: Academic Press.

Donnerstein, E. (1984). Pornography: Its effect on violence against women. In N. Malamuth and E. Donnerstein (Eds.), *Pornography and sexual aggression.* Orlando FL.: Academic Press.

Donnerstein, E., and Barrett, G. (1978). The effects of erotic stimuli on male aggression toward females. *Journal of Personality and Social Psychology,* 36, 180–188.

Donnerstein, E., and Berkowitz, L. (1982). Victim reactions in aggressive-erotic films as a factor in violence against women. *Journal of Personality and Social Psychology,* 41, 710–724.

Donnerstein, E., and Berkowitz, L. (1985). *Role of aggressive and sexual images in violent pornography.* Manuscript submitted for publication.

Donnerstein, E., Donnerstein, M., and Evans, R. (1975). Erotic stimuli and aggression: Facilitation or inhibition. *Journal of Personality and Social Psychology*, 32, 237–244.

Donnerstein, E., and Hallam, J. (1978). Facilitating effects of erotica on aggression against women. *Journal of Personality and Social Psychology*, 36, 1270–1277.

Donnerstein, E., and Linz, D. (1984, January). Sexual violence in the media, a warning. *Psychology Today*, pp. 14–15.

Dworkin, A. (1985). Against the male flood: Censorship, pornography, and equality. *Harvard Women's Law Journal*, 8.

Frodi, A. (1977) Sexual arousal, situational restrictiveness, and aggressive behavior. *Journal of Research in Personality*, 11, 48–58.

Howard, J. L., Liptzin, M. B., and Reifler, C. B. (1973). Is pornography a problem? *Journal of Social Issues*, 29, 133–145.

Liebert, R. M., and Schwartzberg, N. S. (1977). Effects of mass media. *Annual Review of Psychology*, 28, 141–173.

Linz, D., Donnerstein, E., and Penrod, S. (1984). The effects of long-term exposure to filmed violence against women. *Journal of Communication*, 34, 130–147.

MacKinnon, C. A. (1985). Pornography, civil rights, and speech. *Harvard Civil Rights-Civil Liberty Law Review*, 20 (1).

Malamuth, N. (1981a). Rape proclivity among males. *Journal of Social Issues*, 37, 138–157.

———. (1981b). Rape fantasies as a function of exposure to violent-sexual stimuli. *Archives of Sexual Behavior*, 10, 33–47.

Malamuth, N. (1984). Aggression against women: Cultural and individual causes. In N. Malamuth and E. Donnerstein (Eds.), *Pornography and sexual aggression.* Orlando, FL: Academic Press.

Malamuth, N., and Check, J. V. P. (1981). The effects of mass media exposure on acceptance of violence against women: A field experiment. *Journal of Research in Personality*, 15, 436–446.

Malamuth, N., and Check, J. V. P. (1983). Sexual arousal to rape depictions: Individual differences. *Journal of Abnormal Psychology*, 92, 55–67.

Malamuth, N., and Donnerstein, E. (Eds.). (1984). *Pornography and sexual aggression.* New York: Academic Press.

Malamuth, N., and Donnerstein, E. (1982). The effects of aggressive pornographic mass media stimuli. In L. Berkowitz (Ed.), *Advances in experimental social psychology* (vol. 15). New York: Academic Press.

Malamuth, N., Feshbach, S., and Jaffe, Y. (1977). Sexual arousal and aggression: Recent experiments and theoretical issues. *Journal of Social Issues*, 33, 110–133.

Malamuth, N., Haber, S., and Feshbach, S. (1980). Testing hypotheses regarding rape: Exposure to sexual violence, sex differences, and the normality of rape. *Journal of Research in Personality*, 14, 121–137.

Malamuth, N., Heim, M., and Feshbach, S. (1980). The sexual responsiveness of college students to rape depictions: Inhibitory and disinhibitory effects. *Journal of Personality and Social Psychology*, 38, 399–408.

Malamuth, N. M., and Spinner, B. (1980). A longitudinal content analysis of sexual violence in the best-selling erotic magazines. *Journal of Sex Research*, 16(3), 226–237.

Mann, J., Sidman, J., and Starr, S. (1971). Effects of erotic films on sexual behavior of married couples. In *Technical Report of the Commission on Obscenity and Pornography* (vol. 8). Washington, DC: Government Printing Office.

Meyer, T. (1972). The effects of viewing justified and unjustified real film violence on aggressive behavior. *Journal of Personality and Social Psychology*, 23, 21–29.

President's Commission on Obscenity and Pornography. (1970). *Technical report of the Commission on Obscenity and Pornography* (vol. 8). Washington, DC: Government Printing Office.

Russ, J. (1985). *Magic mommas, trembling sisters, puritans and perverts*. New York: The Crossing Press.

Scott, J. (1985). *Sexual violence in* Playboy *magazine: Longitudinal analysis*. Paper presented at the meeting of the American Society of Criminology.

The war against pornography. (1985, March 18). *Newsweek*, pp. 58–62, 65–67.

Wills, G. (1977, November). Measuring the impact of erotica. *Psychology Today*, pp. 30–34.

Zillmann, D. (1971). Excitation transfer in communication-mediated aggressive behavior. *Journal of Experimental Social Psychology*, 7, 419–433.

Zillmann, D. (1979). *Hostility and aggression*. Hillsdale, NJ: Erlbaum.

Zillmann, D. (1984). *Victimization of women through pornography*. Proposal to the National Science Foundation.

Zillmann, D., and Bryant, J. (1982). Pornography, sexual callousness, and the trivialization of rape. *Journal of Communication*, 32, 10–21.

Zillmann, D., and Bryant, J. (1984). Effects of massive exposure to pornography. In N. Malamuth and E. Donnerstein (Eds.), *Pornography and sexual aggression*. New York: Academic Press.

Zillmann, D., and Sapolsky, B. S. (1977). What mediates the effect of mild erotica on annoyance and hostile behavior in males? *Journal of Personality and Social Psychology*, 35, 587–596.

15

Rape, Racism, and the Law*

~

Jennifer Wriggins

THE HISTORY OF RAPE IN THIS COUNTRY has focused on the rape of white women by Black men. From a feminist perspective, two of the most damaging consequences of this selective blindness are the denials that Black women are raped and that all women are subject to pervasive and harmful sexual coercion of all kinds. . . .

The Narrow Focus on Black Offender/White Victim Rape

There are many different kinds of rape. Its victims are of all races, and its perpetrators are of all races. Yet the kind of rape that has been treated most seriously throughout this nation's history has been the illegal forcible rape of a white woman by a Black man.[1] The selective

From Jennifer Wriggins, "Rape, Racism and the Law," *Harvard Women's Law Journal* 6 (Spring 1983): 103–22, 140–41. © 1983 by the President and Fellows of Harvard College. Reprinted by permission of the Harvard Law School Publication Center.

*The word "Black" is capitalized in this chapter when used to denote someone's race. The reason for this has been well stated by Catharine MacKinnon: "Black is conventionally (I am told) regarded as a color rather than a racial or national designation, hence is not usually capitalized. I do not regard Black as merely a color of skin pigmentation, but as a heritage, an experience, a cultural and personal identity, the meaning of which becomes specifically stigmatic and/or glorious and/or ordinary under specific social conditions. It is as much socially created as, and at least in the American context no less specifically meaningful or definitive than, any linguistic, tribal, or religious ethnicity, all of which are conventionally recognized by capitalization." (MacKinnon, "Feminism, Marxism, Method, and the State: An Agenda for Theory," 7 *Signs* 515, 516 [1982]). While a parallel argument could support the capitalization of "white," such a usage would resonate with a long tradition of dominance by whites and is hence rejected.

acknowledgment of Black accused/white victim rape was especially pronounced during slavery and through the first half of the twentieth century. Today a powerful legacy remains that permeates thought about rape and race.

During the slavery period, statutes in many jurisdictions provided the death penalty or castration for rape when the convicted man was Black or mulatto and the victim white. These extremely harsh penalties were frequently imposed.[2] In addition, mobs occasionally broke into jails and courtrooms and lynched slaves alleged to have raped white women, prefiguring Reconstruction mob behavior.

In contrast to the harsh penalties imposed on Black offenders, courts occasionally released a defendant accused of raping a white woman when the evidence was inconclusive as to whether he was Black or mulatto.[3] The rape of Black women by white or Black men, on the other hand, was legal; indictments were sometimes dismissed for failing to allege that the victim was white. In those states where it was illegal for white men to rape white women, statutes provided less severe penalties for the convicted white rapist than for the convicted Black one. In addition, common-law rules both defined rape narrowly and made it a difficult crime to prove.

During slavery, then, the legal system treated seriously only one racial combination of rape—rape involving a Black offender and a white victim. This selective recognition continued long after slavery ended.

After the Civil War, state legislatures made their rape statutes race-neutral, but the legal system treated rape in much the same way as it had before the war. Black women raped by white or Black men had no hope of recourse through the legal system. White women raped by white men faced traditional common-law barriers that protected most rapists from prosecution.

Allegations of rape involving Black offenders and white victims were treated with heightened virulence. This was manifested in two ways. The first response was lynching, which peaked near the end of the nineteenth century.[4] The second, from the early twentieth century on, was the use of the legal system as a functional equivalent of lynching, as illustrated by mob coercion of judicial proceedings, special doctrinal rules, the language of opinions, and the markedly disparate numbers of executions for rape between white and Black defendants.

Between 1882 and 1946 at least 4715 persons were lynched, about three-quarters of whom were Black.[5] Although lynching tapered off after the early 1950s, occasional lynch-like killings persist to this day. The influence of lynching extended far beyond the numbers of Black people murdered because accounts of massive white crowds torturing, burning alive, and dismembering their victims created a widespread sense of terror in the Black community.[6]

The most common justification for lynching was the claim that a Black man had raped a white woman. The thought of this particular crime aroused in many white people an extremely high level of mania and panic. One white woman, the wife of an ex-Congressman, stated in 1898, "If it needs lynching to protect woman's dearest possession from human beasts, then I say lynch a thousand times a week if necessary."[7] The quote resonates with common stereotypes that Black male sexuality is wanton and bestial, and that Black men are wild, criminal rapists of white women.

Many whites accepted lynching as an appropriate punishment for a Black man accused of raping a white woman. The following argument made to the jury by defense counsel in a 1907 Louisiana case illustrates this acceptance:

> Gentlemen of the jury, this man, a nigger, is charged with breaking into the house of a white man in the nighttime and assaulting his wife, with the intent to rape her. Now, don't you know that if this nigger had committed such a crime, he never would have been brought here and tried; that he would have been lynched, and if I were there I would help pull on the rope.[8]

It is doubtful whether the legal system better protected the rights of a Black man accused of raping a white woman than did the mob. Contemporary legal literature used the term "legal lynching" to describe the legal system's treatment of Black men. Well past the first third of the twentieth century, courts were often coerced by violent mobs, which threatened to execute the defendant themselves unless the court convicted him. Such mobs often did lynch the defendant if the judicial proceedings were not acceptable to them. A contemporary authority on lynching commented in 1934 that "the local sentiment which would make a lynching possible would insure a conviction in the courts."[9] Even if the mob was not overtly pressuring for execution, a Black defendant accused of raping a white woman faced a hostile, racist legal system. State court submission to mob pressure is well illustrated by the most famous series of cases about interracial rape, the Scottsboro cases of the 1930s.[10] Eight young Black men were convicted of what the Alabama Supreme Court called "a most foul and revolting crime," which was the rape of "two defenseless white girls." The defendants were summarily sentenced to death based on minimal and dubious evidence, having been denied effective assistance of counsel. The Alabama Supreme Court upheld the convictions in opinions demonstrating relentless determination to hold the defendants guilty regardless of strong evidence that mob pressure had influenced the verdicts and the weak evidence presented against the defendants. In one decision, that court affirmed the trial court's denial of a change of venue on the grounds that the mobs' threats of harm were not imminent enough although the National Guard had been called out to protect the defendants from mob executions. The U.S. Supreme Court later recognized that the proceedings had in fact taken place in an atmosphere of "tense, hostile, and excited public sentiment."[11] After a lengthy appellate process, including three favorable Supreme Court rulings, all of the Scottsboro defendants were released, having spent a total of 104 years in prison.

In addition, courts applied special doctrinal rules to Black defendants accused of the rape or attempted rape of white women. One such rule allowed juries to consider the race of the defendant and victim in drawing factual conclusions as to the defendant's intent in attempted rape cases. If the accused was Black and the victim white, the jury was entitled to draw the inference, based on race alone, that he intended to rape her. One court wrote, "In determining the question of intention, the jury may consider social conditions and customs founded upon racial differences, such as that the prosecutrix was a white woman and defendant was a Negro man."[12] The "social conditions and customs founded upon racial differences" which the jury was to consider included the assumption that Black men always and only want to rape white women, and that a white woman would never consent to sex with a Black man.

The Georgia Supreme Court of 1899 was even more explicit about the significance of race in the context of attempted rape, and particularly about the motivations of Black men. It held that race may properly be considered "to rebut any presumption that might otherwise arise in favor of the accused that his intention was to obtain the consent of the female, upon failure of which he would abandon his purpose to have sexual intercourse with her."[13] Such a rebuttal denied to Black defendants procedural protection that was accorded white defendants.

Judicial attitudes toward the rape of white women by Black men are also manifested in the factual descriptions of the crime in opinions. Courts sometimes created pornographic images of the events of the rape. One court, for example, wrote, "[The victim,]while clad only in her pajamas was forced to a remote spot some two blocks from her home, where battered, bruised, bleeding and exhausted she was overpowered. . . ."[14] The sense of disgusted fascination that such opinions convey is not paralleled in cases where offender and victim are both white.

The outcome of this disparate treatment of Black men by the legal system was often the same as lynching—death. Between 1930 and 1967, thirty-six percent of the Black men who were convicted of raping a white woman were executed. In stark contrast, only two percent of all defendants convicted of rape involving other racial combinations were executed. As a result of such disparate treatment, eighty-nine percent of the men executed for rape in this country were Black.[15] While execution rates for all crimes were much higher for Black men than for white men, the differential was most dramatic when the crime was the rape of a white woman.

The patterns that began in slavery and continued long afterwards have left a powerful legacy that manifests itself today in several ways. Although the death penalty for rape has been declared unconstitutional, the severe statutory penalties for rape continue to be applied in a discriminatory manner. A recent study concluded that Black men convicted of raping white women receive more serious sanctions than all other sexual assault defendants.[16] A recent attitudinal study found that white potential jurors treated Black and white defendants similarly when the victim was Black. However, Black defendants received more severe punishment than white defendants when the victim was white.[17]

The rape of white women by Black men is also used to justify harsh rape penalties. One of the few law review articles written before 1970 that takes a firm position in favor of strong rape laws to secure convictions begins with a long quote from a newspaper article describing rapes by three Black men, who at 3 A.M. on Palm Sunday "broke into a West Philadelphia home occupied by an eighty-year-old widow, her forty-four-year-old daughter and fourteen-year-old granddaughter," brutally beat and raped the white women, and left the grandmother unconscious "lying in a pool of blood."[18] This introduction presents rape as a crime committed by violent Black men against helpless white women. It is an image of a highly atypical rape—the defendants are Black and the victims white, the defendants and victims are strangers to each other, extreme violence is used, and it is a group rape. Contemporaneous statistical data on forcible rapes reported to the Philadelphia police department reveal that this rape case was virtually unique.[19] Use of this highly unrepresentative image of rape to justify strict rape laws is consistent with recent research showing that it is a prevalent, although false, belief about rape that the most common racial combination is Black offender and white victim.[20]

Charges of rapes committed by Black men against white women are still surrounded by sensationalism and public pressure for prosecution. Black men seem to face a special threat of being unjustly prosecuted or convicted. One example is Willie Sanders. Sanders is a

Black Boston man who was arrested and charged with the rapes of four young white women after a sensational media campaign and intense pressure on the police to apprehend the rapist.[21] Although the rapes continued after Sanders was incarcerated, and the evidence against him was extremely weak, the state subjected him to a vigorous twenty-month prosecution. After a lengthy and expensive trial, and an active public defense, he was eventually acquitted. Although Sanders was clearly innocent, he could have been convicted; he and his family suffered incalculable damage despite his acquittal. . . .

From slavery to the present day, the legal system has consistently treated the rape of white women by Black men with more harshness than any other kind of rape. The punishment for Black offender/white victim rape has ranged historically from castration, to death by torture and lynching, to executions. Today, Black men convicted of raping white women receive longer prison sentences than other rape defendants. Innocent Black men also face the threat of racially motivated prosecutions.

This selective focus is significant in several ways. First, since tolerance of coerced sex has been the rule rather than the exception, it is clear that the rape of white women by Black men has been treated seriously not because it is coerced sex and thus damaging to women, but because it is threatening to white men's power over both "their" women and Black men. Second, in treating Black offender/white victim illegal rape much more harshly than all coerced sex experienced by Black women and most coerced sex experienced by white women, the legal system has implicitly condoned the latter forms of rape. Third, this treatment has contributed to a paradigmatic but false concept of rape as being primarily a violent crime between strangers where the perpetrator is Black and the victim white. Finally, this pattern is perverse and discriminatory because rape is painful and degrading to both Black and white victims regardless of the attacker's race.

The Denial of the Rape of Black Women

The selective acknowledgment of the existence and seriousness of the rape of white women by Black men has been accompanied by a denial of the rape of Black women that began in slavery and continues today. Because of racism and sexism, very little has been written about this denial. Mainstream American history has ignored the role of Black people to a large extent; systematic research into Black history has been published only recently. The experiences of Black women have yet to be fully recognized in those histories, although this is beginning to change. Indeed, very little has been written about rape from the perspective of the victim, Black or white, until quite recently. Research about Black women rape victims encounters all these obstacles.

The rape of Black women by white men during slavery was commonplace and was used as a crucial weapon of white supremacy.[22] White men had what one commentator called "institutionalized access" to Black women.[23] The rape of Black women by white men cannot be attributed to unique Southern pathology, however, for numerous accounts exist of northern armies raping Black women while they were "liberating" the South.

The legal system rendered the rape of Black women by any man, white or Black, invisible. The rape of a Black woman was not a crime. In 1859 the Mississippi Supreme Court dismissed the indictment of a male slave for the rape of a female slave less than 10 years old, saying:

> [T]his indictment can not be sustained, either at common law or under our statutes. It charges no offense known to either system. [Slavery] was unknown to the common law . . . and hence its provisions are inapplicable. . . . There is no act (of our legislature on this subject) which embraces either the attempted or actual commission of a rape by a slave on a female slave. . . . Masters and slaves can not be governed by the same system or laws; so different are their positions, rights and duties.[24]

This decision is illuminating in several respects. First, Black men are held to lesser standards of sexual restraint with Black women than are white men with white women. Second, white men are held to lesser standards of restraint with Black women than are Black men with white women. Neither white nor Black men were expected to show sexual restraint with Black women.

After the Civil War, the widespread rape of Black women by white men persisted. Black women were vulnerable to rape in several ways that white women were not. First, the rape of Black women was used as a weapon of group terror by white mobs and by the Ku Klux Klan during Reconstruction. Second, because Black women worked outside the home, they were exposed to employers' sexual aggression as white women who worked inside the home were not.

The legal system's denial that Black women experienced sexual abuse by both white and Black men also persisted, although statutes had been made race-neutral. Even if a Black victim's case went to trial—in itself highly unlikely—procedural barriers and prejudice against Black women protected any man accused of rape or attempted rape. The racist rule which facilitated prosecutions of Black offender/white victim attempted rapes by allowing the jury to consider the defendant's race as evidence of his intent, for instance, was not applied where both persons were "of color and there was no evidence of their social standing."[25] That is, the fact that a defendant was Black was considered relevant only to prove intent to rape a white woman; it was not relevant to prove intent to rape a Black woman. By using disparate procedures, the court implicitly makes two assertions. First, Black men do not want to rape Black women with the same intensity or regularity that Black men want to rape white women. Second, Black women do not experience coerced sex in the sense that white women experience it.

These attitudes reflect a set of myths about Black women's supposed promiscuity which were used to excuse white men's sexual abuse of Black women. An example of early twentieth-century assumptions about Black women's purported promiscuity was provided by the Florida Supreme Court in 1918. In discussing whether the prior chastity of the victim in a statutory rape case should be presumed subject to defendant's rebuttal or should be an element of the crime which the state must prove, the court explained that:

> What has been said by some of our courts about an unchaste female being a comparatively rare exception is no doubt true where the population is composed largely of the Caucasian race, but we would blind ourselves to actual conditions if we adopted this rule where another race that is largely immoral constitutes an appreciable part of the population.[26]

Cloaking itself in the mantle of legal reasoning, the court stated that most young white women are virgins, that most young Black women are not, and that unchaste women are immoral. The traditional law of statutory rape at issue in the above-quoted case provides that women who are not "chaste" cannot be raped. Because of the way the legal system considered chastity, the association of Black women with unchastity meant not only that Black women could not be victims of statutory rape, but also that they would not be recognized as victims of forcible rape.

The criminal justice system continues to take the rape of Black women less seriously than the rape of white women. Studies show that judges generally impose harsher sentences for rape when the victim is white than when the victim is Black.[27] The behavior of white jurors shows a similar bias. A recent study found that sample white jurors imposed significantly lighter sentences on defendants whose victims were Black than on defendants whose victims were white. Black jurors exhibited no such bias.[28]

Evidence concerning police behavior also documents the fact that the claims of Black rape victims are taken less seriously than those of white. A 1968 study of Philadelphia police processing decisions concluded that the differential in police decisions to charge for rape "resulted primarily from a lack of confidence in the veracity of Black complainants and a belief in the myth of Black promiscuity."[29]

The thorough denial of Black women's experiences of rape by the legal system is especially shocking in light of the fact that Black women are much more likely to be victims of rape than are white women.[30] Based on data from national surveys of rape victims, "the profile of the most frequent rape victim is a young woman, divorced or separated, Black and poverty stricken.". . .[31]

Conclusion

The legal system's treatment of rape both has furthered racism and has denied the reality of women's sexual subordination. It has disproportionately targeted Black men for punishment and made Black women both particularly vulnerable and particularly without redress. It has denied the reality of women's sexual subordination by creating a social meaning of rape which implies that the only type of sexual abuse is illegal rape and the only form of illegal rape is Black offender/white victim. Because of the interconnectedness of rape and racism, successful work against rape and other sexual coercion must deal with racism. Struggles against rape must acknowledge the differences among women and the different ways that groups other than women are disempowered. In addition, work against rape must go beyond the focus on illegal rape to include all forms of coerced sex, in order to avoid the racist historical legacy surrounding rape and to combat effectively the subordination of women.

Notes

1. Mann and Selva, "The Sexualization of Racism: The Black as Rapist and White Justice," 3:3 *Black Studies* 168 (1979).

2. H. Catterall, ed., *Judicial Cases Concerning American Slavery and the Negro*, vols. 1–3 (Washington, DC: Carnegie Institution of Washington, 1926–1937); see M. Hindus, *Prison and Plantation: Crime, Justice, and Authority in Massachusetts and South Carolina, 1767–1878* (Chapel Hill: University of North Carolina Press, 1980), 150–61; K. Stampp, *The Peculiar Institution* (New York: Alfred A. Knopf, 1956), 210–11.

3. S. Brownmiller, *Against Our Will* (New York: Simon and Schuster, 1975), 176; Evans, "Rape, Race, and Research," in *Blacks and Criminal Justice*, ed. C. Owens and J. Bell (Lexington, MA: Lexington Books, 1977), 75, 79.

4. A. Raper, *The Tragedy of Lynching* (Chapel Hill: University of North Carolina Press, 1933), 1–2; C. Woodward, *The Strange Career of Jim Crow* (New York: Oxford University Press, 1974), 43; Note, "Constitutionality of Proposed Federal Anti-Lynching Legislation," 34 *Virginia Law Review* 944 (1948).

5. A. Rose, *The Negro in America* (New York: Harper, 1948), 185 (citing a Tuskegee Institute study).

6. A. Rose, *The Negro*, 186–87; J. Hall, "The Mind that Burns in Each Body: Women, Rape, and Racial Violence," in *Powers of Desire: The Politics of Sexuality*, ed. A. Snitow, C. Stansell, and S. Thompson (New York: Monthly Review Press, 1983); C. Hernton, "The Negro Male," in *The Black Male in America*, ed. D. Wilkinson and R. Taylor (Chicago: Nelson-Hall, 1977), 244–46.

7. Reynolds, "The Remedy for Lynch Law," 7 *Yale Law Journal* 20 (1897–98): 20.

8. State v. Petit, 119 La. 1013, 1016, 44 So. 848, 849 (1907).

9. Chadbourn, "Lynching and the Law," *American Bar Association Journal* 20 (1934): 71.

10. Patterson v. State, 224 Ala. 531, 141 So. 195 (1932); Powell v. State, 224 Ala. 540, 141 So. 201 (1932); Weems v. State, 224 Ala. 524, 141 So. 215 (1932).

11. Powell v. Alabama, 287 U.S. 45, 51 (1932).

12. McQuirter v. State, 36 Ala. App. 707, 709, 63 So. 2d 388, 390 (1953).

13. Dorsey v. State, 108 Ga. 477, 480, 34 S.E. 135, 136–37 (1899).

14. Maxwell v. State, 236 Ark. 694, 697, 370 S.W. 2d 113, 115 (1963).

15. Wolfgang, "Racial Discrimination in the Death Sentence for Rape," in *Executions in America*, ed. W. Bowers (Lexington, MA: Lexington Books, 1974), 110–13, 116.

16. G. LaFree, "The Effect of Sexual Stratification by Race on Official Reactions to Rape," *American Sociological Review* 45 (1980): 842, 852.

17. H. Feild and L. Bienen, *Jurors and Rape* (Lexington, MA: Lexington Books, 1980), 117–18.

18. Schwartz, "The Effect in Philadelphia of Pennsylvania's Increased Penalties for Rape and Attempted Rape," *Journal of Criminal Law, Criminology, and Police Science* 59 (1968): 509.

19. M. Amir, *Patterns in Forcible Rape* (Chicago: University of Chicago Press, 1971), 11. Out of 343 rapes reported to the Philadelphia police, 3.3% involved Black defendants accused of raping white women, *id*. at 44; 42% involved complaints of stranger rape, *id*. at 250; 20.5% involved brutal beatings, *id*. at 155–56; 43% involved group rapes, *id*. at 200.

20. In answer to the question, "Among which racial combination do most rapes occur?" 48% of respondents stated Black males and white females, 3% stated white males and Black females, 16% stated Black males and Black females, 33% stated white males and white females. Feild and Bienen, *Jurors*, 80. Recent victim survey data contradicts this prevalent belief; more than four-fifths of illegal rapes reported to researchers were between members of the same race, and white/Black rapes roughly equaled Black/white rapes. L. Bowker, "Women as Victims: An Examination of the Results of L.E.A.A.'s National Crime Survey Program," in *Women and Crime in America*, ed. L. Bowker (New York: Macmillan, 1981).

21. Suffolk Superior Court Indictment No. 025027–36, 025077 (1980).

22. Brownmiller, *Against Our Will*, 165; A. Davis, *Women, Race and Class* (New York: Vintage Books, 1981), 24–27; B. Hooks, *Ain't I a Woman: Black*

Women and Feminism (Boston: South End Press, 1981), 24–27; G. Lerner, *Black Women in White America* (New York: Vintage Press, 1972), 149–50; J. Noble, *Beautiful Also Are the Souls of My Black Sisters* (Englewood Cliffs, NJ: Prentice-Hall, 1978), 35; DuBois, "Divine Right," in *A Documentary History of the Negro People in the United States, 1910–1932*, ed. H. Aptheker (Secaucus, NJ: Citadel Press, 1974), 53.

23. L. Curtis, *Criminal Violence* (Lexington, MA: Lexington Books, 1974), 22.

24. George, a slave, v. State, 37 Miss. 306 (1859).

25. Washington v. State, 38 Ga. 370, 75 S.E. 253 (1912).

26. Dallas v. State, 76 Fla. 358, 79 So. 690 (1918).

27. LaFree, "The Effect of Sexual Stratification by Race," 847–48.

28. Feild and Bienen, *Jurors*, 106.

29. Comment, "Police Discretion and the Judgment That a Crime Has Been Committed—Rape in Philadelphia," 117 *University of Pennsylvania Law Review* (1968): 277, 304.

30. Recent data from random citizen interviews suggest that Black women are much more likely to be victims of illegal rape than are white women. Bowker, "Women as Victims," 164; see Karmen, "Women Victims of Crime: Introduction," 185, 188, in *The Criminal Justice System and Women: Offenders, Victims, Workers*, ed. B. Price and N. Sokoloff (New York: Clark Boardman, 1982).

31. Karmen, "Women Victims," 188.

16

Gender, Ethnicity, and Sexual Assault: Findings from a Los Angeles Study

~

Susan B. Sorenson
Judith M. Siegel

I N THE UNITED STATES TODAY, rates of violent crime reported to the police are highest for persons who live in the inner city, are of lower socioeconomic status, and are members of ethnic minority groups (U.S. Department of Justice, 1988a). Rapes reported to police echo this pattern with one exception—rates are lowest for Hispanics (U.S. Department of Justice, 1988b). Rape is believed to be the most underreported crime, with estimates of nonreporting to police ranging as high as 92% (Russell, 1982). Furthermore, assaults reported to formal agencies differ in important ways from unreported assaults (Ageton, 1983; Williams, 1984), and this fact calls into question the representativeness of law enforcement data. Therefore, the present research employed a probability sample of community-based residents to assess the degree to which gender, minority group membership, and social class are related to sexual assault.

By traditional definition, rape is a crime against women. While sexual assault against women is believed to be more common than against men, men's reports of sexual victimization are gaining increased recognition (Bolton, Morris, & MacEachron, 1989; Hunter, 1990). Some states such as Michigan have removed gender from their sexual assault statutes (Michigan Compiled Laws Annotated, 1986), in part

From Susan B. Sorenson and Judith M. Siegel, "Gender, Ethnicity, and Sexual Assault: Findings from a Los Angeles Study," *Journal of Social Issues* 48, no. 1 (1992): 93–104. © 1992 by the Society for the Psychological Study of Social Issues. Reprinted by permission of the Society for the Psychological Study of Social Issues.

as a recognition of the victimization of men. Because few community-based studies have included men in their samples, whether sexual assault patterns are similar for women and men has received little systematic investigation.

Relatively little research has been conducted on the sexual assault experiences of Hispanics. Research on Hispanic populations is needed for a number of reasons, not the least of which is that Hispanics are expected to comprise the largest minority group in the United States by the year 2000 (Hayes-Bautista, Schink, & Chapa, 1985; Macias, 1977). Data on sexual assault among Hispanics could help address a number of negative stereotypes about the violence in male-female relations in the Hispanic community (e.g., Doyle, 1990; Williams & Holmes, 1981). Moreover, research to date suggests ethnic differences in attitudes regarding rape (Fischer, 1987; Williams & Holmes, 1981).

This paper reviews data concerning the sexual assault experiences of over 3,000 residents of Los Angeles, California. A major feature of this research is a comparison of the prevalence, circumstances, and sequelae of the assault experiences of Hispanics (mostly of Mexican heritage) and non-Hispanic Whites, and of men and women. A number of papers have been published from these data (e.g., Burnam et al., 1988; Siegel et al., 1990). The present article reviews and synthesizes the findings related to gender and ethnicity.

Methods

Respondents were participants in the NIMH-funded Epidemiologic Catchment Area (ECA) project, a national five-site study with the goal of determining rates of mental disorder and use of health services. Supplemental funds permitted data collection on lifetime experiences of sexual assault, the circumstances of assault, and the mental health sequelae.

Space constraints permit only a brief review of the methods; interested readers are referred to Eaton and Kessler (1985) for a detailed description of the methods used in the ECA project.

Sample

Over 3,000 adult (18 years or older) residents of Los Angeles were interviewed in person between June 1983 and August 1984. Two mental health catchment areas served as the initial sampling strata, and respondents were selected using a two-stage cluster sampling technique, with city blocks and households as sampling units. Individual respondents were selected using a modified Kish (1965) procedure. The response rate was 68%, which compares favorably to other large mental health surveys in the city (Frerichs, Aneshensel, & Clark, 1981).

The sample was 47% male and 53% female. A total of 45.6% of the sample were self-identified as Hispanic; 95% of the Hispanics were of Mexican heritage and 56.8% were born in Mexico. Non-Hispanic Whites comprised 41.6% of the sample. The overall median age of respondents was 35 years. Interviews were conducted in Spanish or English, depending on the respondent's preference; among the Hispanics, 45% were interviewed in Spanish, 48% in English, and 8% in a combination of both languages.

Although interviewers and respondents were matched for language facility (Spanish or English), no match was attempted on gender. Not matching on gender had a negligible effect on the prevalence rates obtained (Sorenson et al., 1987).

Definition of Sexual Assault

This research adopted a spectrum definition of sexual assault, which includes but is not limited to rape. Specifically, respondents were asked, "In your lifetime, has anyone ever tried to pressure or force you to have sexual contact? By sexual contact I mean their touching your sexual parts, your touching their sexual parts, or sexual intercourse?" Respondents who answered affirmatively were considered sexually assaulted for the purposes of this research, and were asked a series of questions related to the characteristics of the most recent assault (see Sorenson et al., 1987, for a more complete description).

To obtain the most complete information in a limited time (the interview, which included detailed mental disorder and service use questions, took an average of 2.5 hours to complete), questions about experiences during adulthood were confined to the most recent assault. Restricting questions to the most recent assault, obviously, defines what questions can be addressed using the data (e.g., if the most recent assault was an *attempted* rape, and a previous assault was a rape, the methodology employed would not identify the earlier experience; thus a lifetime prevalence of rape cannot be estimated). When a finding is restricted to the most recent assault, it is clearly identified as such in the subsequent sections.

Analyses

A variety of analytic techniques were used to estimate prevalence rates and risk factors, and to control simultaneously for potentially confounding demographic factors such as age and socioeconomic status. Interested readers are referred to the specific articles cited below for a complete description of the statistical analyses. All findings reported in this article, unless otherwise indicated, are statistically significant at or beyond $p < .05$.

Findings

Prevalence

Consistent with national crime statistics showing lower rates of rapes among Hispanic individuals, the lifetime prevalence of sexual assault among non-Hispanic Whites was 2.5 times that of Hispanics (19.9% vs. 8.1%, $p < .01$; Sorenson et al., 1987). This pattern of ethnic differences was consistent across gender, age, and education levels. Patterns of self-report about the most recent assault were similar for the two groups on many characteristics, including who was most likely to be the assailant (a friend or acquaintance), the use of pressure or force (verbal pressure was most common), and the type of resulting sexual activity (contact including intercourse was the modal outcome). Thus, the difference between the two ethnic groups appeared to be one of frequency of assault rather than characteristics of the assault.

Fewer men than women (9.4% vs. 16.7%, $p < .01$) reported being sexually assaulted at some point in their lives (Sorenson et al., 1987). The gender discrepancy was consistent across ethnicity, age, and education levels. Respondents who reported being assaulted did not differ by gender regarding relation to the assailant; a friend or acquaintance was the most common assailant for both men and women. Women were more likely to be harmed or threatened with harm (73.4% vs. 38.2%, $p < .01$), and men were more likely to be verbally pressured for sexual contact (61.8% vs. 26.71%, $p < .01$). Statistically nonsignificant trends indicated that men were more likely than women to have had their genitals touched by their assailants (26.9% vs. 18.9%, ns), whereas women were more likely than men to have experienced some form of intercourse (50.0% vs. 38.8%, ns).

Multiple sexual victimization was not rare in the present sample; two-thirds of the respondents who were assaulted reported two or more assaults, and the average number of assaults was 3.2 (Sorenson, Siegel, Golding, & Stein, in press). Being Hispanic or male was related to reduced risk of initial victimization. Among persons who had been sexually assaulted, however, neither ethnicity nor gender was related to the number of victimizations (one vs. two or more).

Resistance

A majority (75%) of the respondents reporting a sexual assault indicated that they resisted their most recent assault (Siegel et al., 1989). Among those who mentioned a resistance strategy, verbal strategies were used most often (60%). When an assailant used force, however, physical resistance by the victim (fighting, fleeing) was common. About 10% of the sexually assaulted respondents indicated that they were injured physically in addition to the sexual assault; most of these (79%) were hurt prior to any sexual contact.

Controlling for the context of the assault (use of force by the assailant, age of the respondent at the time of the assault, etc.), Hispanics and non-Hispanic Whites did not differ in their use of resistance strategies. Men were more likely than women to use either verbal resistance (46.9% vs. 31.1%, $p < .01$) or not to resist (31.1% vs. 21.8%, $p < .05$). In contrast, women were more likely than men to use physical resistance strategies (46.6% vs. 22.0%, $p < .01$). These gender differences may be related to the fact that women were more likely than men to be harmed or threatened with harm (as noted above), and perhaps they may have been more likely to resist vigorously.

Reactions

Anger, reported by 59% of the respondents, was the most common emotional reaction to a sexual assault (Siegel, et al., 1990). Other commonly reported reactions were depression (43.0%), anxiety (40.4%), fear (35.1%), guilt (31.8%), and being dishonored or spoiled (29.1%). These findings are consistent with the classic picture of rape trauma syndrome (Burgess & Holmstrom, 1974). Factor analysis of the 15 potential reactions to a sexual assault assessed in the interview produced three components: sexual distress, fear or anxiety, and depression. Physical threat and an assault outcome including oral, anal, or vaginal intercourse were associated with higher levels on each of these components. Young age at assault was associated with greater sexual distress ($p < .001$). Confiding in someone was related to lower levels of fear and anxiety ($p < .05$). Hispanics and non-Hispanic Whites did not differ in their reports of emotional and behavioral reactions to sexual assault.

A significantly greater proportion of women than men reported experiencing 11 of 15 emotional and behavioral responses to sexual assault (Siegel et al., 1990). These were fear (45.5% vs. 15.9%), stopping previous activities (31.8% vs. 15.2%), fear of sex (21.6% vs.

7.9%), loss of sexual interest (32.5% vs. 6.9%), decrease in sexual pleasure (27.1% vs. 8.0%), feeling dishonored or spoiled (33.9% vs. 20.0%), sadness or depression (50.6% vs. 28.8%), anger (72.0% vs. 34.8%), tension or anxiety (49.9% vs. 22.9%), insomnia (25.2% vs. 11.6%), and fear of being alone (23.0% vs. 2.2%). There were no gender differences in self-reports of guilt feelings, change in appetite, or alcohol or drug use. Women's greater likelihood of reporting the above reactions may indicate that women were more distressed than men by the assault. Alternatively, the gender differences may be related to women's greater willingness to tell their symptoms to others (Verbrugge, 1985). . . .

Social Support-Seeking Regarding the Assault

Hispanics and non-Hispanic Whites were about equally likely (61.1% vs. 67.6%, ns) to talk with someone about the sexual assault (Golding et al., 1989). The two groups were equally likely to report the incident to police (9.6% for Hispanics, 10.8% for non-Hispanic Whites, ns), and were very similar regarding with whom they spoke about an assault and from whom they sought social support. The only statistically significant ethnic difference was that non-Hispanic Whites were more than twice as likely as Hispanics to speak with a psychotherapist about the incident (21.2% vs. 8.8%, $p < .05$). Although the difference was not statistically significant, Hispanics were 2.5 times as likely as non-Hispanic Whites to speak with a clergy member about the assault (7.2% vs. 2.9%, ns).

Men and women were about equally likely to speak with someone about the assault (57.3% vs. 69.4%, ns). However, there were differences between the genders regarding to whom they spoke, particularly in terms of contact with the health care and legal systems. Women were more likely than men to talk with mental health professionals (21.6% vs. 5.9%, $p < .01$) and physicians (13.4% vs. 1.6%, $p < .01$). Very few men contacted persons associated with the legal system: women were nearly 20 times more likely than men to speak with police about the assault (15.7% vs. 0.8%, $p < .01$). Only 2.9% of the assaulted women and none of the men spoke with rape crisis centers.

Conclusions and Implications

Ethnicity

In this community sample of Los Angeles adults, non-Hispanic Whites were more likely than Hispanics to report having been sexually assaulted. Although the rates of assault differed for these ethnic groups, the two groups were highly similar in the circumstances and consequences of an assault. Hispanics and non-Hispanic Whites were equally likely to resist assault, to report various specific reactions to the assault, to develop mental disorders subsequent to assault, and to talk to someone about the assault. The only ethnic difference to emerge was that Hispanics talked to psychotherapists about the assault less often than non-Hispanic Whites, a finding that probably reflects the lesser use of health services overall by Hispanics compared to non-Hispanic Whites.

In addition to the possibility of undetected problems in translating the interview instrument from English into Spanish, alternative explanations for the lower rates of sexual assault among Hispanics include the role of specific aspects of acculturation (e.g., the less acculturated may be more reticent to discuss sexual assault), immigration (e.g., persons severely affected by a sexual assault may be less likely to undertake the energy-consuming task of migrating to a new country), and the possibility that there is simply less sexual violence in Mexican cultures. Examination of immigration status indicated that, in general, Mexican-Americans born in the United States reported higher rates of sexual assault than Mexican-Americans born in Mexico (11.4% vs. 3.5%, $p < .05$; Sorenson & Telles, 1991). Assault rates for U.S.-born Hispanics approached the rates reported by U.S.-born non-Hispanic Whites (11.4% vs. 16.2%, ns), suggesting that cultural milieu plays some role in the probability of sexual assault.

Cultural factors may serve to reduce the risk of sexual assault among Hispanics (most of whom were of Mexican heritage). *Machismo*, in addition to its aspects of male dominance, includes strong values of nurturance and dedication to the family. Contemporary U.S. use of the term *macho*, a derivative of *machismo*, focuses almost exclusively on aspects of the concept that are less socially desirable in an egalitarian-striving society. While traditional Mexican culture includes patriarchal notions rejected by feminists, it may also include factors that serve to protect its members from sexual aggression. For example, a girl child often is not allowed to date until late adolescence, and even then her dates are often chaperoned by a member of her family. Such cultural norms may serve to reduce a woman's exposure to situations in which date rape could occur.

This interpretation does not mean that we advocate a more patriarchal social structure as a preventive measure for sexual assault. Similarly, Durkheim (1951), while he did not advocate the values of the Catholic church, found that predominantly Catholic regions had lower rates of suicide than Protestant areas. He hypothesized that, in addition to considering suicide a sin, Catholicism engendered a sense of community and reduced isolation, and these factors helped to prevent individuals from killing themselves. A sense of community may exist in Hispanic groups (specifically, Mexican-Americans) that is similar to that noted by Durkheim. Furthermore, Catholicism is the primary religion of persons of Mexican heritage, and most of the Mexican-Americans in this sample, especially the immigrants, identified themselves as being Catholic and attended church services regularly (e.g., see Sorenson & Golding, 1988). While the constraining aspects of *machismo* and the Catholic church have been well articulated in the past decades, it is possible that each may help to provide a protective environment, to reduce the perception of individual isolation, and to reinforce feelings of belongingness and sense of community.

A possible interpretation is that rape is not simply a function of male dominance or misogyny in a culture, but also a function of a permissive attitude toward violence; thus, a strongly patriarchal culture might have little sexual violence if it decried violence against in-group members. (See Williams & Holmes, 1981, for an in-depth examination of group differences in attitudes toward rape among Anglo, Black, and Mexican-American men and women.) The difference in sexual assault levels for the Mexican-Americans born in the U.S. vs. those born in Mexico suggests a generally higher level of sexual violence in the United States. However, data on other kinds of violence present a different picture; for instance, homicide rates for men in Mexico are nearly three times those of United States men (World Health Organization, 1988, 1989). The complex interaction of social structure and normative (or at least tolerated) violent behavior needs and deserves further study.

In sum, these Los Angeles data suggest that Hispanics are less likely than non-Hispanic Whites to be sexually assaulted. When an assault does occur, however, members of the two ethnic groups are very similar regarding assault circumstances and consequences.

Gender

Women were more likely than men to report that they have been sexually assaulted. In addition, the circumstances of the assault differed. Women were more likely than men to have been harmed or threatened with harm, and to have physically resisted the assault. Women reported numerous specific reactions to assault at a higher frequency than men, but the risk of developing a mental disorder following the assault was similar for the two genders. Men were far less likely than women to speak about the incident to physicians, mental health professionals, police, rape crisis workers, and legal professionals. Regardless of their assault experience, men were less likely than women to use general medical and mental health services.

The gender difference in prevalence of sexual assault may reflect a true difference in the rates. However, there may be a greater tendency for men to underreport assault due to perceived norms of socially desired male behavior and concerns about the reactions of others. The type and frequency of mental disorders following assault were generally similar, despite the fact that women were more likely than men to have been victimized in a physically violent manner.

Implications

The reactions of men and women in this study to sexual assault are consistent with our knowledge of how men and women respond to stress. For example, women use health services more than men, and men more frequently abuse alcohol. Thus, it is appropriate to view sexual assault as a stressor, and to interpret its consequences in the context of social structures and people's location in them (Pearlin, 1989).

Hispanics and non-Hispanic Whites utilized community services about equally, but men and women differed in their use of certain services, such as rape crisis centers. Talking to rape crisis counselors was perceived as helpful by almost all (94.2%) who made use of these services, and rape crisis centers received the highest helpfulness ratings of all possible sources of social support (Golding et al., 1989). However, few of the assaulted respondents (2.9% of the women and none of the men) sought help from rape crisis centers. Perhaps men do not need the services of rape crisis centers, given that they report experiencing specific emotional and behavioral reactions to sexual assault with lesser frequency than women. Alternatively, men may not perceive the services of these centers as appropriate for them even though, ultimately, the services could prove helpful. Individuals and service providers who come into contact with sexually assaulted persons would do well to familiarize themselves with the potential benefits of rape crisis counseling.

In this study reactions to coercive sexual experiences appeared to have certain similar correlates regardless of the victim's ethnicity or gender. The predominant factor in response and outcome was the sexual assault itself, not the ethnicity or gender of the person who was assaulted. While factors unique to Hispanics and to men should be taken into account, their patterns of distressing reactions and mental disorder were generally similar to the model of response developed from previous research predominantly with non-Hispanic White women. Thus, existing models of assault reactions and recovery may be appropriate for application to a broader population. Subsequent research on sexual assault might benefit from using a stress framework and, in particular, a framework that takes into account social and structural variables, such as individuals' exposure to situations that may put them at risk for sexual assault.

References

Ageton, S. S. (1983). *Sexual assault among adolescents*. Lexington, MA: Heath.

American Psychiatric Association. (1980). *Diagnostic and statistical manual of mental disorders* (3rd ed.). Washington, DC: Author.

Bolton, F. G., Morris, L. A., & MacEachron, A. A. (1989). *Males at risk*. Newbury Park, CA: Sage.

Burgess, A. W., & Holmstrom, L. L. (1974). Rape trauma syndrome. *American Journal of Psychiatry*, 131, 981–986.

Burke, J. D. (1986). Diagnostic interview categorization by the Diagnostic Interview Schedule (DIS): A comparison with other methods of assessment. In J. E. Barrett & R. M. Rose (Eds.), *Mental disorder in the community: Progress and challenge* (pp. 255–285). New York: Guilford.

Burnam, M. A., Stein, J. A., Golding, J. M., Siegel, J. M., Sorenson, S. B., Forsythe, A. B., & Telles, C. A. (1988). Sexual assault and mental disorders in a community population. *Journal of Consulting and Clinical Psychology*, 56, 843–850.

Doyle, J. A. (1990). *The male experience*. Dubuque, IA: Brown.

Durkheim, E. (1951). *Suicide*. New York: Free Press. (Original work published in 1897).

Eaton, W. W., & Kessler, L. G. (Eds.). (1985). *Epidemiologic field methods in psychiatry*. Orlando, FL: Academic Press.

Fischer, G. J. (1987). Hispanic and majority student attitudes toward forcible date rape as a function of differences in attitudes toward women. *Sex Roles*, 17, 93–101.

Frerichs, R., Aneshensel, C. A., & Clark, V. A. (1981). Prevalence of depression in Los Angeles County. *American Journal of Epidemiology*, 113, 691–699.

Golding, J. M., Siegel, J. M., Sorenson, S. B., Burnam, M. A., & Stein, J. A. (1989). Social support sources following sexual assault. *Journal of Community Psychology*, 17, 92–107.

Golding, J. M., Stein, J. A., Siegel, J. M., Burnam, M. A., & Sorenson, S. B. (1988). Sexual assault history and use of health and mental health services. *American Journal of Community Psychology*, 16, 625–644.

Hayes-Bautista, D., Schink, W., & Chapa, J. (1985). The Latino population and U.S. social policy: A present and future view. *Border Health*, 1, 7–17.

Hunter, M. (1990). *Abused boys: The neglected victims of sexual abuse*. Lexington, MA: Lexington Books.

Kish, L. (1965). *Survey sampling*. New York: Wiley.

Macias, R. F. (1977). U.S. Hispanics and 2000 AD.: Projecting the number. *Agenda*, 7, 16–20.

Michigan Compiled Laws Annotated. (1986). Secs. 750.520a(a), 750.520b. St. Paul, MN: West.

Pearlin, L. I. (1989). The sociological study of stress. *Journal of Health and Social Behavior*, 30, 241–256.

Robins, L. N., Helzer, J. E., Croughan, J., & Ratcliff, K. (1981). National Institute of Mental Health Diagnostic Interview Schedule: Its history, characteristics, and validity. *Archives of General Psychiatry*, 38, 381–389.

Robins, L. N., Helzer, J. E., Croughan, J., Williams, J. B. W., & Spitzer, R. L. (1982). *NIMH Diagnostic Interview Schedule: Version III*. Rockville, MD: National Institute of Mental Health.

Russell, D. E. H. (1982). The prevalence and incidence of forcible rape and attempted rape of females. *Victimology*, 7, 81–93.

Siegel, J. M., Golding, J. M., Stein, J. A., Burnam, M. A., & Sorenson, S. B. (1990). Reactions to sexual assault: A community study. *Journal of Interpersonal Violence*, 5, 229–246.

Siegel, J. M., Sorenson, S. B., Golding, J. M., Burnam, M. A., & Stein, J. A. (1989). Resistance to sexual assault: Who resists and what happens? *American Journal of Public Health*, 79, 27–31.

Sorenson, S. B., & Golding, J. M. (1988). Prevalence of suicide attempts in a Mexican-American population: Prevention implications of immigration and cultural issues. *Suicide and Life-Threatening Behavior*, 18, 322–333.

Sorenson, S. B., Siegel, J. M., Golding, J. M., & Stein, J. A. (in press). Repeated sexual victimization. *Violence and Victims*.

Sorenson, S. B., Stein, J. A., Siegel, J. M., Golding, J. M., & Burnam, M. A. (1987). The prevalence of adult sexual assault: The Los

Angeles Epidemiologic Catchment Area study. *American Journal of Epidemiology*, 126, 1154–1164.

Sorenson, S. B., & Telles, C. A. (1991). Self-reports of spousal violence in a Mexican-American and non-Hispanic White population. *Violence and Victims*, 6, 3–15.

U.S. Department of Justice. (1988a, March). *Report to the nation on crime and justice* (2nd ed.). Washington, DC: Bureau of Justice Statistics.

U.S. Department of Justice. (1988b, August). *Criminal victimization in the United States, 1986*. Washington, DC: Bureau of Justice Statistics.

Verbrugge, L. M. (1985). Gender and health: An update on hypotheses and evidence. *Journal of Health and Social Behavior*, 26, 156–182.

Williams, J. E., & Holmes, K. A. (1981). *The second assault: Rape and public attitudes*. Westport, CT: Greenwood.

Williams, L. S. (1984). The classic rape: When do victims report? *Social Problems*, 31, 459–467.

World Health Organization. (1988). *World health statistics annual*. Geneva: Author.

World Health Organization. (1989). *World health statistics annual*. Geneva: Author.

V   Strategies for Change

The final section of this volume explores various strategies for ending rape and sexual assault in our society. The articles examine individual, organizational, and structural changes that can be made to prevent rape. A number of social science researchers have conducted studies to identify individual strategies people can pursue to resist sexual assault. In "The Effects of Resistance Strategies on Rape," Janice Zoucha-Jensen and Ann Coyne, scholars in the School of Social Work at the University of Nebraska, Omaha, analyze the effectiveness of various methods to avoid rape, based on an empirical study of 150 women who had been attacked. They find that women who resorted to forceful language, physical resistance, and fleeing from the scene were more likely to avoid rape than those women who offered little or no resistance.

Rape crisis centers have pursued various efforts to address the problem of rape and sexual assault in our society. "Organizational and Community Transformation: The Case of a Rape Crisis Center" examines how one rape crisis center successfully changed the insensitive treatment of rape victims in its community. Patricia Yancey Martin, a sociologist at Florida State University, and her co-authors, Diana DiNitto, Diane Byington, and Sharon Maxwell, found that the center achieved this goal through a strategy of cooperation with, rather than antagonism toward, the mainstream organizations dealing with rape. The rape crisis center influenced police departments, hospitals, and the prosecutor's office to adopt its methods and practices of working with rape victims.

In "Rape and the Law," sociologist and legal scholar Carol Bohmer assesses rape law reform efforts over the last two decades. In the past, rape law and legal practice tended to blame victims for their assault and to make the prosecution and conviction of rapists very difficult. Bohmer discusses how legal reformers have worked to change the criminal justice system's handling of rape in a number of ways, including challenging the "utmost resistance" standard, altering the legal definition of rape, instituting rape shield laws (which deal with the admissibility in court of testimony concerning the prior sexual history of the victim), abolishing the corroboration requirement, and making spousal rape illegal. Bohmer argues that while these changes are important, they have had a limited impact on the legal response to rape because many judges, prosecutors, attorneys, and jury members continue to hold inaccurate, stereotyped beliefs about rape and sexual behavior.

The final chapter addresses broad cultural and structural changes needed to deal with the problem of rape in our society. Michael Kimmel, a sociologist at the State University of New York, Stony Brook, calls in "Clarence, William, Iron Mike, Tailhook, Senator Packwood, Spur Posse, Magic . . . and Us" for a fundamental transformation of the dominant conception of masculinity in our culture, which encourages men to be aggressive, competitive, and emotionally distant in their sexual relationships. This transformation, he argues, is important not only for challenging sexual assault but also for the struggles against sexual harassment and AIDS.

17

The Effects of Resistance Strategies on Rape

~

Janice M. Zoucha-Jensen
Ann Coyne

Introduction

A RAPE IS REPORTED in the United States every 6 minutes. Over the last decade, the rate of reported rapes increased four times as fast as the overall crime rate.[1] Although this statistic is alarming. it substantially underrepresents the true incidence of rape. Government estimates suggest that "for every rape reported to police, 3 to 10 rapes are not reported."[2] Because of these startling statistics, extensive research has been done in the area of rape prevention. However, past research has failed to identify what types of resistance strategies most effectively prevent rape and at what cost. This has led to conflicting advice being offered to women.

Siegel et al.'s interview study, which used randomly selected community residents, found that "resistance, particularly verbal, reduces the probability of sexual contact. Physical resistance, on the other hand, is associated with increased likelihood of contact."[3] Several other researchers reported similar findings with samples of selected subjects who reported the rape to police or sought rape crisis services.[4-6] However, some researchers[7-13] who sampled similar populations found just the opposite to be true. Bart and O'Brien found that "strategies

From Janice M. Zoucha-Jensen and Ann Coyne, "The Effects of Resistance Strategies on Rape," *American Journal of Public Health* 83, no. 11 (November 1993): 1633–34. © 1995 by the American Public Health Association. Reprinted by permission of the American Public Health Association.

associated with avoidance were fleeing or trying to flee, yelling, and using physical force."[7]

Because past research about the effectiveness of various types of resistance has been inconclusive, this research was conducted to determine which resistance strategies were associated with rape avoidance and whether physical resistance in particular was associated with additional physical injury. It was hypothesized that more forceful resistance would be associated with rape avoidance but physical resistance would be associated with additional physical injury.

Methods

Data were collected from the Omaha, Nebraska, Police Department's initial and supplemental reports. The sample consisted of 150 women, aged 16 and older, whose sexual assault occurred between June 1, 1988, and May 31, 1989, and was reported to the Omaha Police Department. Nebraska law requires medical personnel to report to the police any injury sustained because of violence. The sample thus consisted of women who themselves reported the assault to the police or who sought medical attention and whose assault was then reported to the police by medical personnel. It is likely that attacks resulting in injuries, attacks by strangers, and attacks in which resistance was less successful were probably overrepresented in this sample.[8] Despite this inherent bias, however, a finding of a positive association between resistance and rape avoidance with women in this sample should allow us to infer that a similar association would hold for rape attempts not reported to police.

The independent variable, resistance strategy, was defined as any action taken to ward off the attack. This variable was divided into five categories: no resistance; nonforceful verbal resistance (pleading, crying, and/or assertively refusing); forceful verbal resistance (screaming and/or yelling); physical resistance (wrestling/struggling, pushing, striking, biting, and/or using a weapon); and fleeing (running, walking away, and/or fleeing in a car). In cases in which several types of resistance were attempted, this variable was coded as the most forceful resistance strategy attempted.

The dependent variables were outcome of the assault and additional physical injury. Outcome of the assault was divided into two categories, raped and avoided rape. "Raped" was defined as having sustained penile, oral, or digital penetration or penetration by an instrument, in all cases under force or threat of force. "Avoided rape" was defined as having sustained no penetration. "Additional physical injury" was also divided into two categories, injured and not injured.

"Injured" was defined as having sustained any apparent injury or complained of an injury. "Not injured" was defined as not having sustained any apparent injury and not complaining of an injury.

Results

Of the 150 women in the sample, 64.7% were raped and 35.3% avoided rape, with 46.7% incurring an additional physical injury. Physical resistance was the most frequently selected resistance strategy (44.3%).

We analyzed resistance strategy by outcome of the assault using a chi-square test. Forceful verbal resistance, physical resistance, and fleeing were all associated with rape avoidance. No resistance and nonforceful verbal resistance were associated with being raped (x^2 [4, n = 149] = 22.93, $p < .001$) (see table).

Strategy by Outcome of the Assault (n = 149)

| | Outcome of the Assault[a] | |
| | *Raped, %* *(n = 97)* | *Avoided Rape, %* *(n = 52)* |
Resistance Strategy		
No resistance	93.5	6.5
Nonforceful verbal resistance	95.8	4.2
Forceful verbal resistance	50.0	50.0
Physical resistance	45.5	54.5
Running/fleeing	55.0	45.0

[a]x^2 (4, n = 149) = 22.93, $p < .001$.

We analyzed resistance strategy by additional physical injury using a chi-square test. There was no significant relationship between the two variables.

Discussion

This study supports prior research that found an association between physical resistance and rape avoidance.[7-13] It also contradicts other prior research that found an association between less forceful verbal resistance (pleading, crying, etc.) and rape avoidance.[3-6] This study in fact found a negative association between nonforceful verbal resistance (pleading and crying) and rape avoidance but a positive association between forceful verbal resistance (screaming or yelling) and rape avoidance.

The findings of this study, in combination with some past research, provide professionals who are responsible for public health education with direction in planning public educational programs. These findings also counter some prior research on resistance strategies, research that has resulted in inaccurate advice to women to use only nonforceful verbal resistance, or no resistance at all, if faced with a sexual assault. Those types of resistance strategies were shown in this study to be associated with being raped, not with rape avoidance, and they did not reduce the incidence of physical injury.

Because of the contradictory results of past studies, additional research on rape prevention strategies is needed. Special attention should be paid to the temporal sequencing of resistance strategies, outcome, and additional physical injury so that these relationships can be understood. In addition, resistance strategies should be measured so that essentially different strategies are not artificially combined together. For example, if screaming and pleading had been combined into one measure called "verbal resistance," important differences would have been lost. Lastly, future research needs to include women who did not seek medical attention for their injuries or report the assault to the police, women who were not injured, and women who were assaulted by people they knew.

References

1. The mind of the rapist. *Newsweek*. July 23, 1990:46–53.
2. Burgess, A. W. *Rape and Sexual Assault II*. New York, NY: Garland Publishing, Inc; 1988.
3. Siegel, J. M., Sorenson, S. B., Golding, J. M., Burnam, M. A., Stein, J. A. Resistance to sexual assault: who resists and what happens? *Am J Public Health*. 1989; 79:27–31.
4. Block. R., Skogan, W. G. Resistance and nonfatal outcomes in stranger-to-stranger predatory crime. *Viol Victims*. 1986; 1 (4):241–253.
5. Cohen, P. B. Resistance during sexual assaults: avoiding rape and injury. *Victimol: Int J*. 1984; 9 (1):120–129.
6. Quinsey, V. L., Upfold, D. Rape completion and victim injury as a function of female resistance strategy. *Can J Behav Sci/Rev Can Sci Comp*. 1985; 17 (1):40–50.
7. Bart, P. B., O'Brien, P. H. Stopping rape: effective avoidance strategies. *Signs: J Women Cult Soc*. 1984; 10 (1):83–101.
8. Ruback, R. B., Ivie, D. L. Prior relationship, resistance, and injury in rapes: an analysis of crisis center records. *Viol Victims*. 1988; 3 (2) 99–111.
9. Atkeson, B. M., Calhoun, K. S., Morris, K. T. Victim resistance to rape: the relationship of previous victimization, demographics and situational factors. *Arch Sexual Behav*. 1989; 18 (6):497–507.

10. Kleck, G., Sayles, S. Rape and resistance. *Soc Probl.* 1990; 37 (2):149–162.
11. Marchbanks, P. A., Lui, K. J., Mercy, J. A. Risk of injury from resisting rape. *Am J Epidemiol.* 1990; 132 (3):540–549.
12. Ullman, S. E., Knight, R. A. A multivariate model for predicting rape and physical injury outcomes during sexual assaults. *J Consult Clin Psychol.* 1991; 59 (5):724–731.
13. Bart, P. B. A study of women who both were raped and avoided rape. *J Soc Issues.* 1981; 37 (4):123–137.

18

Organizational and Community Transformation: The Case of a Rape Crisis Center

~

Patricia Yancey Martin
Diana DiNitto
Diane Byington
M. Sharon Maxwell

IN THE 1970s THE WOMEN'S MOVEMENT of the United States claimed to have created unique organizational-type feminist organizations (Martin, 1990; Ferree & Hess, 1985). Like other counterculture organizations, feminist organizations were (ideally) collectivist, nonhierarchical, nonbureaucratic, and free of professional and technical elitism (Rothschild & Whitt, 1986). Unlike other counterculture organizations, they emphasized member nurturance and advancement of women as a group (Freeman, 1975, 1979; O'Sullivan, 1978; Riger, 1984; Maxwell, 1987). Early feminist organizers denounced bureaucracy as alienating, elitist, exploitative, and patriarchal (Largen, 1981; Thurston, 1987; Maxwell, 1987; U.S. Department of Justice, 1975).

As a result of such views, many feminists avoided contact with mainstream organizations, including government and the state (Staggenborg, 1989; Leidner, 1991; Reinelt, 1991). (Mainstream organizations provide social welfare services but are not associated with the

From Patricia Yancey Martin, Diana DiNitto, Diane Byington, M. Sharon Maxwell, "Organizational and Community Transformation: The Case of a Rape Crisis Center," *Administration in Social Work* 16, nos. 3–4 (1992): 123–45. © 1992 by the Haworth Press, Binghamton, New York. Reprinted by permission of the Haworth Press.

social movement.) Early rape crisis center (RCC) organizers refused to accept public funds from or interact with organizations such as police, prosecutors, and hospitals (Largen, 1981; O'Sullivan, 1978). They believed such organizations embodied masculinist or patriarchal values, arrangements, and practices that were antithetical to women's well-being and feared that contact with them would undermine their commitment to feminist goals (Ferguson, 1984; Connell, 1987; Bologh, 1990; Reinelt, 1991).

As feminist organizations, rape crisis centers (RCCs) viewed rape victim assistance as a political activity (Largen, 1981; U. S. Department of Justice, 1975; Harvey, 1985; Gornick, Burt, & Pittman, 1985; Koss & Harvey, 1991; Byington et al., 1991). They worried about becoming social service organizations that treated victims rather than remaining true to their political goals of changing society (O'Sullivan, 1978; Simon, 1980; Maxwell, 1987; Freeman, 1975). As a result, many RCCs refused to accept public funding such as that provided by the Law Enforcement Assistance Administration (U.S. Department of Justice, 1975; Simon, 1980). Though most rape crisis centers now accept public funds, they remain wary of mainstream organizations. RCCs and mainstream organizations in many communities are suspicious of, if not hostile towards, each other (Martin et al., 1984; Maxwell, 1987).

The findings of this case study suggest that one RCC transformed itself and other processing organizations in its community by reconceptualizing its boundary, vision of itself, and domain of influence. Rather than being co-opted, it co-opted. By drawing a circle around rather than a line between itself and mainstream organizations, the RCC incorporated the mainstream organizations into its domain of influence. The RCC offered its womanpower, free, to instruct mainstream staff in rape processing skills; assisted mainstream organizations as they developed specialized personnel, practices, and protocols for processing victims; and encouraged mainstream organizations to cooperate and improve rape victim processing in the community. As a result of these changes, the RCC's relations with mainstream organizations and the latter's relations with each other were transformed.

Background and Theoretical Issues

Rape processing. Rape processing refers to organizational activities that move rape victims and their cases through the service network of a community (LaFree, 1989; Holmstrom & Burgess, 1978; Ferraro, 1981). By its nature, it is a multi- and an inter-organizational process because different organizations perform different processing activities. For example, law enforcement secures crime scenes, interviews victims and other witnesses, and arrests assailants. Hospitals perform post-rape exams and treat victims who are injured (Martin et al., 1985; Martin & DiNitto, 1987; DiNitto et al., 1986, 1987, 1989). Prosecutors decide whether to bring charges against alleged assailants and, if so, they prosecute on the state's behalf. Rape crisis centers, the new organizations in the loop, help victims recover from rape and they advocate and intercede for victims with mainstream organizations (Martin et al., 1984; Harvey, 1985; Gornick, Burt, & Pittman, 1985; Koss & Harvey, 1991). RCCs hope to change society to eliminate rape and women's inequality generally (O'Sullivan, 1978; Gornick, Burt, & Pittman, 1985; Harvey, 1985).

Organizational environments: Concrete reality or social construction? An open systems model was the predominant view of organizations in the 1970s and 1980s (Hall, 1986; Martin & O'Connor, 1989). Open systems theory views organizations and their environments as concrete and empirically separate (and separable) phenomena. The successful organization is one that exploits its external environment for scarce resources, secures a niche for itself in the environment, and manages its relations to its environment, including other organizations and state, to its advantage. The open systems model is based on a *positivist* view of social reality. This view can be contrasted with a *social constructionist* view (Burrel & Morgan, 1979). What a positivist perspective claims is factually external is, from a constructionist perspective, neither factual nor external. Social constructionists view organizations as having no inherent or fixed boundaries that separate them from their environment or anything else. Rather, they believe organizational actors actively *constitute or create* an organization, its boundaries, and its environment through the practices in which they engage.

A constructionist view claims that organizations, like other social systems, have no facticity or concrete reality other than that which its members *create* through their actions (Morgan, 1986). Through conceptualizing and acting, organization members *define* the organization's character and boundaries. Different from a positivist view that represents police as factually outside of the rape crisis center, for example, a constructionist view claims that RCC members determine if this is so through their actions. Relations with the police are thus internal or external, depending on the RCC's conceptions and practices.

The distinction between a positivist and social constructionist view (Burrell & Morgan, 1979; Morgan, 1986) is useful for understanding how one RCC transformed itself and its community. Early in its history, the RCC considered mainstream organizations as external to and separate from itself; it viewed itself as the expert and mainstream organizations as a problem. As its relationship to mainstream organizations changed through the task force activity (see below), however, the RCC came to view mainstream organizations as within its domain boundary and, in doing this, transformed itself and the entire processing network.

To understand this transformation, we employ three concepts: Standing outside, allocating blame; revising the domain of influence and boundary; and enacting a new vision.

Standing outside, allocating blame. As noted, many early RCCs avoided contact with mainstream organizations. Worries about cooptation prompted them to pursue a strategy of *standing outside* and *allocating blame* to mainstream organizations when rape victims were mistreated (Largen, 1981; Maxwell, 1987). When a rape victim was mistreated, the RCC denounced the mainstream organization in public rather than working with it in private to protest or negotiate change. A standing outside approach produced some beneficial effects because sheriffs, prosecutors, and hospitals desire a positive public image. Mainstream organizations are supported by tax revenues and need the public's goodwill. Thus, although a standing outside approach produced some positive changes, it also caused mainstream administrators and staff to resent the RCC. The use of a blame allocating strategy suggests that the RCC conceptualized itself *as separate from* mainstream organizations. Such an approach depicts mainstream organizations as inferior to the RCC. Little wonder that mainstream organizations resented this strategy.

Revising the domain of influence: An inclusive boundary. According to a social constructionist view, an organization creates its reality by what its members do and say (Morgan, 1986). Thus, RCCs that view police as the external enemy are not merely *responding* to the police; rather, they are *constituting* the police as *enemy.* If a RCC views the police as within its domain boundary, however, the relationship changes. The RCC then identifies with the police as a part of itself. When this occurs, the RCC's view of police becomes one of "how can we *improve this part of ourselves*?" In the community we studied, a revised domain boundary that defined the police (and other mainstream organizations) and RCC as interdependent rather than separate changed the RCC's strategies and views. The RCC staff were no longer able to view the police and other mainstream organizations as external enemy.

Enacting a new vision. As described below, the RCC's pursuit of a Stop Rape Task Force culminated in a new vision of itself and its relations to mainstream organizations. Through enacting this new vision, it created a new reality. The vision was thus created, enacted, challenged, sustained, and changed through individual and collective action over time (Giddens, 1983, 1984). The process was circular and iterative. In this case, an inclusive vision fostered knowledge, familiarity, and understanding; understanding fostered cooperation and goodwill; cooperation and goodwill fostered knowledge, familiarity, and understanding; and so on. As the RCC enacted its new relationship with law enforcement, prosecutor, and hospital, it developed a new sense of itself in relationship to these organizations. The mainstream organizations were transformed by the RCC's new vision also. In working with the RCC on mutual goals, mainstream organizations revised their internal practices and policies, cooperated more with each other, and reformed their understanding of victims' needs and rights. These organizations were, in a sense, co-opted. They did not conceptualize the RCC as their responsibility (in contrast to the RCC's view of them), but they did become more cooperative with the RCC and each other and they took pride in the new arrangements. While they continued to view the RCC as external to themselves, their changed relationship to the RCC, and to each other, discouraged open criticism, competition, and conflict.

The Case Study

Beach County. Beach County is a fast growing county in the southern half of Florida with a population of 220,000 in 1983. Its largest city, Hermosa (with a population of 50,000+), is tropical, affluent and a popular destination for easterners in the winter tourist season. Hermosa's rape crisis center is housed with a battered women's shelter that serves a three-county area and is funded by a state marriage license fee fund. FBI statistics show that 97 rapes were reported to law enforcement in Beach County in 1983, the year before our visit. The rape index (rapes per 100,000 population) for Beach County is high; it was 124 in 1982 and 90 in 1983, compared to the national index of 39 for comparable urban areas in 1983.

Sample and Data. In the summer of 1984, we interviewed staff in five organizations in Beach County: The rape crisis center, Hermosa city police, Beach County sheriff, the Hermosa hospital, and the state prosecutor's office. (The city, county, other organizations, and all individuals are given pseudonyms to protect anonymity.) Semi-structured, face-to-face interviews with mid- or upper-level administrative personnel lasted from one to two hours and asked about a range of activities about rape victim processing, community relations, outreach to the public, and organizational conditions. Data for the study are taken from interviews, on-site observations, and archival materials from the organizations such as reports, publications, and memoranda. (More information about the methods and sample is in Martin et al., 1984.)

The RCC transformed itself and the community through the establishment of a *permanent working task force of rape processors*. Beach County's permanent Stop Rape Task Force (hereafter referred to as the task force) had been in place for two and one-half years when we interviewed. The task force was a *working* group comprised of employees who processed victims or supervised staff who did rather than a politically appointed, time-limited, fact-finding commission of local officials and citizens. The task force's membership and structure, history and procedures, philosophy, and impact are discussed below.

Membership and Structure

The task force is a problem-solving, policymaking umbrella organization comprised of representatives (one or two) from each processing organization in the area. Task force members process rape victims or they supervise staff who do. A sergeant with authority over investigators and uniformed officers may represent the police but the chief does not. Actual processors and supervisors who know about processing work belong to the task force. Some task force members bring others to meetings on a temporary basis. When we interviewed, a police sergeant was bringing a woman Community Service Aide (see below) from his department. The RCC was represented by the executive director, board president, and counseling director; the Hermosa hospital by two charge nurses; and the prosecutor by an investigator.

Task force stationery listed 15 names of staff from nine processing organizations plus two task force staff, a coordinator and assistant coordinator. The nine organizations included a county sheriff's department, four city police departments, two hospitals, the prosecutor's office, and the RCC. During its first two years, the task force met monthly. At the time we interviewed, it met every six weeks and was moving to an alternate month schedule. In the members' eyes, the need for less frequent meetings was a sign of success. The RCC Board President served as the task force chair. . . .

The idea for the task force came "from the literature." The RCC director and board president read about such a task force in a newsletter of the National Clearing House on Violence Against Women and Children. The RCC board president, accompanied by the RCC director, visited each city and county local government official and director of every processing organization to ask what they thought about starting a task force (like the one they had read about). According to the RCC board president, she and the RCC director said: "We're thinking about doing this. What do you think? [Do you have] any ideas?" To her surprise, everyone said yes. . . .

According to the task force chairwoman (and RCC board president), the response among mainstream staff was positive from the outset:

> I was stunned by the good ideas that emerged, how seriously the task was taken, how much everyone wanted to do something. If we just talk about a problem or issue, it almost immediately helps things get better.

In its initial months, task force meetings dealt with problems of coordination and damage control. How can we alert each other? How can we assure that a mistake doesn't happen again? How can we support the victim and gain her cooperation? What kind of training do we need and how should we provide it? The orientation was to use carrots rather than sticks to gain cooperation and commitment. In discussing the training provided by RCC staff for mainstream organizations, the RCC director said:

> [The RCC] goes in twice a year to every law enforcement program in our county (four police and a sheriff), to two different ERs [of hospitals], and to the state attorney's (prosecutor's) office to do in-service training on rape. This is arranged annually and done routinely. In this way, we are able to assure minimal knowledge of the front-line people who work with victims. Instead of having to fuss at the ER for not doing more training, we say: "Let us do it for you," which is like a gift rather than [an] admonishment. They [staff in the other organizations] actually *like* us.

What produced this unusual, and successful, innovation? Our data suggest that a combination of individuals and community influences were involved. A politically savvy, consensus-building approach was employed in the community, all players were invited to take part, and committed individuals took initiative.

The Individual Actors

The board president. The effort to found the task force was spearheaded by a "graying housewife" (as she described herself) in her sixties who was the RCC board president. Over a decade earlier, Sarah Greene (a pseudonym) had founded the Hermosa RCC and, since then, served as its only board president. As noted earlier, she chairs the Hermosa Stop Rape Task Force. Greene moved to Hermosa in the 1960s from the northeast where, earlier, her daughter had been raped. Greene has a desk and telephone at the RCC and, although she receives no pay for her work on its behalf, regularly spends half days at her desk. She gives guidance, support, and assistance to the RCC president. Greene says her personal brush with rape helps explain her commitment to serving victims and preventing rape crimes. She views communities as political entities and believes sugar is more effective than vinegar in gaining cooperation. She said she seeks ways for "all to win and take credit."

The RCC director. When we interviewed her, the RCC director, Mary Jones, was in her mid-40s. She described herself as ". . . a pragmatic feminist who looks, acts, and talks like a middle-class wife and mother." She was committed to serving rape victims as a top priority. Jones said, "We do whatever it takes to serve women in this area; we do all we can to prevent rapes . . . of girls and women here." Jones became involved with the RCC as a volunteer in 1979, was on the payroll by January of 1980, and became executive director within the year. She and Greene get along well. As Jones and Greene began their visits to discuss the task force with mainstream staff, Jones said that they were not particularly well received at first:

> The police thought we were bra-burning feminists. But we contacted all the agencies and outlined what had to be done. It took her [the task force coordinator] about nine months to bring them all around.

The sheriff's deputy. Jim Dobbs, a tall, burly sheriff's deputy, played a role in the task force story. When he heard about the task force idea, he requested funds from the sheriff to go to Baton Rouge to learn about it first hand. When the sheriff turned him down, Dobbs arranged to pick up a prisoner who was being extradited from Louisiana to Florida, went anyway, and stayed two extra days at his own expense to learn about it from a law enforcement angle.

Dobbs has a distinctive philosophy of rape victim processing. He says he refuses to place himself "above a rape victim . . . so she can start regaining control over her life." By this, he means that he will not tower over a victim; if the victim is standing, he sits; if she is sitting, he will sit on the floor. He hopes to show her she is "back in charge." Yet, like other staff in processing organizations, Dobbs's motives are not pure. His goals are organizational as well as altruistic. According to him, ". . . trusting victims tell more; trusting victims are more cooperative." Dobbs described a woman who held his hand over his shoulder in the car—when he was in the front seat, she in the back. She trusted him completely, he said, and told him everything which, in his opinion, was good for her and the investigation of her case. . . .

The ER nurse. Everyone we interviewed described Penny Adams, a charge nurse (shift supervisor) at Hermosa Hospital's emergency room (ER), as likable and effective. Like Dobbs, Adams has clear views about how rape processing should be done. She thinks victims need to be told in no uncertain terms that rape is not their fault and she thinks doctors rarely do this. She and her supervisor, Joan Townsend, have used annual leave to visit a RCC in a nearby city to learn about the nurse examiner program (Martin et al., 1985; DiNitto et al., 1986; Martin & DiNitto, 1987). At the time we interviewed, she had submitted a proposal to the hospital's administrator and the prosecutor's office asking that nurses be allowed to perform the rape exams. If the hospital and prosecutor approve, Adams and Townsend will supervise the nurse examiners, and MDs will provide back-up treatment for injuries.

Adams says the task force has increased understanding in its male members. "The task force is what is really educating the men . . . and this is changing [their] views [on rape]." A male investigator in the prosecutor's office confirmed her claim. He said, "The task force meetings are really inservice (training, education) because we (his boss who is a male assistant prosecutor and who deals with all sexual battery cases and himself) keep learning and dealing with problems at every meeting."

The Political Strategy

Perhaps the task force succeeded because its initiators *asked* local organizational and political leaders for their opinions and *invited* their suggestions, cooperation, and help. Friendly, personal visits opened communication channels and established common ground for dealing as *equal* partners in a joint activity. The demeanor and style of Sarah Greene, and RCC director Jones, were apparently unthreatening. One police official commented that "they were not as radical or nutty as we had thought." The model upon which the task force was based involved an organization like theirs in Baton Rouge; thus, each organization could look to a sister agency in Baton Rouge for advice, example, and support. Mainstream organizations were spared the necessity of granting superior knowledge to the rape crisis center or other local organizations. The task force allowed each organization to negotiate its niche in the processing system and network.

The hospital charge nurse, Penny Adams, described the task force's philosophy as two-pronged:

> The task force does two things. It emphasizes catching and prosecuting the assailant and emphasizes helping the victim. This makes it very special—and makes everyone relate to it and learn from it.

All respondents noted the value of working together. Task force members agreed to alert each other when a rape occurred. As RCC director Mary Jones said:

> If a rape appears in the newspaper and (the RCC) was not called, I call the law enforcement people and they look into it. When someone in Beach County is raped, everyone involved in serving the victim is immediately notified. I think something like this should be done in every city in Florida.

A police sergeant in Hermosa credited law enforcement's high clearance rate, better than 50 percent, to the philosophy and approach of the task force. He explained, "I think it's because we (staff in all of the processing organizations) establish good rapport [with the victim] and are more involved in the case."

The issue of victims' needs was mentioned repeatedly by task force members. A police sergeant said his department allows uniformed officers to go to the scene and "make a very brief initial investigation" but forbids them from questioning a victim closely because they may be insensitive or ask incorrectly. He said his department has a Victim Processing Protocol that instructs uniformed officers not to request details from rape victims.

> They (uniformed officers) aren't well-trained in the emotions and touchiness of evidence collection. So the tough questions are asked at the police department by an investigator who is better trained in this. The tape statement (the victim's official statement) is a tough time because she is reliving the incident. The investigator has to be very careful . . . The detectives who take the sworn statement . . . they're very sensitive, patient, caring. They really *care*. They're selected for "crimes against persons" because they're very intelligent, nice personality. . . . They're carefully selected.

This department also selects Community Service Aides "for their compassion" and because "they are female." The sergeant whom we interviewed claims that rape victims want to be around women since, because of the rape, they are afraid of men (Martin, 1991). Community Service Aides are hired by the police department to investigate minor crimes, conduct portions of the rape kit exam, and provide emotional and physical support to rape victims before, during, and after the rape kit exam. They stay with the victim during the sworn statement interview also and drive her home when law enforcement is done.

An investigator in the prosecutor's office said: "A special goal is to educate the victim regarding what all is involved. If we're going to do our job, the victim must understand." The prosecutor's office is hiring a victim witness aide who will help victims. According to the investigator, when such an aide is hired, a victim ". . . can call at any time and get through to them (aide) and find out what's going on at any time. It's like calling a bank and saying what's my account like. They (the victim witness aide) will know the victim and the case and can give a more personal response."

The depth of commitment to rape victims is indicated in the comments of RCC director Jones. The RCC receives *no* funds to pay for rape victim services yet it serves victims in many ways. For example, the RCC counsels victims on the phone and in person, meets them at the hospital ER, trains mainstream staff about rape, and so on. Jones said: "[We] . . . fund it (rape victim program) anyway. We do whatever has to be done [to help or serve rape victims]. . . .

Task force members claim that all kinds of training in rape processing are important: about rape as a crime, the aftermath of rape for victims, interviewing victims, the collection of evidence, the development of cases, finding and arresting assailants, the prosecution of cases, the long-term treatment of victims, and so on. Agreement on the value of training may explain the willingness of mainstream organizations to let the RCC provide training twice a year. Task force members see training as beneficial to rape victims as well as their organizations. If people know what they are doing, and how to do it, they are more responsive and effective, less error prone and resentful, and often faster as well (Martin et al., 1984).

Agreement on the goal of providing responsive, coordinated services to victims led to a negotiated division of labor among task force members. A protocol was developed to spell out which organizations should notify others when a rape occurred. The police or sheriff call the hospital and RCC; the RCC call the prosecutor. In most communities, conflict is pervasive over who does rape exams (Martin & DiNitto, 1987) and whether the RCC can have an advocate present during mainstream processing encounters. The Hermosa task force reached an agreement that removed much of the friction from these issues. As a consequence, the police and sheriff have assumed more responsibility for functions that were previously performed by the hospital ER and rape crisis staff (see Martin et al., 1984). Furthermore, they agreed to do so according to RCC-approved standards. This freed the RCC to devote more time to its outreach, fund-raising, community awareness, rape prevention, and social change activities.

Many hospitals, physicians, and nurses dislike doing rape exams (Martin & DiNitto, 1987). Partly because of this, the Hermosa police department offered to take greater responsibility for the exam. It hired and trained three (women) Community Service Aides (CSA) to assist with the exam and victim processing generally. The CSAs were selected for their "compassion and relational skills." The CSAs meet a victim at the hospital ER, talk to and support her, explain the exam and its purposes, and perform the rape exam except for "below the waist" which is done by a physician. The CSA remains with a victim at the hospital until the exam is over and then drives her to the police department where she is interviewed. The CSA sits with the victim during the interview, offering her support. When the victim is free to go, the CSA drives her home (or wherever she wishes), goes into the house with her, and gets her settled before departing. The Beach County sheriff is so impressed with this police department innovation that he has hired some women deputies to play a similar role. Almost unheard of in Florida, the sheriff's office has asked the police department to train its staff.

In Hermosa, as elsewhere, mainstream staff resist RCC requests that a counselor/advocate be allowed to accompany victims during rape exams and law enforcement and prosecutorial interviews. Mainstream staff view RCC advocates as disruptive or intrusive. The task force resolved this problem in one instance by allowing the police department to assume responsibility for counseling and supporting victims. When the CSA arrives at the hospital, she telephones the RCC to report a rape victim is there. When the RCC counselor/advocate arrives at the hospital, she introduces herself to the victim, gives her literature and expressions of support, and makes herself useful in other ways. By agreement with the police department, she does not counsel or interview the victim although she does assist the victim and her family and friends by fetching coffee or Cokes, making phone calls, going for clothing, and so on. The victim/advocate remains at the ER until the victim leaves in case she is wanted and to observe. She encourages the victim to call the RCC at a later time. . . .

The task force has transformed its members in several ways. It has promoted trust and goodwill, fostered the collective ownership of rape, and led to a united front for political action.

As task force participants worked together and became better acquainted, there, they became more respectful of and favorable towards each other. They complimented the staff of other organizations. The sheriff's deputy praised the RCC, saying, "It never drops the ball!" The prosecutor's office praised the hospital ER charge nurse, saying, "She's wonderful." While praise was not universal, little strong criticism was expressed. The police sergeant paid a compliment to the RCC that showed how their relations had improved: "We have excellent relations now. We understand each other's problems. We don't feel they're interfering as much lately." The sheriff and police cooperate with each other in ways that are unique in our research on twenty-five Florida communities (Martin et al., 1984). As noted, the police are training staff for the sheriff's office.

As a result of the task force, mainstream organizations in Hermosa proactively "own" rape crimes. They do not minimize their role in rape processing nor do they try to "give rape away," as mainstream organizations in many other communities do (Martin et al., 1984; Martin, 1991). They view rape as much their concern as the RCC's and, in some cases, believe they do a better job. . . .

The task force is highly regarded in the area. As a sign of its successes, it succeeded in enlisting a statewide agricultural organization to lobby the state legislature on rape victims' behalf. The task force chair asked the statewide organization for its help in the summer of 1982. At its November 1982 meeting, the organization adopted a proposal urging the legislature to enact three "legislative remedies" to help rape victims in Florida. The preamble and remedies read as follows.

> Sexual rape, assault, and battery are increasing at alarming rates in our country. Sexual abuse is an act of violence and hostility and often leaves the victim humiliated, dishonored, and emotionally strained. Rights of the victim must be protected at all levels. Florida law and criminal justice procedures should be such that they encourage victims to report sexual abuse violations and voluntarily cooperate in the investigative [*sic*] and prosecution of said assailants. We support state legislative remedies to: (1) Exempt sexual battery cases from discovery depositions; (2) Repeal requirements that rape victims sign statements that they will prosecute as a condition of state payment for victim's medical care; and (3) Prohibit admission of evidence relative to the sexual assaulted victim's prior sexual activity with persons other than the offender or in prior sexual battery prosecutions.

A joint memorandum, signed by Sarah Greene and the other organization's president, was prepared for the Beach County legislative delegation in January 1983. The second remedy passed the 1983 legislature, along with a dramatically improved sexual battery statute and a version of the rape shield statute described in remedy three. (Florida's rape shield statute gives discretion to judges to decide on the admission of prior sexual activity by the victim.) The first remedy did not pass, however, and rape victims in Florida can still be required to submit to discovery depositions.

Conclusions

Several conclusions are suggested by the case study. First, strategies that facilitate cooperation and goodwill on an interpersonal level can do so on an interorganizational level as well. In asking local leaders and officials for their ideas, support, and help, the RCC gained goodwill and support as well as interest and cooperation. As the task force developed, gained status, developed norms and goals, and asked its members to change for their own and the rape victim's benefit, the effectiveness of an inclusive, consensus-building strategy was confirmed.

Second, the data suggest that rape crisis centers may want to devote considerable energy and attention to mainstream organizations in their communities. Regardless of how excellent its treatment of victims is, a rape crisis center cannot do the job alone; law enforcement, hospital, and prosecutor play necessary roles. The RCC cannot force mainstream organizations to treat victims responsively but in creating a social and political climate of cooperation, goodwill, and responsiveness, it can co-opt mainstream organizations into adopting its practices and goals. Through frequent and extensive—rather than rare and minimal—contact, the RCC can change the system, teach mainstream staff about rape, impart skills and knowledge, and so on. In short, it can transform its processing network and community.

Third, social service and social change goals appear to be less incompatible than the early literature on rape crisis centers suggests (Byington et al., 1991; Maxwell, 1987). RCCs that cooperate with mainstream organizations are not ineluctably co-opted. If they have a vision that takes responsibility for mainstream organizations' treatment of victims, draw their boundary(ies) to include rather than exclude, and avoid standing outside and allocating blame, they may co-opt rather than be co-opted. When they co-opt on behalf of the victims, mainstream organizations may not even mind.

Fourth, rape crisis organizations may want to reexamine their visions and practices to see if they are unwittingly limiting themselves. A limited vision can restrict options and perspectives as much as so-called objective conditions can. Perhaps the success of the RCC in this case study is due to unusual individuals in a unique community. Yet, the circumstances, individuals, and social climate of Beach County and Hermosa are much like those of other Florida communities (Martin et al., 1984). The commitment of the RCC to a vision that drew mainstream organizations into its domain of influence through sustained action was unusual, however. Rape crisis centers, battered women's shelters, and similar social welfare/social movement organizations may want to ask if their vision is one that allows them to achieve the ends to which they aspire.

References

Bologh, R. W. (1990). *Love or greatness: Max Weber and masculine thinking: A feminist inquiry*. London: Unwin Hyman.

Burrell, G., & Morgan, G. (1979). *Sociological paradigms and organizational analysis*. London: Heinemann.

Byington, D., et al. (1991). Organizational affiliation and effectiveness: The case of rape crisis centers. *Administration in Social Work*, 15(3), 83–103.

Connell, R. (1987). *Gender and power: Society, the person, and sexual politics*. Sydney, Australia: Allen & Unwin.

DiNitto, D., et al. (1986). After rape: Who should examine rape survivors? *American Journal of Nursing*, 86, 538–540.

DiNitto, D., et al. (1987). Nurses conduct rape exams. *Response to Violence Against Women and Children*, 10, 10–15.

DiNitto, D., et al. (1989). Rape treatment programs. *Medicine and Law*, 8, 21–30.

Ferguson, K. (1984). *The feminist case against bureaucracy*. Philadelphia: Temple University Press.

Ferraro, X. (1981). Processing battered women. *Journal of Family Issues*, 2, 415–438.

Ferrell, M. M., & Hess, B. (1985). *Controversy and coalition: The new feminist movement*. Boston: Twayne.

Freeman, J. (1975). *The politics of women's liberation*. New York: David Mckay.

Freeman, J. (1979). Resource mobilization and strategy. In M. N. Zald & J. D. McCarthy (Eds.), *The dynamics of social movements*. Cambridge, England: Winthrop.

Giddens, A. (1983). *Central problems in social theory*. Berkeley: University of California Press.

Giddens, A. (1984). *The constitution of society*. Cambridge, England: Polity Press.

Gornick, J., et al. (1985). Structure and activities of rape crisis centers in the 1980s. *Crime and Delinquency*, 31, 247–268.

Hall, R. (1986). *Complex organizations*. Englewood Cliffs, NJ: Prentice-Hall.

Harvey, M. (1985). *Exemplary rape crisis programs*. NCPCP. Washington, DC: U.S. Government Printing Office.

Holmstrom, L. L., & Burgess, A.W. (1978). *The victims of rape: Institutional reactions*. New York: John Wiley.

Koss, M., & Harvey, M. (1991). *The rape victim: Clinical and community interventions.* Newbury Park, CA: Sage Publications.

LaFree, G. D. (1989). *Rape and criminal justice.* Belmont, CA: Wadsworth.

Largen, M. A. (1981). Grass-roots centers and national task forces: A history of the anti-rape movement. *Aegis*, Summer, 46–52.

Leidner, R. (1991). Stretching the boundaries of liberalism. *Signs*, 16, 263–289.

Martin, P. Y. (1990). Rethinking feminist organizations. *Gender & Society*, 4, 182–206.

Martin, P. Y. (1991). Feminism and rape processing. Unpublished manuscript. Sociology Department, Florida State University, Tallahassee.

Martin, P. Y., & O'Connor, G. G. (1989). *The social environment: Open systems applications.* New York: Longman's.

Martin, P. Y., et al. (1984). *Sexual assault: Survivors to rape victims in Florida.* Tallahassee: DHRS, State of Florida.

Martin, P. Y., et al. (1985). Controversies surrounding the rape kit exam. *Crime and Delinquency*, 31, 223–246.

Martin, P. Y. (1987). The rape exam: Beyond the emergency room. *Women & Health*, 12, 5–28.

Maxwell, M. S. (1987). *Rape crisis centers and mainstream human service organizations.* Unpublished doctoral dissertation, Florida State University, Tallahassee.

Morgan, G. (1986). *Images of organizations.* Newbury Park, CA: Sage Publications.

O'Sullivan, E. (1978). What has happened to rape crisis centers? *Victimology*, 3, 45–62.

Reinelt, C. (1991). *Moving into the terrain of the state: The battered women's movement.* Waltham, MA: Brandeis University.

Riger, S. (1984). Vehicles for empowerment. *Prevention in Human Services*, 3, 99–117.

Rothschild, J., & Whitt, A. (1986). *Work without bosses.* Cambridge, England: Cambridge University Press.

Simon, B. L. (1980). In defense of institutionalization. *Journal of Sociology and Social Welfare*, 9, 485–502.

Staggenborg, S. (1989). Stability and innovation in the women's movement. *Social Problems*, 36, 585–606.

Thurston, M. A. (1987). *Feminist women's health centers.* Unpublished doctoral dissertation, Florida State University, Tallahassee.

U.S. Department of Justice. (1975). *Rape and its victims.* Washington, DC: National Institute of Law Enforcement and Criminal Justice.

19

Rape and the Law

~

Carol Bohmer

THE STANDARD STARTING POINT for a discussion of proof of consent in rape law is the resounding pronouncement of Matthew Hale, the British jurist whose description of the common law of England formed the foundation of some of our laws. His statement on rape is the quintessential embodiment of Western society's ambivalence toward rape. "It is true, rape is a most detestable crime, and therefore ought severely and impartially to be punished with death; but it must be remembered that it is an accusation easily to be made and hard to be proved; and harder to be defended by the party accused, though ever so innocent" (Hale, 1680, p. 635).

This ambivalence in the attitudes of the law and those who implement it is nowhere more apparent than in the case of acquaintance rape. The law and those who implement it are extremely punitive toward those cases which they consider "real," but the situation is far different in less clear-cut situations (Estrich, 1987). "Real" rape cases are those perpetrated by a stranger, in circumstances in which no one would consent to sexual intercourse. As a friend who was raped once said, "Who would consent to being raped in a dark alley in January?" It is partly because rape is such a "detestable crime" that it is very difficult for the traditional legal system to put its weight behind what are viewed as questionable charges. One of the situations in which the charges are most likely to be questioned is when the victim and the alleged perpetrator know one another. This is not because of the way the law itself is written but rather how it is interpreted. Rape laws are

From Carol Bohmer, "Rape and the Law" in *Acquaintance Rape: The Hidden Crime*, ed. Andrea Parrot and Laurie Bechhofer (New York: John Wiley and Sons, 1991), 317–27, 329–33. © 1991 by John Wiley and Sons. Reprinted by permission of John Wiley and Sons.

framed in such a way as to cover *all* rapes, whether perpetrated by strangers or by acquaintances. For this reason, most of the legal writing on rape law treats acquaintance and stranger rape together.

The laws themselves are thus only part of the story. The rest of the story is how the courts interpret those laws in order to apply them to a particular set of facts. Predictions about how a court will apply the law are also central to the decision-making process of the actors in the court scene: the police, the prosecution, and the defense attorneys.

This chapter briefly examines the law concerning rape, with special reference to acquaintance rape; the changes that have taken place in the laws of rape in recent years and how those changes have affected cases of acquaintance rape; and how the participants involved in the process of bringing a case to trial function within the legal system.

What Is Rape?

Under traditional law, rape was defined as an act of sexual intercourse undertaken by a man with a woman, not his wife, by force and against her will (Harris, 1976). It included only penile-vaginal intercourse, and required penetration, "be it ever so slight," as the phrase I learned in law school went. Rape was also limited to acts performed by a man on a woman, although a woman could be charged with the crime if she were involved in it, as, for example, holding down another woman while she was raped by a man. This technical exception notwithstanding, neither male on male nor female on female forced sex was included in the definition. Nor were sexual acts other than intercourse covered in the definition, though they might have been covered under other statutes, such as assault or "deviant sex." As we will see, all these aspects of traditional rape law have been subject to criticism by feminists, and all have been changed in one way or another as a result of recent rape reform laws. Nevertheless, most people still think of rape as an offense committed by a man against a woman, which remains statistically true today. For this reason, unless there is a special point to be made, this chapter will refer to the rapist as "he" and the victim as "she."

Susan Brownmiller, whose extensive treatise on rape galvanized feminists when it was published, discussed in detail the history of rape (Brownmiller, 1975). The crime of rape had its origins in property rights, and essentially involved a claim by one man against another for damage to property owned by the claimant. A father whose daughter was raped would have less chance of marrying her off successfully, and a husband's property interest in his wife would be diminished by her having been sullied by another man. The word *rape* comes from the Latin *rapere*, meaning to steal. Rape was originally viewed as an insult to family honor rather than an act that caused trauma to the woman. Despite the fact that rape is now an offense against the woman herself (or against a man, in states that have made their laws applicable to acts against both sexes) rather than against her "owner," vestiges of this old view remain in our current attitudes toward the law of rape.

Traditional attitudes are central in a rape case when the question is whether the event that is the subject of the charge was one to which the victim consented or whether it was forced. As mentioned above, this is particularly true in cases that are not, as Estrich (1987) put it, "real" rape.

Consent

There are four legal defenses to a charge of rape (LaFree, 1989). The first defense a defendant can offer is: "It wasn't me." In this situation, he is not disputing that the events alleged by the prosecution took place, but he is disputing the claim that it was he who perpetrated them. The second defense is that no sex took place, a defense that is relevant under those laws which define rape as intercourse only. A third defense, which is not particularly significant here, is that the defendant is not responsible for his behavior.

The fourth defense is the most significant in acquaintance rape cases. It acknowledges that the sexual encounter took place between the defendant and the victim but argues that it was consensual. In cases of acquaintance rape, the first three defenses are not as central to the rape charge as they can be in stranger rape. The victim is claiming that she was raped by a particular person, and therefore the question of identity has already been decided. The second and third defenses, while possible in acquaintance rape, are dealt with by a law that includes lesser offenses; the third defense is extremely rare. By contrast, the defense of consent is more likely to succeed in acquaintance rape than in stranger rape. For, while we find it hard to believe that someone would consent to sex with a person she has never seen before in her life, the same is not true for someone she knows, however slightly. The better the two people know one another, the easier it is to believe that the encounter was consensual. The only exception to this is in cases where someone is raped by a member of her family. This is usually dealt with under incest statutes but may be charged as rape in some states (LaFree, 1989). The heart of the legal issue in cases of acquaintance rape is consent and its proof. Recognizing this, the recent rape law reform movement has concentrated part of its effort on changes designed to make consent less central in a rape trial.

Lack of consent has been defined in the law by phrases such as "by force" and "against her will," sometimes used synonymously and sometimes as separate elements of consent (Harris, 1976, p. 613). However they are used, these definitions have not proven particularly helpful in aiding judges and juries to decide whether rape or consensual sexual intercourse has taken place.

Sexual encounters, like all social events, have different shades of meaning to each person involved. These social psychological "definitions of reality" make the proof of consent or lack thereof an especially difficult legal issue. To illustrate this, let us look at a hypothetical example. If one is told that a person had intercourse with someone who tied her down, that information would not be enough to decide whether the intercourse was forced. One first needs to know the details of the circumstances whereby the woman was tied down. Did she want to be tied down? Or did she attempt to resist the force used to tie her down against her will? Even asking the participants themselves will not necessarily provide the answer. The woman might say that she did not want to be tied down and the man might say that she did. What she intended as resistance, he interpreted as part of the game he thought they were playing to heighten their sexual pleasure. Both interpretations are plausible; people do engage in the activities described above as part of consensual sexual intercourse. If interpretation of the meaning of behavior is so difficult in this rather extreme example, imagine how difficult it is in more ordinary situations. . . .

The way in which we view sex has a significant impact on the way the courts interpret testimony in rape cases. The law therefore cannot be viewed in the absence of an understanding of these attitudes. For example, American societal norms hold that men should be the initiators in sex and women the responders. A woman who initiates a sexual encounter is seen as "unfeminine," aggressive, and even immoral. By the same token, a woman should not appear too eager in her response to a man who initiates sex. To take this one step further, some people consider it appropriate for a woman to pretend not to be interested and to have to be persuaded to engage in sexual intercourse.

Certain kinds of behavior are considered evidence of sexual provocation and a woman is expected to take the consequences for those actions. This may be particularly true in acquaintance rape situations where the woman is defined as having "asked for it" by showing her availability in a number of ways. A woman who goes to a man's apartment, who dresses too provocatively, who allows herself to get drunk, or who hitchhikes may often find her behavior being interpreted as evidence of her willingness to engage in sex.

In addition, a woman whose lifestyle is deviant—for example, one who drinks a lot, who uses drugs, or who has intercourse outside marriage—may also find that she is unprotected by the law when she is raped. Feminists have argued that these attitudes are a punishment for women who violate appropriate gender-role expectations. Empirical research on this subject supports their view. In acquaintance rape cases, jurors were more influenced by their assessment of the victim's lifestyle than by physical evidence or the seriousness of the event as measured by several variables.

Using opinions about the victim's lifestyle or behavior as a way of deciding whether a rape has taken place is one of several circumstances in which rape cases are evaluated differently than other crimes. A man who gets drunk and flashes his money around in a sleazy neighborhood may be considered to have been stupid when he is mugged. The evidence of his behavior would not, however, be relevant to the proof of the crime at the robbery trial of the mugger.

Just as women risk a charge that they "got what they deserved" by engaging in socially inappropriate behavior, so too are they considered responsible for calling a halt to any foreplay that could result in sexual intercourse. If they wait too long before asking the man to stop, they are expected to take the consequences because men are not supposed to be able to control their raging sexual urges. In such cases the court system is incorporating the legal doctrines of contributory negligence and assumption of risk from the civil law into the criminal law, where they do not belong (Berger, 1979). The criminal law is not supposed to take into account whether the victim was partially responsible for the crime. A theft is a theft regardless of whether the person contributed to it by leaving property in a place that made it available to the thief. In the civil law, on the other hand, the doctrine of contributory negligence is relevant to the assessment of damages. It has nothing to do with deciding whether the event was a crime.

These traditional views about appropriate behavior are clearly not the sexual attitudes of all members of our society. Quite the contrary: the sexual revolution has gone a long way toward making attitudes toward sex more egalitarian, especially among the younger members of our society. The difficulty is that those who administer our criminal justice system are more likely to adhere to traditional attitudes. For this reason, the laws themselves and their interpretation are more likely to embody traditional rather than modern attitudes.

It is easy to see how traditional cultural attitudes feed into misunderstanding of a woman's response to her date's overtures. What she may see as a refusal, he may see as socially appropriate coyness. In such a situation, he may go ahead and press her further. The outcome, sexual intercourse, which she considers forced, may be viewed by him—and by the participants in the courtroom who share his cultural attitudes—as consensual intercourse. Rape laws themselves are not sensitive enough to take into account such variation in interpretation of a single event. As Catherine MacKinnon pointed out, rape laws have assumed that a single objective state of affairs existed (MacKinnon, 1983). A rape occurred or it did not; consent was given or it was not. In fact the reality is often split: "A woman is raped but not by a rapist" (MacKinnon, 1983, p. 654). In focusing on the accused's state of mind, the law concludes that the rape did not happen. In the mind of a woman in an acquaintance rape case, however, rape *did* happen.

The legal definition of consent is usually not very helpful, because it is spare enough to require fleshing out in each individual case. That fleshing out is done in terms of the social attitudes discussed above. The defendant's assertions that he did not mean to force the woman into sexual intercourse focus attention on the woman's behavior. He is arguing that he thought she consented, so the prosecutor then has to refute that argument. This can only be done by convincing the judge or jury that she really did not consent. In the absence of circumstantial evidence or of very convincing testimony on the part of the victim, it is an uphill battle for the prosecution to obtain a conviction in the typical acquaintance rape case.

The victim's own definition of the event is problematic in acquaintance rape cases because the issue of consent is so central. Because of the cultural attitudes discussed above, a victim may not have given a clear signal about whether she wanted to engage in sexual intercourse. Her ambivalent message may have been defined as consent by her date, if not by her. The opposite may also be true. What may in fact have been forced sex is sometimes not defined as such by the victim, who may consider it just an unpleasant encounter.

Closely related to the centrality of traditional attitudes toward sex in determining whether there has been consent, are attitudes toward rape itself. A profusion of myths and incorrect stereotypes about rape exists in our society (Brownmiller, 1975; Feild, 1978). These range from the idea that a woman cannot be raped against her will to the beliefs that all women secretly want to be raped and that most rape complaints are faked. The myths also present rapists as sex-starved men who simply cannot resist following their sexual impulses. All these myths combine to create a climate hostile to rape victims, a climate in which the victim is blamed for the rape. A woman's behavior may be used to reinforce the myth. For example, a woman who goes to a man's apartment or who accepts a ride in the car from him is asking for trouble, since all women secretly want to be raped. In one survey of a cross-section of American adults, 50% agreed with the statement: "A woman who goes to the home or apartment of a man on the first date implies she is willing to have sex" (Wrightsman, 1986).

The definition of whether an event is a rape or consensual intercourse has been shown to be affected by the extent to which a person accepts commonly held rape myths (Burt & Albin, 1981). Although there is no direct research of the extent to which attitudes about sex and rape affect the decisions of judges and juries, it is likely that they have a significant influence. Since juries are composed of the same people on whom the research about rape attitudes and acceptance of rape myths has been conducted, it can safely be assumed that those people will take their attitudes and beliefs into the courtroom when they act as jurors.

Rape Law Reform—Nonconsent

The heavy emphasis on nonconsent and the need to substantiate it with some objective evidence have made conviction extremely difficult in cases that do not fall within the "classic" image of rape: in a dark alley, by a stranger who uses a weapon or inflicts significant injury. Acquaintance rape cases are less likely to have such objective evidence. This leaves little else but the victim's testimony about her behavior and her description of the defendant's actions on which to base a prosecution. Because of these difficulties, many jurisdictions have reformed their law with the intention of moving the attention away from the victim's behavior. . . .

Many states have replaced the rule that a woman had to show nonconsent by resisting "to the utmost" with a rule based on an examination of the acts of the defendant to determine whether force was used. This should be a promising reform for cases like acquaintance rapes in which objective measures of nonconsent are often unavailable. The problem, however, is that force ends up being defined by courts in terms of a woman's resistance, the same old standard that the reforms were designed to avoid (Estrich, 1987). It is also defined in male terms, with the model being that of a fight, in which one is expected to fight back in some way, using one's fists, knees, or elbows. Thus, what is considered "reasonable" in a situation where a woman is about to be raped is in fact not the behavior of a reasonable *woman* at all. As Estrich put it, "their [the judges'] version of a reasonable person is one who does not scare easily, one who is not passive, one who fights back, not cries. The reasonable woman, it seems, is not a schoolboy 'sissy'; she is a real man" (Estrich, 1987, p. 65). The difficulty is that many women do not fight back in the way expected of a reasonable man and in fact are discouraged by our social mores from doing so. Using a male standard in this way, courts may conclude that no force was used because the victim did not fight back.

The issue of consent, always a difficult one in rape cases, is thus doubly difficult in cases of acquaintance rape despite recent reform. As long as society's ambivalent attitudes toward sex and rape are mirrored in our legislatures and courtrooms, and as long as women have difficulty in communicating their wishes and men in honoring those wishes, consent will remain a central issue in the prosecution and trial of such cases.

Other Recent Changes in Rape Law

Over the past 15 years, the women's movement has made rape law reform one of its central goals. The grass-roots movement of the early 1970s led to the establishment of rape crisis centers, the existence of which we almost take for granted now. Part of the purpose of the rape crisis centers was to make the process of reporting a rape and testifying in the subsequent trial less traumatic.

It was clear to women involved in the movement to set up rape crisis centers that they could not effectively minimize the trauma of the rape trial unless the law was changed. As long as attorneys were permitted to engage in what feminists saw as legal character assassination in an attempt to exonerate their clients in court, many would continue to find the trial as much a violation in its own way as the rape itself (Bohmer & Blumberg, 1975). Feminists also believed that the structure of the law reinforced sexist cultural stereotypes of women. Without changes in these laws, they argued, women could never reach equality in other spheres.

Ironically, the impetus for change in rape laws coincided in many states with a movement for general reform in the criminal law. Some changes reflected a need to accommodate changing social attitudes, for example, changes in the age of consent in statutory rape; others reflected a need to strengthen the criminal law in the face of a growing crime rate. Feminist rape law reformers and law and order legislators made strange bedfellows. In part, because of this odd alliance, the rape law reform movement has been only partially successful in achieving the goal of a fairer, less sexist trial experience for rape victims. It also appears that the movement for change in rape laws has now given way to other concerns. Thus, most of the changes took place in the late 1970s and early 1980s.

The legal change in which consent terminology was replaced by a definition based on force has already been discussed above. The other reform of major significance to acquaintance rape cases is that which covers what have come to be known as rape shield laws. These laws deal with the admissibility of testimony concerning the prior sexual behavior of the victim. Traditional rape law allowed evidence to be admitted on this issue, on the grounds that past sexual history was relevant to whether the victim was likely to have consented to the alleged rape. According to this logic, a virgin was less likely to consent to sex than one who had previously engaged in sex, especially if that person were shown to be "promiscuous." . . .

What this argument actually means is that once a woman has had sex, she has thereby reduced, or even (e.g., in the cases of prostitutes) eliminated, any legal protection she might get for future situations in which she does not consent. As in so many other situations, it is the woman who is punished for *her* sexual behavior, rather than the man for *his*.

Prior sexual history is considered relevant not only to the issue of consent, but also to the issue of credibility. Courts continue to believe that a "virtuous" woman is more likely to tell the truth than one who is not "chaste." They believe that the latter is more likely to lie in general because her sexual conduct has shown that she is of low moral character. More specifically, they believe, she might claim that the encounter was a rape as a way of protecting herself from being punished for some inappropriate behavior. For example, a wife who did not want her husband to know that she was having an affair, or a young woman whose parents found out about her sexual activities, would claim that she had been raped, to avoid the ire of husband or father.

Feminists find these arguments not only offensive but also unconvincing. The idea of classifying a woman as chaste or virtuous seems as dated as the bustle. Sex outside marriage is now the norm rather than the exception, so a division of women into good women and bad women is irrelevant. There is also no foundation for the belief that women who are sexually active are more likely to be liars. In addition, given the well-known difficulties in making a rape charge and carrying it through the court process, it is hardly likely that a woman would be more willing to undergo the trauma of a rape trial than be shown to have committed adultery. The empirical evidence is actually quite the opposite. Vast numbers of women who are raped, especially by people they know, choose not to make a complaint to the police, and many who do complain subsequently drop the charges because they decide they cannot bear to go through a trial (LaFree, 1989).

Rape reform statutes have abolished several evidentiary rules that previously singled out rape as a crime to be tried differently from other crimes. Rules that were abolished included the requirement that there be special corroboration in rape cases, proof of resistance, and special instructions to the jury about the need for caution in assessing the testimony of the victim (Berger, Searles, & Neuman, 1988). As discussed above, there have also been changes in the rules about the admissibility of testimony of the prior sexual history of the victim (known as rape shield laws), though they have been much less extensive than feminist reformers would wish. As of 1980, by which time most of this legislative change had take place, more than 40 states had passed statutes that limit in some way the freedom of the defense to introduce evidence about the victim's past (Feild & Bienen, 1980). The most extreme of these statutes totally exclude evidence of the victim's past sexual history with anyone except the defendant. Most states have not gone so far and merely require a hearing to determine whether the judge considers the evidence to be relevant. Defense attorneys have questioned the constitutionality of these new rules, arguing that they violate the defendant's Sixth Amendment right to confront his accuser. Perhaps as a response to this pressure, some states (e.g., Hawaii, Iowa, and North Carolina) have already repealed their rape shield laws (Berger et al., 1988).

Rape shield statutes can operate to the benefit of a victim in an acquaintance rape case if the victim has not had a prior sexual relationship with the defendant. If she has, the evidence will continue to be admissible. In addition, a judge may still decide to admit evidence of the victim's sexual past in those states where the discretion to do so remains.

Another area in which there has been much legislative activity has been that of redefining rape. Some states no longer have a crime of rape but rather a series of graded offenses with penalties depending on such variables as the amount of coercion, the infliction of injury, and the age of the victim (Feild & Bienen, 1980). The purpose of this change was to try to increase the conviction rate, on the assumption that juries might convict more defendants on a wider range of offenses if the definitions and the penalties were more closely tailored to fit the circumstances. The replacement of the term *rape* with *sexual assault* or, in some cases, *assault* alone was also designed to emphasize that rape was a violent rather than a sexual crime. Some feminists do not agree with this goal, while others doubt whether the change has had the intended effect (MacKinnon, 1987; Tong, 1984).

The definition of rape has also been extended by making the laws gender-neutral and by expanding the acts that constitute the crime of rape. Sexual assault between people of the same sex, either by males or females, is now covered in some of the new statutes; in others it is dealt with under statutes that cover deviant sexual behavior. The acts covered under the new laws include oral and anal penetration, sexual penetration with objects, and, in some cases, touching of intimate body parts (Berger et al., 1988).

The Impact of Rape Reform Laws

Preliminary studies of the impact of changes in rape laws indicate that many of these reforms have had limited effect on the experience of the victim or the likelihood that there will be a conviction. Court personnel seem still to be wedded to traditional assumptions regarding sexual behavior and the conduct of a rape trial and apparently do not always comply with the spirit of the new statute (Berger et al., 1988; Feild & Bienen, 1980). For example, in those states with discretionary rape shield laws, a trial judge may continue to believe that the victim's past sexual behavior is relevant both to consent and credibility. In this situation, he or she will exercise discretion and admit that evidence.

To date, those few studies that have been undertaken on the impact of the rape reform laws have found that there has been no significant increase in the percentage of rape complaints that have resulted in conviction, nor in the reporting or arrest rates (Loh, 1980, 1981; Polk, 1985). The only significant change has been an increased likelihood that a defendant, once convicted of rape, would receive an institutional sentence (Polk, 1985). This difference is probably one example of more punitive sentencing in general, rather than for rapists in particular, since felons other than rapists are also receiving tougher sentences.

The lack of change in the conviction rate comes as a setback especially for those reformers who believed that a redefinition of the crime of rape as one of varying degrees of criminal sexual assault would result in more convictions. This redefinition has been adopted in a number of states, the most important of which is Michigan, which has been used by other states as a model (Feild & Bienen, 1980). In addition to its anticipated benefits in conviction rates, the reform was seen by its exponents as a way of downplaying the issues of consent which have been so troublesome. By making changes in the definition and description of rape, it was hoped that the focus in a trial would be less influenced by the traditional notions of acceptable female behavior discussed above (Tong, 1984). In a trial to prove that the defendant had committed a kind of assault, the victim's prior sexual history becomes as irrelevant as any other aspect of her life or as irrelevant as it would be in any other kind of assault. These benefits are particularly significant in the case of acquaintance rape, in which traditional attitudes toward sexual behavior frequently make a conviction all but impossible. Empirical research has not yet revealed whether incorporating rape law into that of criminal assault has indeed had any effect on the conviction rate of acquaintance rape per se. . . .

The Use of Discretion and the Limits of the Law

As discussed above, the law reforms that have been initiated have to some extent been limited in their usefulness by the reluctance of the courts to exercise discretion in such a way as to benefit the victim in the courtroom. Indeed, the negative effect of discretion exercised by various actors in the legal system actually begins long before the case gets to court, if it ever does. After a rape victim files a complaint, the police may decide that the case is not worth pursuing and the case will go no further. In police terminology the decision is made to "unfound" the case, a graphic if ungrammatical term. Police officers believe that rape complaints are generally less valid than other complaints (LaFree, 1989). Rape is the only serious crime for which the FBI calculates an unfounding rate (Hilberman, 1976). The police argue that the rate of "unfounded" rape cases is an indication that women press charges in circumstances that are not really rape or women are using the process for inappropriate reasons (Estrich, 1987). But that very exercise of discretion is based on traditional attitudes, which define as rape only those events that fit the (male) police officer's perception of a rape case (LaFree, 1989). Evidence in support of this interpretation of the exercise of discretion comes from the New York and Philadelphia police departments. When they added a woman to the investigative team, the rate of cases considered suitable for unfounding was reduced (Brownmiller, 1975).

Some cases of acquaintance rape will not even get as far as a prosecutor who could exercise his (or her) discretion as to whether to proceed; the cases will have already been unfounded by the police. A higher proportion of acquaintance rape cases meet this fate than do cases of stranger rape (Chappell & Singer, 1977, p. 260).

Prosecutors are involved in exercising their discretion in much the same way as the police and are strongly influenced by the police (LaFree, 1989). They will decide, based on various factors, including whether the victim and assailant knew one another, whether it is worth expending scarce resources to try to get a conviction (Estrich, 1987). Another way in which the prosecutor exercises discretion (using the same variables) is in the process of plea bargaining. Most studies show that approximately 90% of all cases are dealt with by plea bargaining and do not therefore result in a trial. The figures for rape are likely to be similar.

The legal process in rape cases, even more than in other crimes, is a vast funnel that gets narrower as fewer and fewer cases are retained. This exercise of discretion at every stage in the process puts into perspective the limits of law reform in another way. Most of the reforms are involved with the conduct of the trial. Since most cases are either dropped or plea bargained to a guilty plea, these reforms have a tiny impact on the role of the law in any rape case, especially an acquaintance rape case.

Acquaintance Rape and the Civil Law

A central tenet of our legal system (often missed by those concerned about the treatment of victims in court) is that, in a criminal case, the victim's status is that of the prosecuting witness for the state's case against the defendant. She is not a party to the suit and thus her only legal rights are as a witness. The only way in which a victim can become a plaintiff in a suit against her assailant is if she herself initiates a civil lawsuit against him. Since an acquaintance rape victim by definition knows her assailant, she has no difficulty naming her defendant. She must still prove that the rape was without her consent and that she suffered damage as a result of it. She risks suffering the same kind of humiliation at the hands of the defense attorney as she might experience in a criminal case. Since rape shield laws apply only to criminal cases, the defense attorney can introduce any kind of evidence she or he can prove is relevant to the plaintiff's claim, which could include evidence of her past sexual history.

The standard of proof required in a civil case ("preponderance of probability") is a lower one than in a criminal case (proof beyond a reasonable doubt). This lower standard might make it possible for an acquaintance rape victim to win in civil litigation, even when the defendant has not been convicted in a criminal court.

For many if not most victims, this is not a very attractive option. The problems of negative treatment in court still exist whether the victim is the state's witness or a plaintiff in her own right, and the chance that she can extract monetary damages from her attacker may be slight even if she wins. But apart from any psychological satisfaction a victim might get from winning a civil judgment in court, this option may offer her the opportunity to sue someone in addition to her assailant. If the victim can prove that a third party can be held responsible for the rapist's behavior (as, for example, the college attended by both parties), that party can be named as a defendant. In one recently filed case, a student has sued Colgate University and a fraternity there, claiming that they were responsible for a sexual attack on her which took place at a party in a fraternity house. Her argument is that the university should have prohibited the fraternity from holding the party because the fraternity had already been found guilty of violating the school's alcohol policies. She is also arguing that the guards at the party should have stopped fraternity members from serving alcohol to underage members ("Colgate student sues university," 1989). The case has not yet been heard.

It is fairly difficult to prove such third-party responsibility, especially in a campus dating situation that turns into an acquaintance rape. The case law on this subject is sketchy, partly because of the dearth of suits and also because when a lawsuit is filed, the college or other third party has a great interest in minimizing the negative publicity and in settling without a court case that might provide a legal precedent. Although such settlements may extract silence from the victim as a price, they are likely to serve at least one very useful function: sensitizing institutions to their responsibility to educate their students about appropriate sexual behavior.

Conclusion

Legal changes that have taken place since the early 1970s have not had a great deal of impact on the way rape is treated by the law. Clearly, there is little interest in making further legal changes, both because they do not seem to have much effect and because our society is now involved in other issues which are seen as more urgent. Even the field of rape research and scholarship provides evidence of this. There is still a great deal we do not know about how rape cases in general and acquaintance rape cases in particular fare in our legal system. However, the scholarly research peaked in the late 1970s and early 1980s, when public interest was at its height and there was more funding available. Since then, many of the gaps in knowledge remain unfilled. Thus, it has not been possible to provide empirical data about many aspects of acquaintance rape. The FBI and other agencies that keep crime statistics do not distinguish between cases of stranger rape and those of acquaintance rape. Research is needed to provide this information. So far, very little of this kind of research has been undertaken. What we do know is that our legal system remains an inhospitable environment for the trial and prosecution of rape.

The law that applies to acquaintance rape, like rape in general, is closely related to social attitudes about appropriate sexual behavior.

As long as sex and rape are seen in traditional ways, the likelihood is that a woman (or a man) who is raped by an acquaintance is at the mercy of the whole legal system's interpretation as to whether a crime was committed. There is much less need to change the law in the area of rape, and especially acquaintance rape, than there is to change the way we view sexual behavior.

References

Berger, R. J., Searles, P., & Neuman, W. L. (1988). The dimensions of rape reform legislation. *Law and Society Review*, 22, 329–357.

Berger, V. (1979). Man's trial, woman's tribulation: Rape cases in the courtroom. *Columbia University Law Review*, 77, 1–103.

Bohmer, C., & Blumberg, A. (1975). Twice traumatized: The rape victim and the legal process. *Judicature*, 58, 390–399.

Brownmiller, S. (1975). *Against our will: Men, women, and rape*. New York: Simon & Schuster.

Burt, M. R., & Albin, R. S. (1981). Rape myths, rape definitions, and probability of conviction. *Journal of Applied Social Psychology*, 11, 212–230.

Chappell, D., & Singer, S. (1977). Rape in New York City: A study of material in the police files and its meaning. In D. Chappell, R. Geis, & G. Geis (Eds.), *Forcible rape* (pp. 245–271). New York: Columbia University Press.

Colgate student sues university and fraternity. (1989, June 12). *Ithaca Journal*, p. 7A

Estrich, S. (1987). *Real rape*. Cambridge, MA: Harvard University Press.

Feild, H. S. (1978). Attitudes toward rape: A comparative analysis of police, rapists, crisis counselors, and citizens. *Journal of Personality and Social Psychology*, 36, 166–179.

Feild, H. S., & Bienen, L. B. (1980). *Jurors and rape*. Lexington, MA: Lexington Books.

Hale, M. (1680). *History of the pleas of the crown* (Vol. 1). (Emlyn ed., 1847).

Harris, L. R. (1976). Towards a consent standard in the law of rape. *University of Chicago Law Review*, 43, 613–645.

Hilberman, E. (1976). *The rape victim*. New York: Basic Books.

LaFree, G. D. (1989). *Rape and criminal justice*. Belmont, CA: Wadsworth.

Loh, W. D. (1980). The impact of common law and reform rape statutes on prosecution: An empirical study. *Washington Law Review*, 55, 543–652.

Loh, W. D. (1981). Q: What has reform of rape legislation wrought? A: Truth in criminal labelling. *Journal of Social Issues*, 37, 28–52.

MacKinnon, C. (1983). Feminism, marxism, method and the state. Toward feminist jurisprudence. *Signs: Journal of Women in Culture and Society*, 8, 635–658.

MacKinnon, C. (1987). *Feminism unmodified*. Cambridge, MA: Harvard University Press.

Polk, K. (1985). Rape reform and criminal justice processing. *Crime and Delinquency*, 31, 191–205.

Tong, R. (1984). *Women, sex, and the law*. Totowa, NJ: Rowman & Allanheld.

Wrightsman, L. S. (1986). *Psychology and the legal system*. Monterey, CA: Brooks/Cole.

20

Clarence, William, Iron Mike, Tailhook, Senator Packwood, Spur Posse, Magic . . . and Us

~

Michael S. Kimmel

THE 1990s MAY BE REMEMBERED as the decade in which America took a crash course on male sexuality. From the national teach-in on sexual harassment that emerged from Clarence Thomas's confirmation hearings, to accusations about sexual harassment against Senator Robert Packwood, to the U.S. Navy Tailhook scandal, to Magic Johnson's revelation that he is infected with the HIV virus, to William Kennedy Smith and Mike Tyson's date rape trials, to the trials of lacrosse players at St. John's University and high school athletes at Glen Ridge, New Jersey, we've had a steady discussion about male sexuality, about a sexuality that is more about predatory conquest than pleasure and connection.

And there's no end in sight—which explains the title of this essay. In the immediate aftermath of the Clarence Thomas confirmation hearings, the media claimed, as if with one voice, that the hearings would have a "chilling effect" on American women—that women would be far less likely to come forward and report incidents of sexual harassment for fear that they would be treated in the same shameful way as Anita Hill was by the Senate Judiciary Committee. Have the media ever been more wrong?

From Michael S. Kimmel, "Clarence, William, Iron Mike, Tailhook, Senator Packwood, Spur Posse, Magic . . . and Us," in *Transforming a Rape Culture*, ed. Emilie Buchwald, Pamela R. Fletcher, and Martha Roth (Minneapolis: Milkweed Editions, 1993), 119–38. References omitted. © 1993 by Michael S. Kimmel. Reprinted by permission of Michael S. Kimmel.

Since then, we've had less of a "chilling effect," and more of a national thaw, as women have come forward in record numbers to report cases of sexual harassment, date rape, and acquaintance rape. "Every woman has her Clarence Thomas," commented one woman, sadly surveying the workplace over the past two decades. In an op-ed essay in the *New York Times*, novelist Mary Lee Settle commented that Anita Hill had, "by her heroic stance, given not only me but thousands of women who have been silenced by shame the courage and the need to speak out about what we have tried for so long to bury and forget."

Currently, corporations, state and local governments, universities, and law firms are scrambling to implement procedures to handle sexual harassment. Most seem motivated more out of fear of lawsuits than out of general concern for women's experiences; thus, they are more interested in adjudicating harassment after the fact than in developing mechanisms to prevent it. In the same way, colleges and universities are developing strategies to handle the remarkable rise in date and acquaintance rape, although only a few are developing programs on prevention.

With more women coming forward now than ever before, many men have reacted defensively; "Men on Trial" has been the common headline linking Smith and Thomas in the media. But it's not *men* on trial here, it's *masculinity*, or, rather, a definition of masculinity that leads to certain behaviors that we now see as problematic and often physically threatening. Under prevailing definitions, men have been and are the "politically incorrect" sex.

But why have these issues emerged now? And why are issues such as sexual harassment and date rape the particular issues we're facing? Since it is certain that we will continue to face these issues for the rest of the decade, how can we understand these changes? And, most important, what can we do about it? How can we change the meanings of masculinity so that sexual harassment and date rape will disappear from our workplaces and our relationships?

The Social Construction of Male Sexuality

To speak of transforming masculinity is to begin with the way men are sexual in our culture. As social scientists now understand, sexuality is less a product of biological urges and more about the meanings that we attach to those urges, meanings that vary dramatically across cultures, over time, and among a variety of social groups within any particular culture. Sexual beings are made, not born. John Gagnon, a well-known theoretician of this approach, argues in his book *Human Sexualities* that

People learn when they are quite young a few of the things that they are expected to be, and continue slowly to accumulate a belief in who they are and ought to be through the rest of childhood, adolescence, and adulthood. Sexual conduct is learned in the same ways and through the same processes; it is acquired and assembled in human interaction, judged and performed in specific cultural and historical worlds.

And the major item in that assemblage, the chief building block in the social construction of sexuality, is gender. We experience our sexual selves through a gendered prism. The meanings of sex to women and to men are very, very different. There really are a "his" and "hers" when it comes to sex. Just one example: think about the difference in the way we view a man or a woman who has a lot of different partners—the difference, say, between a stud and a slut.

The rules of masculinity and femininity are strictly enforced. And difference equals power. The difference between male and female sexuality reproduces men's power over women, and simultaneously, the power of some men over other men, especially of the dominant, hegemonic form of manhood—white, straight, middle-class—over marginalized masculinities. Those who dare to cross over—women who are sexually adventurous and men who are sexually passive—risk being seen as *gender*, not sexual, nonconformists. And we all know how homophobia links gender nonconformity to homosexuality. The stakes are high if you don't play along.

Sexual behavior confirms manhood. It makes men feel manly. Robert Brannon has identified the four traditional rules of American manhood: (1) No Sissy Stuff: Men can never do anything that even remotely suggests femininity. Manhood is a relentless repudiation and devaluation of the feminine. (2) Be a Big Wheel: Manhood is measured by power, wealth, and success. Whoever has the most toys when he dies, wins. (3) Be a Sturdy Oak: Manhood depends on emotional reserve. Dependability in a crisis requires that men not reveal their feelings. (4) Give 'Em Hell: Exude an aura of manly daring and aggression. Go for it. Take risks.

These four rules lead to a sexuality built around accumulating partners (scoring), emotional distance, and risk taking. In locker rooms and on playgrounds across the country, men are taught that the goal of every encounter with women is to score. Men are supposed to be ever ready for sex, constantly seeking sex, and constantly seeking to escalate every encounter so that intercourse will result, since, as one of my students once noted, "It doesn't count unless you put it in.". . .

Risk taking is a centerpiece of male sexuality. Sex is about adventure, excitement, danger. Taking chances. Responsibility is a word that seldom turns up in male sexual discourse. And this of course has serious medical side effects; the possibilities include STDs, impregnation, and AIDS—currently the most gendered disease in American history.

To rein in this constructed male "appetite," women have been assigned the role of asexual gatekeeper; women decide, metaphorically and literally, who enters the desired garden of earthly delights, and who doesn't. Women's sexual agency, women's sense of entitlement to desire, is drowned out by the incessant humming of male desire, propelling him ever forward. A man's job is to wear down her resistance. One fraternity at a college I was lecturing at last year offered seminars to pledges on dating etiquette that appropriated the book of business advice called *Getting to Yes.*

Sometimes that hum can be so loud that it drowns out the actual voice of the real live woman that he's with. Men suffer from socialized deafness, a hearing impairment that strikes only when women say "no.". . .

Date Rape and Sexual Predation, Aggression, and Entitlement

As women have clamed the right to say "yes," they've also begun to assert their rights to say "no." Women are now demanding that men be more sexually responsible and are holding men accountable for their sexual behaviors. It is women who have changed the rules of sexual conduct. What used to be (and in many places still is) called male sexual etiquette—forcing a woman to have sex when she says no, conniving, coercing, pushing, ignoring efforts to get you to stop, getting her so drunk that she loses the ability (or consciousness) that one needs to give consent—is now defined as date rape.

In one recent study, by psychologist Mary Koss at the University of Arizona, forty-five percent of all college women said that they had had some form of sexual contact against their will. A full twenty-five percent had been pressed or forced to have sexual intercourse against their will. And Patricia Bowman, who went home with William Kennedy Smith from Au Bar in Palm Beach, Florida, knows all about those statistics. She testified that when she told Smith that she'd called her friends, and she was going to call the police, he responded, "You shouldn't have done that. Nobody's going to believe you." And, indeed, the jury didn't. I did.

I also believed that the testimony of three other women who claimed they were sexually assaulted by Smith should have been allowed in the trial. Such testimony would have established a pattern not of criminal assault, but of Smith's obvious belief in sexual *entitlement*, that he was entitled to press his sexual needs on women despite their resistance, because he didn't particularly care what they felt about it.

And Desiree Washington knows all about men who don't listen when a woman says no. Mike Tyson's aggressive masculinity in the boxing ring was sadly translated into a vicious misogyny with his ex-wife Robin Givens and a predatory sexuality, as evidenced by his behavior with Desiree Washington. Tyson's "grandiose sense of entitlement, fueled by the insecurities and emotions of adolescence," as writer Joyce Carol Oates put it, led to a behavior with women that was as out of control as his homosocial behavior inside the ring.

Tyson's case underscores our particular fascination with athletes, and the causal equation we make between athletes and sexual aggression. From the St. John's University lacrosse team, to Glen Ridge, New Jersey, high school athletes, to dozens of athletic teams and individual players at campuses across the nation, we're getting the message that our young male athletes, trained for fearless aggression on the field, are translating that into a predatory sexual aggression in relationships with women. Columnist Robert Lipsyte calls it the "varsity syndrome—winner take all, winning at any cost, violence as a tool, aggression as a mark of masculinity." The very qualities we seek in our athletes are exactly the qualities we do not want in young men today. Rather, we want to encourage respect for others, compassion, the ability to listen, and attention to process rather than the end goal. Our task is to make it clear that what we want from our athletes when they are on the playing field is *not* the same as what we want from them when they are playing the field.

I think, though, that athletes only illustrate a deeper problem: the problem of men in groups. Most athletes play on teams, so much of their social life and much of a player's public persona is constructed through association with his teammates. Another homosocial preserve, fraternities, are the site of most gang rapes that occur on college campuses, according to psychologist Chris O'Sullivan, who has been studying gang rape for several years. At scores of campus and corporate workshops over the past five years, women have shared the complaint that, while individual men may appear sympathetic when they are alone with women, they suddenly turn out to be macho louts capable of the vilest misogynistic statements when they are in groups of men. The members of the U.S. Navy Tailhook Association are quite possibly decent, law-abiding family men when they are alone or with their families. But put them together at a convention, and they become a marauding gang of hypermasculine thugs who should be prosecuted for felonious assault, not merely slapped on their collective wrists.

I suppose it's true that the members of Spur Posse, a group of relatively affluent Southern California adolescent boys, are also "regular guys." Which makes their sexual predation and homosocial competition as chilling as it is revealing of something at the heart of American masculinity. Before a large group of young women and girls—one as young as ten!—came forward to claim that members of Spur Posse had sexually assaulted and raped them, these guys would have been seen as typical high school fellas. Members of the group competed with one another to have sex with the most girls and kept elaborately coded scores of their exploits by referring to various athletes' names as a way of signifying the number of conquests. Thus a reference to "Reggie Jackson" would refer to 44, the number on his jersey, while "David Robinson" would signify 50 different conquests. In this way the boys could publicly compete with one another without the young women understanding that they were simply the grounds for homosocial competition.

When some of these young women accused the boys of assault and rape, many residents of their affluent suburb were shocked. The boys' mothers, particularly, winced when they heard that their fifteen-year-old sons had had sex with 44 or 50 girls. A few expressed outrage. But the boys' fathers glowed with pride. "That's my boy," they declared in chorus. They accused the girls of being sluts. And we wonder where the kids get it from?

Spur Posse is only the most recent example of the way masculine sexual entitlement is offered to boys as part of their birthright. Transforming a rape culture is going to mean transforming a view of women as the vessels through which men can compete with one another, trying to better their positions on the homosocial ladders of success and status.

What is it about groups that seems to bring out the worst in men? I think it is because the animating condition for most American men is a deeply rooted fear of other men—a fear that other men will view us as less than manly. The fear of humiliation, of losing in a competitive ranking among men, of being dominated by other men—these are the fears that keep men in tow and that reinforce traditional definitions of masculinity as a false definition of safety. Homophobia (which I understand as more than the fear of homosexual men; it's also the fear of other men) keeps men acting like men, keeps men exaggerating their adherence to traditional norms, so that no other men will get the idea that we might really be that most dreaded person: the sissy.

Men's fear of being judged a failure as a man in the eyes of other men leads to a certain homosocial element within the heterosexual encounter: men often will use their sexual conquest as a form of currency to gain status among other men. Such homosocial competition contributes to the strange hearing impairment that men experience in any sexual encounter, a socialized deafness that leads us to hear "no" as "yes," to escalate the encounter, to always go for it, to score. And this is occurring just at the moment when women are, themselves, learning to say "yes" to their own sexuality, to say "yes" to their own desire for sexual pleasure. Instead of our socialized deafness, we need to become what Langston Hughes called "articulate listeners": we need to trust women when they tell us what they want, and when they want it, and what they don't want as well. If we listen when women say "no," then they will feel more trusting and open to saying "yes" when they feel that. And we need to listen to our own inner voices, our own desires and needs. Not the voices that are about compulsively proving something that cannot be proved, but the voices that are about connection with another and the desires and passions that may happen between two equals.

Escalating a sexual encounter beyond what a woman may want is date rape, not sex; it is one of the most important issues we will face in the 1990s. It is transforming the sexual landscape as earlier sexual behaviors are being reevaluated in light of new ideas about sexual politics. We have to explore the meaning of the word *consent*, explore our own understandings, and make sure that these definitions are in accord with women's definitions.

From the Bedroom to the Boardroom

Just as women have been claiming the right to say "yes" and demanding the right to say "no" and have it listened to and respected in the sexual arena, they've also transformed the public arena, the workplace. As with sexuality, the real revolution in the past thirty years has been women's dramatic entry into the labor force in unprecedented numbers. Almost half of the labor force is female. I often demonstrate this point to my classes by asking the women who intend to have careers to raise their hands. All do. Then I ask them to keep their hands raised if their mothers have had a career outside the home for more than ten years. Half put their hands down. Then I ask them to keep their hands raised if their grandmothers had a career for ten years. Virtually no hands remain raised. In three generations, they can visibly see the

difference in women's working lives. Women are in the work force to
stay, and men had better get used to having them around.

That means that the cozy boys' club—another homosocial arena—
has been penetrated by women. And this, just when that arena is more
suffused with doubt and anxieties than ever before. We are, after all, a
downwardly mobile culture. Most Americans are less successful now
than their parents were at the same age. It now takes two incomes to
provide the same standard of living that one income provided about a
generation ago. And most of us in the middle class cannot afford to
buy the houses in which we were brought up. Since men derive their
identity in the public sphere, and the primary public arena where masculinity is demonstrated is the workplace, this is an important issue.
There are fewer and fewer big wheels and more and more men who
will feel as though they haven't made the grade, who will feel dam-
aged, injured, powerless—men who will need to demonstrate their
masculinity all over again. Suddenly, men's fears of humiliation and
domination are out in the open, and there's a convenient target at which
to vent those anxieties.

And now, here come women into the workplace in unprecedented
numbers. It now seems virtually impossible that a man will go through
his entire working life without having a woman colleague, co-worker,
or boss. Just when men's economic breadwinner status is threatened,
women appear on the scene as easy targets for men's anger. Thus,
sexual harassment in the workplace is a distorted effort to put women
back in their place, to remind women that they are not equal to men in
the workplace, that they are still just women, even if they are in the
workplace. . . .

If an employer asks an employee for a date, and she declines, perhaps he has forgotten about it by the time he gets to the parking lot.
No big deal, he says to himself. You ask someone out, and she says
"no." You forget about it. In fact, repairing a wounded male ego often
requires that you forget about it. But the female employee? She's now
frozen, partly with fear. What if I said yes? Would I have gotten promoted? Would he have expected more than a date? Will I now get
fired? Will someone else get promoted over me? What should I do?
And so, she will do what millions of women do in that situation: she
calls her friends, who counsel her to let the matter rest and get on with
her work. And she remembers for a long, long time. Who, therefore, is
likely to have a better memory: those in power or those against whom
that power is deployed?

This is precisely the divergence in experience that characterizes
the controversies spinning around Senator Bob Packwood. Long a
public supporter of women's causes, Senator Packwood also appar-

ently chased numerous women around office desks, clumsily trying to have affairs with them. He claims, now, that alcoholism caused this behavior and that he doesn't remember. It's a good thing that the women remember. They often do.

Sexual harassment is particularly volatile because it often fuses two levels of power: the power of employers over employees and the power of men over women. Thus, what may be said or intended as a man to a woman is also experienced in the context of superior and subordinate, or vice versa. Sexual harassment in the workplace results from men using their public position to demand or exact social relationships. It is the confusion of public and private, bringing together two arenas of men's power over women. Not only are men in positions of power in the workplace, but we are socialized to be the sexual initiators and to see sexual prowess as a confirmation of masculinity.

Sexual harassment is also a way to remind women that they are not yet equals in the workplace, that they really don't belong there. Harassment is most frequent in those occupations and workplaces where women are new and in the minority, like surgeons, firefighters, and investment bankers. "Men see women as invading a masculine environment," says Louise Fitzgerald, a University of Illinois psychologist. "These are guys whose sexual harassment has nothing whatever to do with sex. They're trying to scare women off a male preserve.". . .

Although men surely do benefit from sexual harassment, I believe that we also have a stake in ending it. First, our ability to form positive and productive relationships with women colleagues in the workplace is undermined by it. So long as sexual harassment is a daily occurrence and women are afraid of their superiors in the workplace, innocent men's behaviors may be misinterpreted. Second, men's ability to develop social and sexual relationships that are both ethical and exciting is also compromised. If a male boss dates a subordinate, can he really trust that the reason she is with him is because she *wants* to be? Or will there always be a lingering doubt that she is there because she is afraid not to be or because she seeks to please him because of his position?

Currently, law firms and corporations all over the country are scrambling to implement sexual harassment policies, to make sure that sexual harassment will be recognized and punished. But our challenge is greater than admonition and post hoc counseling. Our challenge will be to prevent sexual harassment *before* it happens. And that means working with men. Men must come to see that these are not women who happen to be in the workplace (where, by this logic, they actually don't belong), but workers who happen to be women. . . .

AIDS as a Men's Disease

Surely, men will benefit from the eradication of AIDS. Although we are used to discussing AIDS as a disease of gay men and IV drug users, I think we need to see AIDS as a men's disease. Over ninety percent of all AIDS patients are men; AIDS is now the leading cause of death for men aged thirty-three to forty-five nationwide. AIDS is American men's number one health problem, and yet we rarely treat it as a men's issue. But AIDS is also the most gender-linked disease in American history. No other disease has attacked one gender so disproportionately, except those to which only one sex is susceptible, such as hemophilia or uterine or prostate cancer. AIDS *could* affect both men and women equally (and in Africa that seems to be closer to the case). But in the United States, AIDS patients are overwhelmingly men.

(Let me be clear that in no way am I saying that one should not be compassionate for women AIDS patients. Of course one must recognize that women are as likely to get AIDS from engaging in the same high-risk behaviors as men. But that's precisely my point. Women don't engage in those behaviors at rates anything like men.)

One is put at risk for AIDS by engaging in specific high-risk behaviors, activities that ignore potential health risks for more immediate pleasures. For example, sharing needles is both a defiant flaunting of health risks and an expression of community among IV drug users. And the capacity for high-risk sexual behaviors—unprotected anal intercourse with a large number of partners, the ability to take it, despite any potential pain—are also confirmations of masculinity.

And so is accumulation—of money, property, or sexual conquests. It's curious that one of America's most lionized heroes, Magic Johnson, doesn't seem to have been particularly compassionate about the possibility of infection of the twenty-five women he reported that he slept with. Johnson told *Sports Illustrated* that as a single man, he tried to "accommodate as many women as I could, most of them through unprotected sex." Accommodate? When he protested that his words were misunderstood, he told the *New York Times*, "I was a bachelor, and I lived a bachelor's life. And I'm paying the price for it. But you know I respect women to the utmost." (I suppose that Wilt Chamberlain, who boasted in his autobiography that he slept with over twenty thousand women, respected them almost ten times as much.)

As sociologists have long understood, stigmatized gender identity often leads to exaggerated forms of gender-specific behavior. Thus, those whose masculinity is least secure are precisely those most likely to enact behavioral codes and hold fast to traditional definitions of masculinity. In social science research, hypermasculinity as compensation for insecure gender identity has been used to explain the propensity for homophobia, authoritarianism, racism, anti-Semitism, juvenile delinquency, and urban gangs.

Gay men and IV drug users—the two largest risk groups—can be seen in this light, although for different reasons. The traditional view of gay men is that they are not "real men." Most of the stereotypes revolve around effeminacy, weakness, passivity. But following the Stonewall riots of 1969, in which gay men fought back against a police raid on a gay bar in Greenwich Village, New York, and the subsequent birth of the Gay Liberation Movement, a new gay masculinity emerged in major cities. The "clone," as the new gay man was called, dressed in hypermasculine garb (flannel shirts, blue jeans, leather); had short hair (not at all androgynous) and a mustache; and was athletic, highly muscular. In short, the clone looked more like a "real man" than most straight men.

And the clones—who comprised roughly one-third of all gay men living in the major urban enclaves of the 1970s—enacted a hypermasculine sexuality in steamy back rooms, bars, and bathhouses, where sex was plentiful, anonymous, and very hot. No unnecessary foreplay, romance, or post-coital awkwardness. Sex without attachment. One might even say that, given the norms of masculinity (that men are always seeking sex, ready for sex, wanting sex), gay men were the only men in America who were getting as much sex as they wanted. Predictably, high levels of sexual activity led to high levels of sexually transmitted diseases, such as gonorrhea, among the clones. But no one could have predicted AIDS.

Among IV drug users, we see a different pattern, but with some similar outcomes when seen from a gender perspective. The majority of IV drug users are African-American and Latino, two groups for whom the traditional avenues of successful manhood are blocked by poverty and racism. More than half of the black men between eighteen and twenty-five in our cities are unemployed, and one in four is in some way involved with the penal system (in jail, on probation, under arrest). We thus have an entire generation structurally prevented from demonstrating its manhood in that most traditional of ways—as breadwinners.

The drug culture offers an alternative. Dealing drugs can provide an income to support a family as well as the opportunity for manly risks and adventure. The community of drug users can confirm gender identity; the sharing of needles is a demonstration of that solidarity. And the ever-present risk of death by overdose takes hypermasculine bravado to its limits.

Who Asked for It?

The victims of men's adherence to these crazy norms of masculinity—AIDS patients, rape victims, victims of sexual harassment—did not become victims intentionally. They did not "ask for it," and they certainly do not deserve blame. That some women today are also sexual predators, going to swank bars or waiting outside athletes' locker rooms or trying to score with male subordinates at work, doesn't make William Kennedy Smith, Mike Tyson, Magic Johnson, or Clarence Thomas any less predatory. When predatory animals threaten civil populations, we warn the population to stay indoors until the wild animals can be caught and recaged. When it's men on the prowl, women engage in a voluntary curfew, unless they want to risk being attacked.

And the men—the date rapists, the sexual harassers, the AIDS patients—are not "perverts" or "deviants" who have strayed from the norms of masculinity. They are, if anything, overconformists to destructive norms of male sexual behavior. Until we change the meaning of manhood, sexual risk-taking and conquest will remain part of the rhetoric of masculinity. And we will scatter the victims, both women and men, along the wayside as we rush headlong toward a testosterone-infected oblivion.

The Sexual Politics of Safety

What links the struggle against sexual harassment, date and acquaintance rape, and AIDS is that preventing all of them require that *safety* become the central term, an organizing principle of men's relationships with women, as well as with other men. The politics of safety may be the missing link in the transformation of men's lives, in their capacity for change. Safety is more than the absence of danger, although that wouldn't be such a bad thing itself. Safety is proactive, the creation of a space in which all people, women and men, gay and straight, and of all colors, can experience and express the fullness of their being.

Think for a moment about how the politics of safety affects the three areas I have discussed in this essay. What is the best way to prevent AIDS? To use sterile needles for intravenous drug injections and to practice "safer sex." Sterile needles and safer sex share one basic characteristic: they both require that men act responsibly. This is not one of the cardinal rules of manhood. Safer sex programs encourage men to have fewer partners, to avoid certain particularly dangerous practices, and to use condoms when having any sex that involves the exchange of bodily fluids. In short, safer sex programs encourage men to stop having sex like men. To men, you see, "safer sex" is an oxymoron, one of those juxtapositions of terms that produce a nonsensical outcome. That which is sexy is not safe, that which is safe is not sexy. Sex is about danger, risk, excitement; safety is about comfort, softness, and security.

Seen this way, it is not surprising to find, as some researchers have found, that one-fourth of urban gay men report that they have not changed their unsafe sexual behaviors. What is, in fact, astonishing is that slightly more than three-fourths *have* changed and are now practicing safer sex.

What heterosexual men could learn from the gay community's response to AIDS is how to eroticize that responsibility—something that women have been trying to teach men for decades. Making safer sex into sexy sex has been one of the great transformations of male sexuality accomplished by the gay community. And straight men could also learn a thing or two about caring for one another through illness, supporting one another in grief, and maintaining a resilience in the face of a devastating disease and the callous indifference of the larger society.

Safety is also the animating condition for women's expression of sexuality. While safety may be a turnoff for men (comfort, softness, and security are the terms of postorgasmic detumescence, not sexual arousal), safety is a precondition for sexual agency for women. Only when women feel safe can they give their sexuality full expression. For men, hot sex leaves a warm afterglow; for women, warmth builds to heat, but warmth is not created by heat.

This perspective helps explain that curious finding in the sex research literature about the divergence of women's and men's sexualities as they age. We believe that men reach their sexual peak at around eighteen, and then go into steady, and later more precipitous, decline for the rest of their lives, while women hit their sexual stride closer to thirty, with the years between twenty-seven and thirty-eight as their peak years. Typically, we understand these changes as having to do with differences in biology—that hormonal changes find men feeling soft and cuddly just as women are getting all steamed up. But aging does not produce such changes in every culture; that is, biology doesn't seem to work the same way everywhere.

What biological explanations leave out is the way that men's and women's sexualities are related to each other, and the way that both are shaped by the institution of marriage. Marriage makes one's sexuality more predictable—the partner, the timing, the experience—and it places sex *always* in the context of the marital relationship. Marriage makes sex safer. No wonder women find their sexuality heightening—they finally feel safe enough to allow their sexual desires to be expressed. And no wonder men's sexuality deflates—there's no danger, risk, or excitement left.

Safety is a precondition for women's sexual expression. Only when a woman is certain, beyond the shadow of a doubt, that her "no" means "no," can she ever say "yes" to her own sexual desires. So if we men are going to have the sexual relationships with exciting, desiring women that we say we want, then we have to make the environment safe enough for women to express their desires. We have to make it absolutely certain to a woman that her "no" means "no"—no matter how urgently we feel the burning of our own desires.

To do this we will need to transform the definition of what it means to be a real man. But we have to work fast. AIDS is spreading rapidly, and date rape and sexual harassment are epidemic in the nation's colleges and workplaces. As AIDS spreads, and as women speak up about these issues, there are more and more people who need our compassion and support. Yet compassion is in relatively short supply among American men, since it involves the capacity of taking the role of the other, of seeing ourselves in someone else's shoes, a quality that contradicts the manly independence we have so carefully cultivated.

Sexual democracy, just like political democracy, relies on a balance between rights and responsibilities, between the claims of the individual and the claims of the community. When one discusses one's sexual rights—that each person, every woman and man, has an equal right to pleasure—men understand immediately what you mean. Women often look delighted and a little bit surprised. Add to the Bill of Sexual Rights a notion of responsibility, in which each of us treats sexual partners as if they had an integrity equal to our own, and it's the men who look puzzled. "Responsibility? What's that got to do with sex? I thought sex was about having fun."

Sure it is, but it's also political in the most intimate sense. Sexual democracy doesn't have to mean no sex. It means treating your partner as someone whose lust is equal to yours and also as someone whose life is equally valuable. It's about enacting in daily life one's principles, claiming our rights to pleasure, and making sure that our partners also feel safe enough to be able to fully claim theirs. This is what we demand for those who have come to America seeking refuge—safety—from political tyranny. Could we ask any less of those who are now asking for protection and refuge from millennia of sexual tyranny?

Suggested Readings

Abbey, Antonia, Lisa Thomson Ross, Donna McDuffie, and Pam McAuslan. "Alcohol and Dating Risk Factors for Sexual Assault among College Women." *Psychology of Women Quarterly* 20 (1996): 147–69.

Allison, Julia A., and Lawrence S. Wrightsman. *Rape: The Misunderstood Crime*. Newbury Park, CA: Sage Publications, 1993.

Baron, Larry, and Murray A. Straus. *Four Theories of Rape in American Society*. New Haven: Yale University Press, 1989.

Bart, Pauline B., and Patricia H. O'Brien. *Stopping Rape: Successful Survival Strategies*. New York: Pergamon, 1985.

Bart, Pauline B., and Eileen Geil Moran. *Violence against Women: The Bloody Footprints*. Newbury Park, CA: Sage Publications, 1993.

Beneke, Timothy. *Men on Rape*. New York: St. Martin's Press, 1982.

Berger, Ronald J., Patricia Searles, and W. Lawrence Neuman. "The Dimensions of Rape Reform Legislation." *Law and Society Review* 22 (1988): 329–57.

Brownmiller, Susan. *Against Our Will: Men, Women, and Rape*. New York: Simon and Schuster, 1975.

Buchwald, Emilie, Pamela R. Fletcher, and Martha Roth, eds. *Transforming a Rape Culture*. Minneapolis: Milkweed Editions, 1993.

Burgess, Ann Wolbert, ed. *Rape and Sexual Assault: A Research Handbook*. New York: Garland Publishing, 1985.

———. *Rape and Sexual Assault II*. New York: Garland Publishing, 1988.

Burt, Martha R. "Cultural Myths and Support for Rape." *Journal of Personality and Social Psychology* 38 (1980): 217–30.

Byington, Diane, Patricia Yancey Martin, Diana DiNitto, and M. Sharon Maxwell. "Organizational Affiliation and Effectiveness: The Case of Rape Crisis Centers." *Administration in Social Work* 15 (1991): 83–103.

Caringella-MacDonald, Susan. "Marxist and Feminist Interpretations of the Aftermath of Rape Reforms." *Contemporary Crisis* 12 (1988): 125–44.

Clark, Lorenne, and Debra Lewis. *Rape: The Price of Coercive Sexuality*. Toronto: Women's Press, 1977.

Davis, Angela. "The Myth of the Black Rapist." In *Women, Race and Class*, 172–201. New York: Random House, 1981.

Ellis, Lee. *Theories of Rape: Inquiries into the Causes of Sexual Aggression*. New York: Hemisphere, 1989.

Estrich, Susan. *Real Rape*. Cambridge, MA: Harvard University Press, 1987.

Fairstein, Linda A. *Sexual Violence: Our War against Rape*. New York: William Morrow, 1993.

Finkelhor, David, and Kersti Yllo. *License to Rape: Sexual Abuse of Wives*. New York: Holt, Rinehart, and Winston, 1985.

Frieze, Irene H., and Angela Browne. "Investigation into the Causes and Consequences of Marital Rape." *Signs* 8 (1983): 532–53.

Gilbert, Neil. "The Phantom Epidemic of Sexual Assault." *Public Interest* (Spring 1991): 54–65.

Goldberg-Ambrose, Carole. "Unfinished Business in Rape Law Reform." *Journal of Social Issues* 48 (1992): 173–86.

Gornick, Janet, Martha R. Burt, and Karen J. Pittman. "Structure and Activities of Rape Crisis Centers in the 1980s." *Crime and Delinquency* 31 (1985): 247–68.

Grauerholz, Elizabeth, and Mary A. Koralewski, eds. *Sexual Coercion: A Source Book on Its Nature, Causes, and Prevention*. Lexington, MA: D. C. Heath, 1991.

Griffin, Susan. "Rape: The All-American Crime." *Ramparts* 10 (1971): 26–35.

Groth, Nicholas A., and Ann Wolbert Burgess. "Male Rape: Offenders and Victims." *American Journal of Psychiatry* 137 (1980): 806–10.

Groth, Nicholas A., and H. Jean Birnbaum. *Men Who Rape: The Psychology of the Offender*. New York: Plenum Press, 1979.

Hanmer, Jalna, and Mary Maynard, eds. *Women, Violence, and Social Control*. Basingstoke: Macmillan, 1987.

Harlow, Caroline Wolf. *Female Victims of Violent Crime*. Washington, DC: U.S. Department of Justice, 1991.

Herman, Dianne. "The Rape Culture." In *Women: A Feminist Perspective*, 4th edition, edited by Jo Freeman, 20–44. Mountain View, CA: Mayfield, 1989.

Jackson, Stevi. "The Social Context of Rape: Sexual Scripts and Motivation." *Women's Studies International Quarterly* 1 (1978): 27–38.

Johnson, Allen Griswold. "On the Prevalence of Rape in the United States." *Signs* 6 (1980): 136–46.

Kanin, Eugene. "Date Rape: Unofficial Criminals, Victims." *Victimology* 9 (1984): 95–108.

Koss, Mary P., Christine A. Gidycz, and Nadine Wisniewski. "The Scope of Rape: Incidence and Prevalence of Sexual Aggression and

Victimization in a National Sample of Higher Education Students."
Journal of Consulting and Clinical Psychology 55 (1987): 162–
70.

Koss, Mary P., and Mary R. Harvey. *The Rape Victim: Clinical and Community Interventions*. Second edition. Newbury Park, CA: Sage Publications, 1991.

Koss, Mary P., et al. *No Safe Haven: Male Violence against Women*. Washington, DC: American Psychological Association, 1994.

LaFree, Gary. "The Effect of Sexual Stratification by Race on Official Reactions to Rape." *American Sociological Review* 45 (1980): 842–54.

———. "Male Power and Female Victimization: Towards a Theory of Interracial Rape." *American Journal of Sociology* 88 (1982): 311–28.

———. *Rape and Criminal Justice: The Social Construction of Sexual Assault*. Belmont, CA: Wadsworth, 1989.

Levine-MacCombie, Joyce, and Mary P. Koss. "Acquaintance Rape: Effective Avoidance Strategies." *Psychology of Women Quarterly* 10 (1986): 311–20.

Linz, Daniel, Edward Donnerstein, and Steven Penrod. "The Effects of Multiple Exposure to Filmed Violence against Women." *Journal of Communications* 34 (1984): 130–47.

Lonsway, Kimberly A., and Louise R. Fitzgerald. "Rape Myths in Review." *Psychology of Women Quarterly* 18 (1994): 133–64.

MacKinnon, Catherine A. "Feminism, Marxism, Method and the State: Toward Feminist Jurisprudence." *Signs* 8 (1983): 635–58.

———. *Feminism Unmodified: Discourses on Life and Law*. Cambridge, MA: Harvard University Press, 1987.

Malamuth, Neil M., and Edward Donnerstein, eds. *Pornography and Sexual Aggression*. Orlando, FL: Academic Press, 1984.

Malamuth, Neil M., and John Briere. "Sexual Violence in the Media: Indirect Effects on Aggression against Women." *Journal of Social Issues* 42 (1986): 75–92.

Marcus, Sharon. "Fighting Bodies, Fighting Words: A Theory and Politics of Rape Prevention." In *Feminists Theorize the Political*, edited by Judith Butler and Joan W. Scott, 385–403. New York: Routledge, 1992.

Marsh, Jeanne C., Alison Geist, and Nathan S. Caplan. *Rape and the Limits of Law Reform*. Boston: Auburn House, 1982.

Matthews, Nancy A. *Confronting Rape: The Feminist Anti-Rape Movement and the State*. London: Routledge, 1994.

Meyers, Michael R. "Men Sexually Assaulted as Adults and Sexually Abused as Boys." *Archives of Sexual Behavior* 18 (1989): 203–15.

Mezey, Gillian C., and Michael B. King, eds. *Male Victims of Sexual Assault*. Oxford: Oxford University Press, 1992.

Muehlenhard, Charlene L. "Misinterpreted Dating Behaviors and the Risk of Date Rape." *Journal of Social and Clinical Psychology* 34 (1988): 20–37.

Muehlenhard, Charlene L., Debra E. Friedman, and Celeste M. Thomas. "Is Date Rape Justifiable? The Effects of Dating Activity, Who Initiated, Who Paid, and Men's Attitudes toward Women." *Psychology of Women Quarterly* 9 (1985): 297–310.

Muehlenhard, Charlene L., and Melaney A. Linton. "Date Rape and Sexual Aggression in Dating Situations: Incidence and Risk Factors." *Journal of Counseling Psychology* 34 (1987): 186–96.

Norris, Jeanette, Paula S. Nurius, and Linda A. Dimeff. "Through Her Eyes: Factors Affecting Women's Perception of and Resistance to Acquaintance Sexual Aggression Threat." *Psychology of Women Quarterly* 20 (1996): 123–45.

Parrot, Andrea, and Laurie Bechhofer, eds. *Acquaintance Rape: The Hidden Crime*. New York: John Wiley and Sons, 1991.

Pirog-Good, Maureen A., and Jan E. Stets, eds. *Violence in Dating Relationships: Emerging Social Issues*. New York: Praeger, 1989.

Rapaport, Karen, and Barry R. Burkhart. "Personality and Attitudinal Characteristics of Sexually Coercive College Males." *Journal of Abnormal Psychology* 93 (1984): 216–21.

Roiphe, Katie. *The Morning After: Sex, Fear, and Feminism on Campus*. Boston: Little, Brown, 1993.

Russell, Diana E. H. *The Politics of Rape: The Victim's Perspective*. New York: Stein and Day, 1975.

———. *Rape in Marriage*, revised edition. Bloomington: Indiana University Press, 1990.

———. *Sexual Exploitation: Rape, Child Sexual Abuse, and Workplace Harassment*. Beverly Hills, CA: Sage Publications, 1984.

Russell, Diana E. H., and Nancy Howell. "The Prevalence of Rape in the U.S. Revisited." *Signs* 8 (1983): 68–95.

Sanday, Peggy Reeves. *Fraternity Gang Rape: Sex, Brotherhood, and Privilege on Campus*. New York: New York University Press, 1990.

Schwendinger, Julia R., and Herman Schwendinger. *Rape and Inequality*. Newbury Park, CA: Sage Publications, 1983.

Scully, Diana. *Understanding Sexual Violence: A Study of Convicted Rapists*. Boston: Unwin Hyman, 1990.

Scully, Diana, and Joseph Marolla. "Convicted Rapists' Vocabulary of Motives: Excuses and Justifications." *Social Problems* 31 (1984): 530–44.

Sheffield, Carole J. "Sexual Terrorism." In *Women: A Feminist Perspective*, 4th edition, edited by Jo Freeman, 3–19. Mountain View, CA: Mayfield, 1989.

Sorenson, Susan B., Judith A. Stein, Judith M. Siegel, Jacqueline M. Golding, and M. Audrey Burnam. "The Prevalence of Adult Sexual Assault: The Los Angeles Epidemiologic Catchment Area Project." *American Journal of Epidemiology* 126 (1987): 1154–64.

Spohn, Cassia, and Julie Horney. *Rape Law Reform: A Grass-Roots Revolution and Its Impact*. New York: Plenum Press, 1992.

Ullman, Sarah E., and Raymond Knight. "Fighting Back: Women's Resistance to Rape." *Journal of Interpersonal Violence* 7 (1992): 31–43.

Ward, Colleen A. *Attitudes toward Rape: Feminist and Social Psychological Perspectives*. Thousand Oaks, CA: Sage Publications, 1995.

Warshaw, Robin. *I Never Called It Rape*. New York: Harper & Row, 1988.

Waterman, Caroline K., Lori J. Dawson, and Michael J. Bologna. "Sexual Coercion in Gay Male and Lesbian Relationships: Predictors and Implications for Support Services." *Journal of Sex Research* 26 (1989): 118–24.

Wyatt, Gail Elizabeth. "The Sociocultural Context of African American and White American Women's Rape." *Journal of Social Issues* 48 (1992): 77–92.

Suggested Films

The Accused (1988; 110 minutes) Feature Film
Compelling drama about the gang rape of a young woman and the trial of her assailants, inspired by a real-life case. The victim, in a powerful performance by Jodie Foster, challenges an indifferent legal system and social stereotypes of rape in her pursuit of justice.

The Color Purple (1985; 125 minutes) Feature Film
This Stephen Spielberg film, based on Alice Walker's Pulitzer Prize-winning book, focuses on the life and struggles of a courageous black woman in the South who suffers rape at the hands of her stepfather and her husband.

The Confrontation: Latinas Fight Back against Rape (1983; 37 minutes)
Women Make Movies, Inc., Sales and Rentals Department, 462 Broadway, Suite 500 C, New York, NY 10013 (212) 925-0606

One controversial response to rape is confronting the rapist in a public place. In this docudrama, Marta and a group of friends and counselors decide to take this approach after Marta is raped on the way home from a party.

Dating Rites: Gang Rape on Campus (1993; 28 minutes)
Filmmakers Library, 124 East 40th Street, New York, NY 10016 (212) 808-4980

In this documentary Meg Davis, a survivor of gang rape, discusses her assault, which took place eight years ago, and explains why it still affects her life. Next, a convicted rapist is interviewed, providing insights into the mind of the perpetrator. This film also includes a reenactment of a gang rape.

Dreamworlds (1995; 55 minutes)
The Media Education Foundation, 26 Center Street, Northampton, MA 01060 (800) 659-6882

One of the most pervasive forms of popular culture today is the music video. This film examines the representation of women in music videos and how these images affect both how men think about women sexually as well as how women think about themselves.

Finding Out: Date Rape (1990; 30 minutes)
The National Center for Drug Abuse, Violence, and Recovery, P.O. Box 9, 102 HWY 81 N., Calhoun, KY 42327-0009 (800) 962-6662

Recommended by the producers for freshman orientation sessions, this film demonstrates to students why date rape is prevalent on many college campuses as well as advises them on reducing "at-risk" behavior. The producers note that the film contains adult language and that an edited version is available.

Five Out of Five (1987; 7 minutes)
Women Make Movies, Inc., Sales and Rentals Department, 462 Broadway, Suite 500 C, New York, NY 10013 (212) 925-0606

Featuring New York Women Against Rape's Acting Out Teen Theatre, this short rap rock video examines child and teen sexual abuse. In this accessible video, teens talk about sex-role stereotypes and abuses of power as well as their own experiences with sexual assault.

Four Men Speak Out (1991; 28 minutes)
The National Center for Drug Abuse, Violence, and Recovery, P.O. Box 9, 102 HWY 81 N., Calhoun, KY 42327-0009 (800) 962-6662

Recognizing that sexual violence also affects males, this film explores the experiences of four men who survived sexual assault. The film examines the long and short-term effects of the abuse as well as recovery strategies.

From Victim to Survivor (1989; 29 minutes)
Produced by the Boulder County Rape Crisis Team.
Filmmakers Library, 124 East 40th Street, New York, NY 10016 (212) 808-4980

Physical survival is only the first step in recovering from rape. This film follows the survival story of two women and one man who share their experiences of emotional healing.

Home Avenue (1989; 17 minutes)
Women Make Movies, Inc., Sales and Rentals Department, 462 Broadway, Suite 500 C, New York, NY 10013 (212) 925-0606

Jennifer Montgomery retells her own personal story of rape through the lens of a Super 8 camera. She retraces the events that occurred nine years ago when she was raped at gunpoint while traveling from her boyfriend's dorm to her parents' house. She also explores the reactions she received from her family and from the criminal justice system.

Men, Sex, and Rape (1992; 50 minutes)
The National Center for Drug Abuse, Violence, and Recovery, P.O. Box 9, 102 HWY 81 N., Calhoun, KY 42327-0009 (800) 962-6662

Host Peter Jennings raises questions about men and rape, such as where does the idea of rape begin and what are the differences between what we all agree is rape and what some believe is normal behavior.

No Visible Bruises: The Katie Koestner Story
The National Center for Drug Abuse, Violence, and Recovery, P.O. Box 9, 102 HWY 81 N., Calhoun, KY 42327-0009 (800) 962-6662

As a college freshman, Katie accused a fellow student of rape. By examining Katie's story, this film confronts the issue of acquaintance rape on college campuses.

Open Letter: Grasp the Bird's Tail (1992; 16 minutes)
Women Make Movies, Inc., Sales and Rentals Department, 462 Broadway, Suite 500 C, New York, NY 10013 (212) 925-0606

This poignant film by Brenda Joy Lem examines the implications of rape in a racist society. Using the metaphor of a contortionist trapped in a box, Sylvester (played by Lem) writes a letter to her new lover explaining that while she cares for him, she also feels vulnerable due to her experiences of sexual and racial violence.

Rape: An Act of Hate (1986; 30 minutes)
Films for the Humanities and Sciences, P.O. Box 2053, Princeton, NJ 08543-2053 (800) 257-5126

Hosted by Veronica Hamel, this film examines why rape occurs and offers advice to help women protect themselves from rape. By interviewing experts in the field and dispelling rape myths, the program shows that rape is ultimately an act of violence.

Rape: Face to Face (1985; 55 minutes)
Filmmakers Library, 124 East 40th Street, New York, NY 10016 (212) 808-4980

This documentary explores the trauma of rape and examines its causes and consequences. In a confrontation between rapists and victims of rape (though not by these particular men), the rape survivors reveal the depth of their emotional scars. The men, who are in therapy at the Washington State Hospital, seem surprised at the emotional wounds that the women experienced.

Rape and DNA Testing (28 minutes)
Films for the Humanities and Sciences, P.O. Box 2053, Princeton, NJ 08543-2053 (800) 257-5126

In this specially adapted Phil Donahue segment, experts examine the usefulness of DNA testing in rape cases.

Rape by Any Name (1990; 60 minutes)
Women Make Movies, Inc., Sales and Rentals Department, 462 Broadway, Suite 500 C, New York, NY 10013 (212) 925-0606

Although the majority of rapes occur between individuals who know one another, acquaintance rape continues to be underreported and difficult to prosecute. This film features interviews with rape survivors, counselors, and college students as well as examines the boundaries between consensual and coercive sex.

Rape Stories (1989; 25 minutes)
Women Make Movies, Inc., Sales and Rentals Department, 462 Broadway, Suite 500 C, New York, NY 10013 (212) 925-0606

Two weeks after being raped in the elevator of her apartment building, Margie Strosser asked a friend to interview her about the assault. Now, ten years later, she looks back on the experience, revealing the range of emotions evoked by the memories.

Surviving Rape: A Journey through Grief (1992; 27 minutes)
The National Center for Drug Abuse, Violence, and Recovery, P.O. Box 9, 102 HWY 81 N., Calhoun, KY 42327-0009 (800) 962-6662

Five survivors of sexual assault discuss their recovery processes, revealing the five stages through which many rape victims suffer (denial, anger, depression, bargaining, and acceptance).

20/20 Foresight: Rape Awareness and Self-Defense (1990; 48 minutes)
The National Center for Drug Abuse, Violence, and Recovery, P.O. Box 9, 102 HWY 81 N., Calhoun, KY 42327-0009 (800) 962-6662

Focusing on self-defense techniques to help women avoid rape, this film helps women learn how to be street smart and recognize their options if they are confronted with an assault.

Twice a Victim (1993; 23 minutes)
The National Center for Drug Abuse, Violence, and Recovery, P.O. Box 9, 102 HWY 81 N., Calhoun, KY 42327-0009 (800) 962-6662

This drama portrays the story of a college woman who is raped at the end of a date by a fellow student. The young women sees a doctor for her physical injuries but refuses to disclose her attacker's identity. Instead of seeking counseling, she pretends the rape never occurred. She ultimately breaks her silence by identifying the rapist in an anonymous message on the wall of the women's restroom. Afterwards, she joins a support group, where she begins to recognize that date rape is all too common on college campuses.

Waking Up to Rape (1985; 35 minutes)
Women Make Movies, Inc., Sales and Rentals Department, 462 Broadway, Suite 500 C, New York, NY 10013 (212) 925-0606

This film examines the personal trauma of rape through interviews with three rape survivors (Black, Chicana, and white) who courageously describe their experiences (acquaintance rape, incest, and stranger rape). Also featuring scenes with women police officers, counselors, and self-defense instructors, this film exposes societal attitudes about rape as well as the problem of racism in the criminal justice system.